70 Days for 70 Years

Remember the Past
to Build the Future

EDITED BY

Rabbi Aubrey Hersh, Rabbi Andrew Shaw
& Naomi Cowan

US
Living &
Learning

In memory of the six million

First published in Great Britain 2015 by

THE UNITED SYNAGOGUE

305 Ballards Lane, Finchley

London N12 8GB

REGISTERED CHARITY NUMBER: 242552

ENQUIRIES: info@theus.org.uk

WEBSITE: www.theus.org.uk

ISBN: 978-1-909004-02-3

EDITORIAL TEAM: Rabbi Aubrey Hersh, Rabbi Andrew Shaw,
                Naomi Cowan

BOOK DESIGN & LAYOUT: Raphaël Freeman, Renana Typesetting

Preface
The 70 Days for 70 Years Project

70 years ago, six million of our people had been murdered in the darkest period of our history. In the world, paraphrasing chapter 3 of *Kohelet* (Ecclesiastes), there is a time for everything under the sun: a time to be silent and a time to speak, a time to refrain and a time to learn, a time to remember and a time to forget. Now is the time to remember, to learn, to speak and to be involved for the sake of the past, the present, and the future.

In 1985, Rabbi Shapira from Netanya attended the commemoration of Thereisenstadt concentration camp, 40 years after its liberation. Two thoughts struck him. First, could anything positive be taken from such a tragedy? The second thought was more worrying. He, an orphan of the Holocaust, could personally remember the dark years of 1939–1945, but what about his children and their children. How would they remember?

He returned to Israel and contacted Yad Vashem. They supplied the names of 30 children who died in the Holocaust. He gave these names to 30 children in his home city and asked each of them to learn in memory of one of those child victims of the Holocaust.

It was this idea that inspired me to embark on the project "50 Days for 50 Years" when working for the Union of Jewish Students in 1995.

Five thousand Jewish students across the United Kingdom received the name of a victim of student age and were asked to learn in their memory for 50 days: a chance to remember the past to build the future.

Along with the name, students also received a pocket book containing fifty questions and ideas about various aspects of Judaism chosen by students from across the country. The answers were provided by scholars, rabbis and professors from around the world.

Ten years on, in 2005, the "60 Days for 60 Years" project became an even greater success with over 100,000 participants worldwide, each receiving a book of essays and a memorial card to learn for one victim of the Holocaust. Communities across the United Kingdom, South Africa, Australia, Canada, Israel, and the USA were engaged in a global project to remember the past to build the future.

Another ten years have now passed since that project. However, the idea remains as alive and relevant today as it was back in 1995. Then we remembered five thousand, ten years on we remembered hundreds of thousands. Today we hope to remember millions.

There are several other differences from ten years ago.

Firstly with the advent of social media, we will be providing abilities for global interaction through Twitter, Facebook and our website. We hope to link people worldwide as we collectively learn and remember during the 70 days. With our interactive 70 Days website at the heart of the project, we believe it will enhance your connection to the concepts and ideas you are reading and discussing with additional readings and videos. It will also allow you, via a link to the Yad Vashem Central Database of Shoah Victims' Names, to learn more about the person in whose memory you are learning.

Secondly, and more importantly, the world is unfortunately different from ten years ago. With extremism rising across Europe and the Middle East and a return to the 'world's oldest hatred' – antisemitism – it is time to remind ourselves about the end result of fanatical antisemitism and to steel ourselves to combat the delegitimisation of our people and our land.

The message of the 70 Days project is engagement with our heritage, to remind ourselves what being Jewish is all about and how despite what many have tried for millennia to destroy we continue to build.

This new book contains 70 thought-provoking questions, ideas, stories and articles which provide entry points to issues which are crucial to our religion and people. The book is divided into seven themes, one for each day of the week, covering a wide range of Jewish topics from cultural to historical and religious. As you will see, each essay is clearly labelled thematically. We hope this will add to your overall 70 Days for 70 Years learning experience.

The articles reflect the authors' own personal viewpoint. It is up to you, the reader, to take the study further, to find out what it means to be a Jew today, a journey which I hope this book will facilitate.

As you begin the 70 days of commemoration, consider the following. There are Jews reading this who are teenagers, there are Jews reading this who are in their 70s and 80s. There are Jews reading this in America, there are Jews reading this in South Africa, there are Jews reading this in Switzerland. There are Jews reading this in French, there are Jews reading this in English, there are Jews reading this in Hebrew. This is truly a global project for a global people.

70 years ago, an evil movement that rose up to destroy us was itself destroyed. 70 years on, we are learning in memory of those who were murdered and to learn for our future as well. These 70 days should be used as a time of commemoration for the person in whose memory you are learning and for the place they came from. People who had similar dreams, hopes and aspirations, until their lives were tragically cut short. Let us reclaim their lives from the Holocaust; let us, as Rabbi Lord Sacks says, "give them a living memorial."

For these 70 days I urge you to get involved. Not just for a Jewish life that was tragically cut short, but also for us, Jews in 2015, who are the guardians of our 3,000-year-old heritage. Be a part of one of the most ambitious and inspiring concepts ever attempted in the Jewish world. We all have a chance in the next ten weeks to remember a past that no longer is, and in those same ten weeks we have a chance to help build a future. The Jewish future. Our future.

Rabbi Andrew Shaw
Director, 70 Days for 70 Years and US Living and Learning
January 2015 / Shevat 5775

Contents

The Ziff Family

A key feature of the 70 Days for 70 Years project and its two predecessors is the concept of focussing on names and not numbers, of taking an individual and learning in his or her memory. Not only is every life precious, but every individual is a world in itself. Tragically, as a result of the Shoah, the individuals whom we are learning in memory of had their lives cut short. We, who are blessed to live in freedom, need to be reminded how much can be achieved in a lifetime by each and every one of us.

The late Arnold Ziff was an individual who achieved a significant amount in his lifetime alongside his devoted wife, Marjorie. As well as being a successful and respected businessman, his life featured impressive contributions to and engagement with the Jewish and non-Jewish worlds. His and Marjorie's passions were education, welfare, youth and Israel. For the Ziff family as a whole those areas of interest have always been and continue to be at the centre of their work.

Arnold was both President of the Leeds Jewish Welfare Board and the Leeds Jewish Housing Association. He worked tirelessly for Israel, a country he loved. For the wider community in Leeds and beyond, he devoted much time and energy, as well as philanthropic support. He was active in supporting a plethora of projects including helping to create the Leeds International Piano Competition and the Tropical World Garden in Roundhay Park.

Marjorie and her children, Michael, Ann and Edward, have

carried on his charitable ideals. They are actively involved in charity ventures both locally in Leeds and wider afield. They fundraised for and helped the procurement of the Marjorie & Arnold Ziff Community Centre in North Leeds which is now a focal point for much of the communal life in the city. They also continue to be involved with the Leeds Jewish Welfare Board.

In recent years, Marjorie has been awarded an MBE for her services to the community and Honorary Doctorates have been bestowed upon the family from the Universities of Leeds and Bradford and Leeds Becket University. The relationship the family enjoys with the University of Leeds goes even further with the Marjorie and Arnold Ziff building on campus. The family is also closely connected with Oncology research at Leeds Children's Hospital.

The Ziff family name is linked to a myriad of projects across the Jewish world, such as the Maccabi organisation, the dormitories at Kfar Galim School in Israel and The Zone Youth Centre in Leeds. These three projects again demonstrate the family's commitment to education, youth, social welfare and Israel.

In 2008 the family supported the previous 60 Days for 60 Years Israel project. At the launch of the project in Jerusalem, Marjorie spoke passionately about the connection of the family to the 60 Days Israel project and linked it also to the 60 Days Holocaust project of 2005. She said, "Whilst saying Kaddish for Arnold, we were inspired by the 60 Days for 60 Years project. It was a journey that gave us hope at a time when we needed it." The family's generous support for the 70 Days project will enable hundreds of thousands across the Jewish world to be inspired by the initiative and will provide a fitting memorial for the victims of the Shoah.

May the 70 Days for 70 Years project perpetuate Arnold's memory and give honour to Marjorie, children Michael, Ann and Edward, 13 grandchildren and 14 great grandchildren who continue the family legacy. May they continue to be a source of blessing to British Jewry, particularly their beloved Leeds, to Israel and to all the Jewish people.

Chief Rabbi Ephraim Mirvis

Acknowledgements

For a project of such magnitude, there are so many people to thank. The compilation of this book and the running of the project have taken months of work from so many quarters. It is impossible to thank every person who has contributed to making the 70 Days project a reality; however, the following deserve special mention:

- Rabbi Shapira from Netanya, whose ideas 20 years ago were the catalyst for the original project.
- Rabbi Maurice Hool, formerly of Kingsbury United Synagogue, who gave me the inspiration for the 50 Days concept in 1994.
- Chief Rabbi Ephraim Mirvis, our 70 Days President, for being such a driving force behind 70 Days.
- The Ziff family, whose generosity allowed 70 Days to get off the ground and flourish and whose constant engagement inspired us to take 70 Days to a far wider audience than we originally thought possible.
- Suzanne Goodman, whose belief in the project right at the start allowed us to begin the work and whose continual ideas and guidance have been invaluable. Her passion, patronage and commitment to 70 Days has been an inspiration. Her generosity has allowed the *70 Days* website to come to fruition.
- Rabbi Lord Jonathan Sacks, who has been a friend and strong supporter from the start of the original project 20 years ago, and whose support continues to this day, as our International President.
- Yad Vashem, for being a phenomenal resource and working with us closely, so that we can memorialise the six million in a meaningful and positive way.
- Rabbi Aubrey Hersh, for giving up so many days and nights to be an invaluable help with editing the essays – we could not have done it without him.
- David Kaplan, for his input into and passion for this project.
- Dayan Elimelech Vanzetta, for spreading the project globally and coordinating resources.

- Naomi Cowan, for liaising with our authors and compiling the book.
- Rabbi Johnny Solomon for compiling the Resource Pack for the project.
- Our website resource team: Rabbi Yisroel Binstock, Rebbetzin Ilana Epstein, Rebbetzin Lauren Levin, Rabbi Nicky Liss and Rabbi Nissan Wilson.
- Yossi Fachler, for his enormous efforts in helping bring this project to realisation.
- David Collins, for coordinating both our work with the Orthodox Union and with Tribe.
- Ian Myers, Richard Marcus, and the marketing team of the United Synagogue for all their guidance, help, and promotion.
- Michelle Kramer and Joanna Rose for their logistical assistance for the project.
- Ari Jesner and the Office of the Chief Rabbi for their support.
- Dan Sacker and Joanna Benarroch for all their help with the involvement of Rabbi Sacks.
- Rabbi Baruch Davis and the Rabbinical Council of the United Synagogue (RCUS) Executive and Committee and Rabbi Mordechai Ginsbury of P'eir for their amazing support and collegiality.
- Gaby Godfrey and the Tribe Israel team, for all their help with 70 Days in Israel.
- Rabbi Doron (Laurence) Perez and World Mizrachi, for their support and dedication to both the 60 Days and the 70 Days projects.
- Kerry Rosenfeld for her key involvement in bringing 70 Days to life.
- Raphaël Freeman at Renana Typesetting, for his unique design for the book.
- Rabbi YY Rubinstein, working on the project in the USA.
- Liz Fishel, for coordinating our efforts in the USA.
- Rabbi Davey Blackman and Lindi Stein, for driving the project 'down under' in Australia.
- Jonny Lipczer and Lesley Schwartz, for their dedication to bringing 70 Days to Canada.

- Rabbi Steven Weil and the Orthodox Union, for bringing 70 Days to their communities across America.
- Rabbi Hershel Becker, whose enthusiasm brought 70 Days to the USA.
- Yad Vashem UK, for their support, advice and partnership.
- All our donors and supporters, for their help in making 70 Days possible.
- Creative & Commercial, especially Barry Frankfurt and Charlotte Gillis, for their contribution to the website and social media.
- Ivor Rosenthal and the staff at Kellmatt, for printing and distribution.
- And finally, Matti Fruhman, for his wonderful management of the project. His determination and perseverance have turned the dream into reality.

Rabbi Andrew Shaw
Director, 70 Days for 70 Years and US Living and Learning.

LETTERS OF SUPPORT

Office *of* The
CHIEF RABBI

I would like to congratulate all who are responsible for bringing the "70 Days for 70 Years" project to fruition. Many thousands of people will be significantly informed and inspired by this publication.

With the passing of each year, more survivors of the most terrible crime in human history are gathered into the company of those they lost. We must soon contemplate a world in which first-person testimony is available only in archives, and when the last efforts have been made to record the most painful of memories for the sake of truth and for posterity.

We remember not just the wrongs and the sufferings and the losses of our people, but also their achievements, the culture, the scholarship, the charitable and educational institutions they created, the values they lived by, and the loving homes they built.

This volume will form part of a remarkable and sacred project, to hand on the lessons of the past in order to inspire the future. May it help us to understand the enduring gift that a lost generation managed, against all odds, to pass on to us: a fine example and a set of Jewish ideals that form an essential part of our identity. May their memory be for a blessing.

By studying the content of this book, we will ensure that the victims of the Shoah are not forgotten. Through celebrating our Judaism and committing ourselves to live by our timely and timeless values, we will achieve what the victims were so cruelly prevented from doing. We carry with us the legacy of the past and its inspiration for the future. Armed with information and education, we can face the future with confidence and commitment.

Chief Rabbi Ephraim Mirvis
Chief Rabbi of the United Hebrew
Congregations of the Commonwealth

The US

This project has inspired thousands of people across numerous countries and of all ages. Many families in our community have lost relatives and friends in the Holocaust and we feel very close to the victims. Sadly, there are fewer and fewer people still with us who survived the concentration camps and can give us first hand testimony, so it is now up to the next generation to keep the memories alive.

"70 Days for 70 Years" is a very effective way of achieving this. The idea of learning each day for 70 days in the memory of someone who perished in the Holocaust means that that person is not forgotten. Learning for a period of 70 days from the time of the liberation of Auschwitz to the first night of Passover helps us to remember the importance of freedom to us all.

I would like to congratulate the United Synagogue Living and Learning department for generating this excellent idea and relentlessly pursuing every detail until it became a reality. So many people have been involved that it is hard to single out individuals, but I do know that this would not have happened without the dedication of Rabbi Andrew Shaw. I would like to take this opportunity to thank all the generous donors who made this project feasible and in particular the Ziff family.

I am so pleased that the United Synagogue has been able to inspire other communities across the Jewish world to join this initiative. We have shown how we can lead the way in this project and in so many other areas of Jewish life.

My contemporaries and I realise we are part of a very fortunate generation that missed the First and Second World Wars – but that good fortune comes with a sacred obligation – to do whatever we can to remember those who died so we can enjoy our freedom today.

Stephen Pack
President
United Synagogue

ראש הממשלה
Prime Minister

August 18, 2014
כ״ב אב, תשע״ד

Dear Friends,

As we commemorate the 70th anniversary of the liberation of Auschwitz, we recommit ourselves to ensuring that the unparalleled tragedy of the Holocaust is never forgotten.

The 70 Days for 70 Years project aims to educate about that dark period of Jewish history. In so doing, you will not only be preserving the memory of those who were murdered in the Holocaust, but also reminding us that we must remain ever vigilant in the face of anti-Semitism and other forms of hatred.

I commend all those involved in this important project.

Sincerely,

Benjamin Netanyahu

Jerusalem, Israel

Yad Vashem

Remembering the People behind the Names

"I should like someone to remember that there once lived a person named David Berger..."

David Berger, from Przemysl, Poland, was shot in Vilna in July 1941, at the age of 22.

From the moment a person is born, their name becomes their identity. The mere mention of a name evokes memories of an individual's character and achievements long after his or her death. In the aftermath of the Shoah, many victims were left with no tombstones or descendants to be named after them; each victim represents an unending potential chain of creation that was lost to the Jewish people and all humanity. Realizing our moral imperative to salvage their memory, we seek to collect and document the victims' names and to commemorate the lives that were so brutally cut short.

Contrary to myth, in most cases, the Germans did not create orderly lists of the Jews that they murdered. Generally, names were ignored and replaced with numbers, in a systematic effort to annihilate not just the victims themselves, but also their identities. Since the 1950s, Yad Vashem has encouraged surviving relatives and friends to fill out Pages of Testimony – unique forms containing the biographical details and, when available, photographs of Holocaust victims, which are then stored for perpetuity in Yad Vashem's Hall of Names. These pages represent our effort to redeem the individual identities of every Jew lost in the Holocaust.

These private memorials have been transformed into public commemoration for the Jewish people and all of mankind. This ceaseless endeavour has to date identified more than four million names of Shoah victims, which are now documented in the Central Database of Shoah Victims' Names (www.yadvashem.org). Roughly half of the victims' names in the database were derived from a variety of archival sources and post-war commemoration projects. The rest are recorded on "Pages of Testimony" submitted by relatives and others who knew of the victims. The outstanding universal value of the Pages of Testimony Memorial Collection has been recognized by UNESCO, which inscribed it this year in its prestigious Memory of the World Register.

I encourage you, the participants of "70 Days for 70 Years," to utilize the vast information available in the Names Database in order to learn more about the lives of the individuals whose memories you are commemorating. In addition, I call upon you and members of your community to search for the names of relatives or others you may know of who were victims of the Shoah, and to submit a Page of Testimony for each previously unregistered victim to Yad Vashem.

These names are a vital part of our shared legacy and national heritage. Please help us to preserve them in the collective memory of the Jewish People for generations to come.

Avner Shalev
Chairman of the Yad Vashem Directorate

ORTHODOX UNION
תורה ומצוות
Enhancing Jewish Life

"70 Days for 70 Years" is a collection of fascinating insights into multiple topics associated with Jewish philosophy, the Jewish calendar, Jewish ethics, and issues confronting thinking human beings. The essays that I have read are not only stimulating, but will provoke meaningful conversation, and are substantive, thoughtful, and educational. Ten years ago, when Tribe published "60 Days for 60 Years," thousands of individuals used that volume as a source for daily learning, Shabbat table discussions, and study sessions. Many individuals and communities have used the work over the last decade, and it is my feeling that the success of "70 Days for 70 Years" will be even more impactful.

As an American Jew, it is a great honour to partner with my peers on the other side of the pond, to learn from them, and experience the impact they are having on world Jewry. This work is a gift that will have meaning to Jews of all backgrounds and will serve as a catalyst for many stimulating conversations.

Kol HaKavod to all those involved in its production and to those communities and individuals participating in the learning experience of "70 Days for 70 Years."

Sincerely,

Rabbi Steven Weil
Senior Managing Director of the Orthodox Union

MIZRACHI
WORLD MOVEMENT העולמית המזרחי

In Buchenwald 70 years ago, stood one of the concentration camps youngest survivors – Lulec Lau. Young Lulec lost his parents and almost every member of his family. Remarkably, though, as we all know, Lulec grew up to be Chief Rabbi Yisrael Meir Lau, a Chief Rabbi of the modern State of Israel. His story is the story of our nation. Fittingly, Chief Rabbi Lau will be the one launching the global initiative in Jerusalem for 70 Days for 70 Years.

The World Mizrachi Movement is enormously privileged to be a partner of the United Synagogue for this launch, as well as a global partner in this wonderful project. Equally, our Mizrachi UK branch is privileged to be a partner of the local UK edition.

Out of the depths of the most unimaginable and horrific suffering, the Jewish people chose the greatest form of vengeance – a reaffirmation of life. Countless people dedicated themselves to rebuilding the Torah world that was lost, and to recreating Jewish sovereignty in our homeland. Two astounding facts testify to their miraculous success. Firstly, there are over six million Jews living in Israel today – an incredibly significant number. Those who attempted to destroy Jewish life inadvertently aided its greatest affirmation. Secondly, Israel's largest yeshiva, the Mir Yeshiva has larger numbers of yeshiva students than all the Yeshivot of pre-war Europe put together. There are arguably more people studying Torah today than any time in Jewish history. Those who wished to destroy the Jewish way of life inadvertently gave impetus to its rebirth. The miraculous resurgence of both Torah and Israel is the astounding story of our generation.

Yishar Koach to the United Synagogue for this extraordinary project: bringing together Israel and Diaspora communities, Jews from all backgrounds, merging the memory of the past with a vision for the future and connecting us all through the power of Torah learning.

Steven Blumgart
Chairman – Mizrachi UK

Rav Doron (Laurence) Perez
Director General – World Mizrachi

RABBI
SACKS

Ten years ago, as Chief Rabbi, I was involved with a wonderfully imaginative project by the United Synagogue called "60 Days for 60 Years." Its success and impact across Anglo-Jewry has led to the revival of the project – "70 Days for 70 Years" – that seeks to reach beyond the UK and impact Jewish communities around the world.

As International President, I am delighted to be associated with the "70 Days for 70 Years" initiative, not only because of the ongoing importance of Holocaust remembrance, but because behind it lies a set of profound Jewish ideas.

The first is remembering for life: the idea that we take the tragedies of Jewish history and turn them into lessons for the future. What the victims of the Shoah died for, we commit ourselves to live for. We cannot bring the dead back to life, but we can bring their memory back to life and ensure that they are not forgotten – and that we undertake in our lives to do what they were so cruelly prevented from doing.

The second is learning as a bond between the living and the dead. The words of Torah are beyond time, and through them we are connected with all previous generations of Jews. Learning in the name of one of the victims of the Shoah symbolically rewrites their letter into the Torah scroll of the Jewish people.

The third is the act of rededication. One-third of our people died in the Shoah, but the Jewish people as a whole refused to die. A mere three years after the Shoah, it created the greatest single collective affirmation of Jewish life in 2000 years: the State of Israel. Every Jew today carries the legacy of the past and its hopes for the future. The most important thing we can possibly do is to ensure that Judaism and the Jewish people face the future with confidence and commitment. That is our gift to the past – and its challenge to us.

So: congratulations to all those who have brought this project to fruition – and thanks to you for taking part. May your 70 days of study turn the memory of one of the victims of the Shoah into a blessing.

With blessings and best wishes,

Rabbi Lord Jonathan Sacks
International President, 70 Days for 70 Years

JEWISH LEADERSHIP
C O U N C I L

I am particularly pleased to write in support of the "70 Days for 70 Years" project, as I am in the midst of the work of the Holocaust Commission, set up by the Prime Minister, the RT. Hon. David Cameron MP, which is tasked with making recommendations for how best we can create a permanent and lasting remembrance of the Holocaust in the United Kingdom, as the number of survivors dwindles year by year, and ensure that future generations of British citizens understand the Holocaust and take forward its lessons into their lives. We look forward to presenting our recommendations to the Prime Minister in the next few months and, as I think about our work, I am drawn to this great initiative for our community.

This book, "70 Days for 70 Years," enables members of the community to engage in learning, self-development, and Jewish education, in the merit and memory of a victim of the Holocaust over a 70-day period, culminating in Pesach this year. This, in itself, provides a lasting and positive legacy and a permanent remembrance of the Holocaust.

I remember the precursor to this project, "60 Days for 60 Years." I know of many people who, like me, benefited from learning and exploring more about their Jewish identity, and I know that it provided a tangible, personally enriching, and meaningful way to remember the individual victims of the greatest human crime that mankind has ever committed.

The enormity of the Holocaust is often brought home to us when we talk of it in terms of the deaths of six million Jews. However, while it is right to think about the calamity that befell us, and indeed mankind, in terms of its unimaginable magnitude, we must never forget that this happened to individual Jews; it is their humanity that we must cherish in our memory. Each was an individual, with a family, with friends, with people who loved them, with hopes, dreams, and aspirations. It is right therefore to learn and perpetuate our rich Jewish life in memory of the individual victim and not just the collective tragedy. "70 Days for 70 Years" gives us all the opportunity to improve our learning and our knowledge whilst also holding and cherishing the memory of one individual victim.

In recent months, it has been shameful to hear and read of individuals who invoke imagery, language, and ideology from the Holocaust when criticising the policies of the Israeli government. This has no place in a free and tolerant society. With projects such as "70 Days for 70 Years," we can demonstrate that as Jews, our aim is to honour the memory of those whose lives were cruelly extinguished by helping to create a better and more caring world, and by enriching our own personal knowledge of peace, Jewish values, and kindness.

I wish this project every success and look forward to the inspiration and enrichment that this book will provide.

Sincerely,

Mick Davis
Chair of Trustees, Jewish Leadership Council,
Chair, Prime Minister's Holocaust Commission

THE BOARD
OF DEPUTIES OF BRITISH JEWS
Proud to represent the community

I am delighted to support the "70 Days for 70 Years" project. The Holocaust is not merely one of the most dramatic events in Jewish history, but it is also one of the main elements in the identity of British Jews today. However, with the passage of time, as fewer survivors are left to tell their stories, it is passing from memory to history, and the challenge of keeping the recollection alive becomes ever greater.

The best way to meet that challenge is by doing precisely what the architects of that tragedy were trying to prevent – by promoting the continued existence and vitality of Jewish life. We know that the Nazis, while hating all Jews, showed particular viciousness and cruelty toward religious Jews by humiliating them, mocking their practises, and frequently forcing them to breach fundamental religious principles, thus adding vicious insult to deadly injury.

That is why a learning project stretching from just before the date of the commemoration of the liberation of Auschwitz to *Seder* night, the date of our redemption in the Bible and the anniversary of the Warsaw Ghetto uprising, is such an inspired idea. To demonstrate, in a graphic way, our ongoing commitment to our tradition and history shows, with complete clarity, that the Nazis – though they succeeded in bringing misery to millions on a scale never seen before in history – failed in their objective to put an end to our tradition.

The United Synagogue is to be applauded for this marvellous initiative.

Vivian Wineman
President, The Board of Deputies of British Jews

Our identity lies within our memory; without the collective recall of our past trials and triumphs, we would have no sense of who we are. The Jewish people have, therefore, always drawn their national consciousness from history. To the Jew, two thousand years ago is as relevant as yesterday. We live in the present, with a past that is ever-alive before us. Thus, the days of old are never old, but simply, *yemei kedem* – "days which came before."

At the end of Moses' life, he spoke to the Children of Israel and left them words of advice and caution. Perhaps the most prominent and famous of these was his charge: "Remember the days that came before, understand the years of each generation" (Deuteronomy 32:7). When we wish to cultivate a robust identity, we are careful not to be selective with our memories. We remember both the painful and pleasant times and we grow from seeing ourselves connected to and emerging from them.

The "70 Days for 70 Years" project comes from the awareness of this ideal. For our memories to remain vibrant and relevant, they require active recall and thought. This project aims to accomplish this in a deeply meaningful way by connecting to our memories with study. It is a project that fulfils not only the memory of the dark and harrowing days of the Holocaust, but also attempts to better *contemplate* that generation and its events in a way that brings growth to our lives.

We pray that through this endeavour, we, the "cinders saved from the fire," may honour and further hallow the memory of the six million holy victims.

Joseph Dweck
Senior Rabbi to the Spanish and Portuguese Jews' Congregation

"And to them will I give in my house and within my walls a memorial and a name (a *"yad va-shem"*)...that shall not be cut off" (Isaiah 56:5).

As the Jewish people's living memorial to the Holocaust, Yad Vashem safeguards the memory of the past and imparts its meaning for future generations. Established in 1953, as the world centre for documentation, research, education, and commemoration of the Holocaust, Yad Vashem is today a dynamic and vital place of intergenerational and international encounter.

The Holocaust was the murder of six million Jews by Nazi Germany. While the Nazi persecution of the Jews began in 1933, the mass murder was committed during World War II. It took the Germans and their accomplices four and a half years to murder six million Jews. They were at their most efficient from April to November 1942 – 250 days in which they murdered some two and a half million Jews. They never showed any restraint, they slowed down only when they began to run out of Jews to kill, and they only stopped when the Allies defeated them.

There was no escape. The murderers were not content with destroying the communities; they also traced each hidden Jew and hunted down each fugitive. The crime of being a Jew was so great, that every single one had to be put to death – the men, the women, the children, the committed, the disinterested, the apostates, the healthy and creative, the sickly, and the lazy – all were meant to suffer and die, with no reprieve, no hope, no possible amnesty, nor chance for alleviation.

Most of the Jews of Europe were dead by 1945. A civilization that had flourished for almost 2,000 years was no more. The survivors – one from a town, two from a host – dazed, emaciated, bereaved beyond measure, gathered the remnants of their vitality and the remaining sparks of their humanity, and rebuilt. They never meted out justice to their tormentors – for what justice could ever be achieved after such a crime? Rather, they turned to rebuilding new families, forever under the shadow of those absent; new life stories, forever warped by the wounds; new communities, forever haunted by the loss.

"70 years ago, a nation rose up to gather us together to destroy us. 70 years on, we are gathering together to learn in memory of those who were murdered and to learn for our future."

Yad Vashem – UK Foundation is proud to be associated with the vision of this project.

"70 days for 70 years" will mean that there will be Jews of all ages from all over the world connecting, to remember the past to build the future.

Simon Bentley
Chairman
Yad Vashem – UK Foundation

REMEMBER THE PAST

Remember the Past to Build the Future

Rabbi Lord Jonathan Sacks
International President 70 Days for 70 Years

The Holocaust is a black hole in human history. There was never anything like it before, and if humanity is to be worthy of its existence, there will never be anything like it again.

At some time in the spring or early summer of 1941, Hitler issued an order for a "Final Solution to the Jewish Question," a brutal euphemism for the planned, systematic destruction of the Jewish people. Four years later, as World War II came to an end, the first soldiers to enter the concentration camps began to realise what had been done, and they did not believe it. Six million human beings, among them one and a half million children, had been shot, gassed, burned, or buried alive for no other reason than that they were Jews. Where once there had been community after community of sages and scholars, poets and mystics, intellectuals and visionaries, there was the stench of death. As Jews, we mourn and, still today, we refuse to be comforted.

The Holocaust raises many questions. In an essay entitled "*Kol Dodi Dofek*," the late Rabbi Joseph Soloveitchik made a profound distinction between two Jewish responses to suffering. There is the metaphysical question, "Why did this happen?" But there is also the halachic question, "What then shall I do?" The halachic response invites us to react to tragedy not as objects, but as subjects, not as figures of fate, but as masters of our destiny. We are not defined by what happens to us, but by how we respond.

Judaism has never sought to deny the existence of evil. But, equally, it has not sought to come to terms with it by explaining it away, mystically or metaphysically. "There is," says Rabbi Soloveitchik, "a theological answer to 'Why did this happen?'" But it must always elude us, for we are not God, nor can we see events from the perspective of eternity. Halachah summons us not to understand

and thus accept the existence of evil, but instead to fight it, as partners with God in the process of redemption.

In this mode of Jewish spirituality, there is a profound insistence on human dignity, often in the face of immense and unfathomable suffering. The halachic response is not naïve. It does not hide from questions, but it is courageous. It says: we must continue to affirm Jewish life even in the absence of answers. In that, there is a faith that defies even the Angel of Death.

One of the most important halachic responses to tragedy is the act of remembering, *Yizkor*. More than it has history, the Jewish people has memory. There is no word for history in the *Tanach*, and modern Hebrew had to borrow one, *historiah*. But the word *zachor* (remember), occurs no fewer than 169 times in the Hebrew Bible. The difference between them is this: history is someone else's story; memory is my story. In history, we recall what happened. Through memory, we identify with what happened so that it becomes part of us and who we are. History is the story of a past that is dead. Memory is the story of a future. We cannot bring the dead to life, but we can keep their memory alive. That is what the Jewish people always did for those who died as martyrs *al kiddush Hashem* (sanctifying God's name). They never forgot them, as we must never forget the victims of the Holocaust.

But there is a specifically Jewish way of remembering. When the word *yizkor* is mentioned in the Torah, it refers not to the past, but to the present and to renewal. "*Va-yizkor Elokim et Rachel*" (God remembered Rachel) and gave her a child, and thus new life. "*Va-yizkor Elokim et berito*" (God remembered His covenant) and began the process of rescuing the Israelites from Egypt. When we remember as Jews, we do so for the sake of the future, so that those who died may live on in us.

Commemorating the 70 years that have passed with 70 days of study, linking individuals with Holocaust victims, and communities with communities that perished – this is the Jewish way of remembering. Few things could do more to give those who died a living memorial.

At the core of Judaism is an affirmation of life. Unlike other religions we do not venerate death. In Judaism, death defiles. Moses asked the Israelites to "choose life," and his words still echo today.

One-third of our people died because they were Jews. The most profound Judaic affirmation we can make is to live because we are Jews – to live as Jews, affirming our faith with courage, our identity with pride, refusing to be traumatised by evil, or intimidated by antisemitism.

Whenever, through indifference or fear, we drift away from living as Jews, the Holocaust claims yet more belated victims. Hitler's antisemitism was not accidental. Hitler declared that "conscience is a Jewish invention," and he was right. Nazi Germany was intended to demonstrate the triumph of everything Jews had fought against since the days of Abraham and Sarah: might as against right, power as against justice, racism as opposed to the respect for human dignity, violence as opposed to the sanctity of human life. Jews have always lived by and for a different set of values and, as a result, we have always been called on to have the courage to be different. We need that courage now. It is not too much to say that humanity needs it now.

If each of us in the coming year makes a significant personal gesture to show that Judaism is alive and being lived, there can be no more momentous signal to humanity that evil does not have the final victory, because *Am Yisrael Chai*, the Jewish people lives.

One Person, One Name

Chief Rabbi Yisrael Meir Lau
Former Chief Rabbi of Israel,
Chief Rabbi of Tel Aviv and Chairman of Yad Vashem

It wasn't until I came to the American Society for Yad Vashem's annual dinner that I finally realized how to convey the horror of the Holocaust to the next generation.

What was the reason survivors kept quiet for decades following the war? It was because nobody could understand six million deaths. It was too big a number to comprehend.

At eight years old, I was the youngest survivor of Buchenwald. When I was ten years old, I picked up *The Diary of Anne Frank*. I wanted to see what everybody was talking about. I was astonished. That's all? The whole book is not to be compared to one day in Buchenwald. Where is the concentration camp, the torture, the killings? I couldn't understand why people were so excited about this book.

When I got older, I realised that the book's success lay in the fact that it didn't speak about millions. It was one person's story. With one human being you can identify.

For the first time I understood what Yad Vashem means. As it says in Isaiah: "I will give them *yad va-shem* – a hand and a name." One hand, one name. If it is single, it will convince you. You cannot bear millions of deaths, but one name you can understand.

That was why Anne Frank's diary was so powerful – it was the story of one individual. Anyone can identify with another single human being. And that is why 70 Days for 70 Years is so powerful – we each can identify with one victim and learn in their memory – one person, one name.

Pictures from the Past

With thanks to Ganzach Kiddush Hashem, Yad Vashem & USHMM for permission to print these photos. Photo research by Rabbi Aubrey Hersh.

These photos are both a chronological record of the Holocaust as well as a window onto the religious persecution and strength of the Jews.

Munich – 1933. *Hitler meets with admirers in the Braune Haus. Hitler had great appeal to the German people and was elected democratically in the 1930s.*

Vienna – 1938. *Jews humiliated by being forced to clean the streets, while onlookers crowd around and laugh. These scenes took place immediately after the German Anschluss in March 1938.*

Baden-Baden – 1938. *Jews ordered to walk in the street after Kristall-nacht on 10th November 1938, holding a sign which read: "God does not forgive us." The Germans were determined to both denegrate the Jews as well as desecrate Judaism itself.*

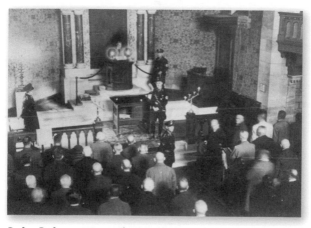

Baden-Baden – 1938. *Jews forced to stand in a synagogue bare-headed and listen to an antisemitic speech.*

Warsaw – 1940. *Jewish men in the Ghetto being rounded up for slave labour.*

Warsaw – 1941. *Even with constant starvation and poverty, Jews in the Ghetto still practised giving charity where possible.*

Warsaw – 1941. *Outdoor prayers on Yom Kippur.*

לִפְנֵי אֲכִילַת חָמֵץ יֹאמַר בְּכַוָּנַת הַלֵּב :
אָבִינוּ שֶׁבַּשָּׁמַיִם הִנֵּה גָּלוּי וְיָדוּעַ לְפָנֶיךָ שֶׁרְצוֹנֵנוּ לַעֲשׂוֹת
רְצוֹנֶךָ וְלַחֹג אֶת חַג הַפֶּסַח בַּאֲכִילַת מַצָּה וּבִשְׁמִירַת אִסּוּר
חָמֵץ. אַךְ עַל זֹאת דָּאֲבָה לִבֵּנוּ שֶׁהַשִּׁעְבּוּד מְעַכֵּב אוֹתָנוּ
וַאֲנַחְנוּ נִמְצָאִים בְּסַכָּנַת נְפָשׁוֹת. הִנְנוּ מוּכָנִים וּמְזֻמָּנִים
לְקַיֵּם מִצְוָתְךָ וְחַי בָּהֶם וְלֹא שֶׁיָּמוּת בָּהֶם וְלִזָּהֵר מֵאַזְהָרַת
הִשָּׁמֶר לְךָ וּשְׁמֹר נַפְשְׁךָ מְאֹד. עַל כֵּן תְּפִלָּתֵנוּ לְךָ
שֶׁתְּחַיֵּנוּ וּתְקַיְּמֵנוּ וְתִגְאָלֵנוּ בִּמְהֵרָה לִשְׁמֹר חֻקֶּיךָ
וְלַעֲשׂוֹת רְצוֹנֶךָ וּלְעָבְדְּךָ בְּלֵבָב שָׁלֵם אָמֵן

Bergen-Belsen – April 1944. *An incredible prayer of faith, composed by prisoners in the concentration camp, in which they state that they will eat chametz over Pesach – brokenheartedly – because the mitzvah to remain alive is more important than the transgression of eating chametz.*

The last sentence reads: "We pray that You sustain us and redeem us soon, so that we can once again observe Your commandments"

Auschwitz-Birkenau – May 1944. *Part of a transport of Jews from Hungary, who have just been selected to be gassed and cremated, walking towards Crematoria II.*

Budapest – November 1944. *Jews being rounded up by the pro-Nazi Arrow Cross guards in a desperate attempt to murder the remaining 250,000 Jews of Budapest before the war ended*

Buchenwald district – May 1945. *A case of wedding rings belonging to Jewish victims that was found by the allies in Germany after WWII. It is estimated that the Nazis plundered 100 tons of gold during the war.*

Bergen-Belsen – May 1945. *British Army Chaplain Rev Hardman (see Essay 28), in front of a mass grave of Jews who died of illness and malnutrition, shortly after the liberation of the camp in April 1945.*

70 DAYS FOR 70 YEARS

Rabbi Lord Jonathan Sacks

Surviving Exile

In her book, *The Watchman's Rattle*, subtitled 'Thinking Our Way
Out of Extinction,"[1] Rebecca Costa delivers a fascinating account
of how civilizations die. Their problems become too complex.
Societies reach what she calls a cognitive threshold. They simply
can't chart a path from the present to the future.

The example she gives is the Mayans. For a period of 3,500 years,
between 2600 BCE and 900 CE, they developed an extraordinary
civilization, spreading over what is today Mexico, Guatemala,
Honduras, El Salvador, and Belize with an estimated population
of 15 million people.

Not only were they master potters, weavers, architects, and
farmers, but they also developed an intricate calendar system, with
celestial charts to track the movements of the stars and predict
weather patterns. They had their own unique form of writing and
advanced mathematics. Most impressively, they developed a wa-
ter-supply infrastructure involving a complex network of reservoirs,
canals, dams, and levees.

Then, suddenly, for reasons we still don't fully understand, the
entire system collapsed. Some time between the middle of the
eighth and ninth century, the majority of the Mayan people simply
disappeared. There have been many theories as to why it happened:
drought, overpopulation, epidemics, war, or a combination of
these and other factors. One way or another, having survived for
35 centuries, Mayan civilization became extinct.

Rebecca Costa's argument is that whatever the causes, the
Mayan collapse, like the fall of the Roman Empire and the Khmer

---

1. See Rebecca Costa, *The Watchman's Rattle: Thinking Our Way Out of
Extinction*. New York: Vanguard Press, 2010.

Empire in Cambodia, occurred because problems became too many and complicated for the people of that time and place to solve. There was cognitive overload, and systems broke down.

It can happen to any civilization. It may, she says, be happening to ours. The first sign of breakdown is gridlock. Instead of dealing with what everyone can see are major problems, people continue as usual and simply pass their problems on to the next generation. The second sign is a retreat into irrationality. Since people can no longer cope with the facts, they take refuge in more extreme religious consolations.

Which makes the case of Jews and Judaism fascinating. It is difficult at this distance in time to realise the depth of the crisis represented by the destruction of the Second Temple in the year 70 CE, and the later suppression of the disastrous Bar Kochba revolt (132–135 CE). The very foundations of Jewish existence had been destroyed. There was now no Temple or Jewish sovereignty, and Jerusalem had been razed to the ground and rebuilt as a Roman city, *Aelia Capitolina,* in which Jews were forbidden to live.

Centuries earlier, following the destruction of the First Temple, the people had come close to despair. A psalm from that period has left us with an indelible record of their mood: 'By the rivers of Babylon we sat and wept when we remembered Zion... How can we sing the songs of the Lord in a strange land?' That moment, though, brought its own consolation. There were prophets of the stature of Jeremiah and Ezekiel to assure the people that they would return. The exile would be finite, temporary. There was no such assurance in Roman times. To be sure, great figures like Rabbi Akiva were confident that redemption would come. But his hopes were also invested in Bar Kochba, and when that uprising failed, so too did any hope that Israel's fortunes would be restored in the foreseeable future.

A midrash on Jacob's dream of a ladder and angels tells us something of the mood of those times:

> The Holy One, blessed be He, showed Jacob the angel of Babylon ascending and descending, the angel of Media ascending and descending, the angel of Greece ascending and descending, and the angel of Rome ascending [but not descending].

Jacob was afraid. He thought: Is it possible this one will never descend? The Holy One, blessed be He, said to him: Fear not, My servant Jacob.

Every other exile had a finite duration, but the fall of Israel under Rome seemed to extend indefinitely into the future.

What happened next is one of the great, if quiet, dramas of history. The Jewish people, so bound to time and space – seeing God in history and their home in a specific land – reconstituted itself as a nation *outside* time and space. Prayer took the place of sacrifice. Repentance, which had been an addition to the great ritual of atonement performed by the High Priest in the Holy of Holies, became its substitute. The synagogue – a building that could be anywhere – became a fragment of the Temple in Jerusalem. The Jewish people itself, once a nation in its own land, became a virtual community scattered through space, bound now by a mystical sense of collective responsibility ('Israel,' said Rabbi Shimon bar Yochai, is 'like a single body with a single soul: when one is afflicted, all feel the pain.'). In exile everywhere, they were at home in a text. 'The Torah,' said the German poet Heinrich Heine, 'became the portable homeland of the Jew.'

These developments did not happen overnight. In a sense, Jews had been preparing them ever since the Persian exile. It was then, beginning with Ezra, that a succession of scribes, scholars, and sages began to reshape Israel from the People of the Land to the People of the Book. They neither abandoned their past, nor clung to it. They thought through the future and created institutions like the synagogue and house of study and school that could be built anywhere and sustain Jewish identity even in the most adverse conditions.

The result was that Jews succeeded in doing what no other people had ever done. They sustained their identity and way of life through almost 2,000 years of exile. Despite the hostility showed to them – Max Weber once described them as a 'pariah people' – they kept their dignity and self-respect. Through some of the worst sufferings ever experienced by a group, they preserved their hope: 'Next year in Jerusalem; next year, free.'

That is no small achievement. The world's greatest civilizations have all, in time, become extinct, while Judaism has always survived. In one sense, that was surely Divine Providence. But in another it was the foresight of our Sages who resisted cognitive breakdown, created solutions today for the problems of tomorrow, who did not seek refuge in the irrational, and who quietly built the Jewish future.

Surely there is a lesson here for the Jewish people today. Plan generations ahead. Think at least 25 years into the future. Contemplate worst-case scenarios. Ask "what would we do, if...?" What saved the Jewish people throughout the darkest moments of their history was an ability, despite their deep and abiding faith, never to let go of rational thought, and, despite their loyalty to the past, to keep planning for the future. That is how to ensure the triumph of faith over circumstance.

Rabbi Dr Abraham Twerski

Defining Spirituality

Spirituality is a frequently used term, but one that is rather difficult to describe. I would like to share a definition which I have used professionally for many years, although our journey should begin by stating what Jewish spirituality is *not*. It is *not* withdrawing from society, eating the bare minimum, and spending the entire day in meditation; the Torah does not advocate these. We are permitted to eat meat and drink wine judiciously; we are required to marry and have families. In short, we are to lead normal lives, but all the activities of normal living should be within the scope of spirituality.

Let us perhaps define a more elementary term: *humanity*. You may say that this has been adequately described in science where we learned that the human being is *Homo sapiens*, a classification which is universally accepted. And, indeed, in Latin, this appellation sounds both sophisticated and innocent, but to understand it, we need to translate it. *Homo* refers to a genus, a family of animals of which man is a member, and he shares this genus with others, such as monkeys, gorillas and baboons. Man is distinct from the other members of his group by being a species of *Homo* which is *sapiens*, a term that essentially refers to intellect. *Homo sapiens* thus means "an ape with intellect."

Yet, while intellect is an important and distinct trait of man, it is not the only feature which distinguishes him from animals. There are a number of other elements that are unique and which, alongside intellect, form that definition.

A human being has the capacity to *learn from the past*. Animals may, indeed, learn from previous experiences, but they are unable to learn from the experiences of past generations. Suppose a race horse runs the Kentucky Derby and loses by just a neck. Were this horse to sire a foal who grows to be a race horse, this second generation horse could not study the race its father lost, to discover where he had erred, and avoid this mistake.

A second feature that is uniquely human *is the capacity to think about the purpose of one's existence*. It is safe to assume that animals do not reflect on the purpose of their existence, and while some people may not do so either, they nevertheless have the ability and capacity to do so.

One might perhaps challenge this and ask: "How do you make such assumptions about animals? Perhaps they do have these capacities, but we are unaware of them." To this I would respond, how do you know that animals are not *sapiens*? Perhaps they have the equivalent of the dialogues of Plato of which we are unaware, just as they are undoubtedly unaware of human knowledge. Inasmuch as no one seems to challenge the scientific assumption that intellect is unique to man, we reasonably have the same right to make these assumptions about other capacities which we do not observe in animals.

Another important unique feature is man's *capacity to volitionally improve himself*. It is unlikely that a cow, for example, ever thinks, "What must I do to become a better cow?" Only a human being can reflect upon and implement self-improvement. Animals are born essentially complete, and change by growing larger and stronger. There can be some rather radical changes, such as when the caterpillar becomes a beautiful butterfly, but these changes are not something which the caterpillar decides to do volitionally. A caterpillar is certainly not capable of deciding that it is afraid of heights and does not wish to become a butterfly. It is programmed to change.

Additionally, an animal does not have *the capacity to delay gratification*. Whatever an animal desires, it will attempt to get, unless it fears immediate consequence, such as an attack. And, whereas human beings also have desire, they are able to postpone it if they choose. This is also expressed in their *capacity to control anger*. An enraged animal acts promptly out of anger, whereas a person is able to suppress emotion, by overcoming natural reaction and making decisions contrary to instinct.

Humans are also able *to reflect upon the consequences of their actions,* and how it will affect themselves and others in the future. This is because man is the only living creature that can be considered *truly free.* Animals, even in the wild, are not free because they are under the domination of their body and instinct and cannot make a free choice.

Obviously not all human decisions are made in the spirit of free will. People may sometimes quell a desire because of fear of retribution. Yet when there is no possibility of detection, and the person, nevertheless, suppresses the desire, and restrains themselves simply because it is morally and ethically wrong, they are exemplifying a uniquely human trait.

Taking *all* the traits that are unique to man and grouping them together gives a sum total of what I refer to as the *spirit.* We believe that the spirit was instilled in man by God at the time of man's creation. Those who do not believe that God created man must, nevertheless, agree that man has a spirit, but they may contend that these features were somehow developed in the process of human evolution. *That man has a spirit is thus independent of one's belief.*

Man may or may not put these capacities to use. If he does, he is implementing the spirit and can, therefore, be said to be *spiritual.* There can be varying degrees or levels of spirituality depending on how much one exercises these uniquely human capacities. *Spirituality* is thus nothing more than the implementation of these capacities, hence *spirituality can be seen as being synonymous with humanity.* To the degree that a person is lacking in spirituality, to that degree he is lacking in humanity.

Many of us can recall that as children we were often admonished, "Be a *mentsch,*" or "Act like a *mentsch.*" Although we walked upright and verbalised words and concepts, we were not yet a "*mentsch.*" What was being asked of us is that we develop those traits that are the hallmark of a human being, the spiritual traits that elevate him above the level of *Homo sapiens.*

Extract from: Rabbi A Twerski, *Twerski on Spirituality*

Sara Yoheved Rigler

Yom Kippur: The Crime
I Didn't Commit

On a recent visit to Michigan, I stayed with Circuit Court Judge Alice Gilbert and was intrigued by her brilliant idea of requiring every person convicted in her courtroom to confront the consequences of their actions by writing an essay answering four questions: How did my crime affect me? How did it affect my family? My community? And what can be done to prevent such crimes in the future?

She had two boxes of essays (with names deleted) and I picked out the most severe crimes: a drunken driver who had killed a teenage girl; a high school student who had given birth to a baby, stuffed him into her closet and gone off to school, etc. I sat down to read these dramatic confrontations of human beings with their shadow selves and the epiphanies that ensued.

What I read, instead, was essay after essay explaining why the writer was not *really* guilty of the crime. Totally ignoring the judge's four questions, each convict wrote at length how events had conspired to produce the horrific outcome and that it was absolutely not the fault of the writer.

The drunk driver wrote that it was the fault of the weather; it was the fault of the girl herself; it was even the fault of the police. As for the high school girl and the dead baby, she didn't realise she was pregnant until the baby started coming out, and anyway she did everything she could to save the baby's life, and ... Why is it so hard for people to admit they did wrong?

The first step in the process of *teshuvah* (of returning to God through repentance) is to admit, "I did it!" A Jew confesses transgressions not to a priest or any other human being, but to God – in the privacy of his or her own home. This is where the process of change begins, but trying to change without admitting wrong-doing is like trying to ski without snow.

THE SHREK FALLACY

Three major obstacles keep us humans from that simple act of admitting wrong-doing. The first is a sense of "I'm as rotten as my sins."

The human ego is too wobbly a table to load it up with a couple hundred pounds of wrong-doings. If I admit that I cheated on my exams, then I'm a despicable, dishonest cheat. If I admit that my outbursts of anger traumatise my children, then I'm an out-of-control, savage ogre. My wrong actions are not simply the garments that clothe my essential self; they become my image of who I really am.

This misconception derives from the "Shrek fallacy." Shrek famously declared, "Ogres are like onions. They have layers," meaning that they are complex beings with multiple layers of personality components. Since human beings, too, have layers, the faulty syllogism is that human beings are like onions. This is a lethal analogy because, if you take an onion apart, layer by layer, in the end you will find . . . nothing.

This fear – that really we are nothing but the sum total of our personality traits and actions, with nothing inside – leads to the existential angst that fuels justification and rationalisation at the expense of truly admitting our faults. And justification and rationalisation are splintery boards to bolster up the wobbly table.

Judaism counters the Shrek fallacy with the assertion that a human being is essentially a divine soul. If you take off the layers of personality and actions, you will find shining within, a perfect, pure, immutable, divine soul.

The soul is like a candle flame. It cannot be tarnished or stained in any way. Transgressions are simply curtains strung around the flame. Many layers of thick curtains, especially room darkening curtains, can shroud the flame so that its light is totally invisible, but the flame itself is unaffected.

The more a person – through the spiritual practices of the Torah – identifies with this inner core of spirituality, the more courage the person will have to admit wrongdoing. He or she realises that sin adheres to the essential self as little as dirt adheres to fire – which is to say, not at all. Thus, *teshuvah* is predicated on establishing a sense of oneself as a soul, on connecting to one's inner core of good. Confession is the first step in taking down the curtains that veil the soul.

THE "I CAN'T CHANGE" FALLACY

My daughter Pliyah Esther and I were planning a trip to Hawaii. I spent hours on the Internet, comparing, researching and reading. I would never have invested so much time and energy if I didn't believe that we would eventually get to Hawaii. If I were toying with travel to an impossible destination, I would not have spent the time planning the journey.

To plunge into the journey called *teshuvah* and admit your wrongdoings requires a belief that you can actually arrive at the destination – called "real change." This conviction is, therefore, undermined by the fallacy that your actions are determined by heredity and environment, and you cannot change.

If *teshuvah's* destination is a fantasy Shangri-La location, you'll never embark on the journey.

Countering this fallacy, Judaism insists that human beings have free-will in the moral sphere. Yes, everything is determined by God *except* your choices between right and wrong. You can choose not to cheat on your exams, not to yell at your children, not to gossip, not to carry a grudge, etc.

The "I Can't Change" fallacy is fuelled by your past failures in trying to reach your desired destination. Mark Twain quipped, "Quit smoking? It's easy! I've done it hundreds of times." If you have tried to stop smoking (or yelling or cheating or gossiping) many times, and each time you succumbed to the habit, then you are easy prey for the "I Can't Change" fallacy.

I personally know people who – through the Jewish ethical practice of *Musar* – changed themselves from screaming banshees who yelled at their kids several times a day to parents who almost never yell at their kids.

THE "GOD IS TOO SMALL" FALLACY

The third obstacle to honestly admitting our transgressions is our hopelessness that the mess we made can ever be cleaned up.

But the life-altering process of *teshuvah* changes who we are so fundamentally that God erases our past. The result of our *teshuvah* is that God performs the miracle of expunging our sins. It's as if they never happened. If we do the requisite steps of confession, regret, and making a concrete plan to change (and, when another person was involved, asking forgiveness and making restitution), then God cleans up the mess.

Years ago, a woman, whom I'll call Beth, came to Jerusalem bearing a deep dark secret. Beth enrolled in a programme that teaches Judaism. When the month of Elul (preceding Rosh Hashanah and Yom Kippur) rolled around and Beth started learning about *teshuvah,* she recoiled. She had committed a sin so grievous that she was sure that *teshuvah* was impossible.

When Beth was 19 years old, she had had an affair with one of her college professors. This professor was married with children. For young Beth, the affair was an escapade, but it turned out that the professor was serious about their relationship. He divorced his wife. Beth ditched the professor, but he did not return to his family. As the years passed, Beth was haunted by what she had done. She was sure that there was no way to cleanse from her soul the stain of destroying an entire family.

One of Beth's teachers took her to a prominent rabbi. He told her, "Your problem is that you think God is too small to forgive big sins." He explained that her sin was, indeed, big, but she had to realise that God is bigger. Beth protested that she could not possibly fix the damage she had caused. The rabbi advised her to learn the laws of *lashon ha-ra* (proper speech). When other women saw that Beth never gossiped or divulged secrets, they would come to her to confide their conflicts. Eventually a woman who was grappling with the same temptation would confide in her, and Beth would be able to guide the woman away from committing that sin. That would be her expiation.

With an infinite God, *teshuvah* is always possible.

Once we realise that our sins do not define us, that we can, indeed, change, and that God can absolve us for even the worst misdeeds, we can be brave enough to admit that we did wrong. That's the beginning of *teshuvah*.

Professor Laurence Rees

The Nazis

How was it possible that during the 20th century people from Germany, a cultured nation at the heart of Europe, perpetrated such crimes?

In my attempt to answer this, I was helped by two accidents of history. The first was that I met many former Nazis at exactly the moment when most of them had nothing to lose by speaking openly. Fifteen years earlier, holding down influential jobs and pillars of their communities, they would not have spoken. The second fortuitous circumstance was the fall of the Berlin Wall and the access to Eastern Europe – not just to the archives but the people as well.

As I travelled, however, I became aware that the question was not confined to Germany. In the newly liberated countries of Eastern Europe, I encountered something frightening: virulent antisemitism. I had expected people to tell me how much they hated the Communists. But to hate Jews? It seemed ludicrous, especially since there were hardly any Jews left in the places I was visiting – the Nazis had seen to that. Yet the old man in the Baltic States who had helped the Nazis shoot Jews in 1941 still thought he had done the right thing. And even some of those who had fought against the Nazis held wild antisemitic beliefs. One Ukrainian veteran, who had fought bravely for the Ukrainian Nationalist partisans against both the Nazis and the Red Army and had been persecuted as a result, asked me: "What do you think of the view that there is an international conspiracy of Jewish financiers operating out of New York which is trying to destroy all non-Jewish governments?" I looked at him for a second. Not being Jewish myself, it is always something of a shock to encounter naked antisemitism from an unexpected source. "What do I think of that view?" I replied finally,

"I think it's total garbage." The old partisan took a sip of vodka. "Really," he said, "That's your opinion. Interesting."

Those who think that this history is of little relevance today, or that the corrosive antisemitism was somehow confined to the Nazis, would do well to remember that the extermination of the Jews was not somehow imposed by a few mad people upon an unwilling Europe. Indeed, there was nothing 'uniquely exterminatory' about German society before the Nazis came to power and many Jews had fled *to* Germany in the 1920s to seek sanctuary.

And having questioned a significant number of perpetrators from all of the three totalitarian regimes of World War II: the Nazis, Stalin, and the Japanese, and having written comprehensively about all three dictatorships, I can confirm that the Nazi war criminals I met were different.

In the Soviet Union, the climate of fear under Stalin was pervasive in a way it never was in Germany under Hitler. Whereas in Nazi Germany, unless you were a member of a specific risk group, the Jews, the Communists, the gypsies, homosexuals and, indeed, anyone who opposed the regime – you could live comparatively free from fear. People felt personally secure and happy enough that they would have voted to keep Hitler in power if there had been free and fair elections. By contrast, in the Soviet Union, not even Stalin's closest, most loyal colleagues, ever felt they could sleep securely.

What appears in the minds of many Nazi war criminals is encapsulated by the interview with Hans Friedrich who admits to having personally shot Jews, as a member of an SS unit in the East. Even today, with the Nazi regime long defeated, he is not sorry for what he did. The easy course for him would be to hide behind the "acting under orders" or "I was brainwashed by propaganda" excuses, but such is the strength of his own internal conviction that he does not. At the time, he believed it was right to shoot Jews, and he gives every appearance of still believing it today. It is a loathsome, despicable position – but nonetheless an intriguing one. And the contemporary evidence shows that he is not unique. At Auschwitz, for example, there is not one case in the records that shows that an SS man was prosecuted for refusing to take part in the killings, whilst there is plenty of material showing that the real discipline problem in the camp – from the point of view of the SS leadership – was theft.

Thus, the conclusion I reached, from interviews, archival research and discussions with researchers, was that there was a greater likelihood of individuals who committed crimes within the Nazi system taking personal responsibility for their actions ("I thought it was the right thing to do"), rather than an external one ("I was ordered to do it"), in marked contrast to war criminals who served Stalin or Hirohito.

One obvious reason for this is that the Nazis carefully built on pre-existing convictions. Antisemitism existed in Germany long before Adolf Hitler, and plenty of people blamed the Jews, falsely, for Germany's defeat in World War 1. Such that when the Depression gripped Germany in the early 1930s, millions of Germans voluntarily voted for the Nazi party as a solution to the country's ills.

Another reason was the work of Dr Josef Goebbels, who was the most effective propagandist of the 20th century. He is often dismissed as a crude polemicist, infamous for *Der ewige Jude* (the eternal Jew), a notorious film in which shots of Jews were intercut with pictures of rats. But, in reality, the vast majority of his work was much more sophisticated and much more insidious.

It is also important to convey the excitement that the leading Nazis felt at serving a man who dared to dream in epic terms. Hitler dreamt of defeating France in weeks – the very country in which the German army had been struck for years during World War 1 – and succeeded. He had dreamt of conquering the Soviet Union, and, in the summer and autumn of 1941, it looked almost certain that he would win. And he dreamt of exterminating the Jews, which in some ways was to prove the easiest task of all.

Furthermore, there was no blueprint for extermination which was imposed from above. Individual Nazis were not coerced by crude threats to commit murder. It was a collective enterprise owned by thousands of people who made the decision themselves, not to just take part, but to contribute initiatives in order to kill human beings and dispose of their bodies on a scale never attempted before. As we follow the journey upon which both the Nazis and those whom they persecuted embarked, we also gain a great deal of insight into the human condition. By observing how people behaved in some of the most extreme conditions in history, there is a great deal we can learn about ourselves.

Toivi Blatt, who was forced by the Nazis to work in Sobibor and then risked his life to escape, says: "People asked me, 'what did you learn?' and I think I'm only sure of one thing – nobody knows themselves."

What the survivors taught me (and the perpetrators too) is that human behaviour is fragile and unpredictable and often at the mercy of the situation. Every individual still has, of course, the choice how to behave; it is just that for many people the situation is a key determinant in that choice. Even those individuals such as Hitler himself, who appear to be masters of their own destiny, were to a considerable extent created by their response to previous situations. The Adolf Hitler known to history was substantially formed by the interaction between the pre-war Hitler, who was a worthless drifter, and the events of World War 1.

However, this history also shows us that if individuals can be buffeted around by the situation, then groups of human beings working together can create better cultures, which in turn can help individuals to behave more virtuously.

In the end, though, there is a profound sense of sadness around this subject that cannot be reduced. Throughout the time I was working on this project, the voices I heard loudest were those of the people whom we could not interview: the 1.1 million human beings who were murdered in Auschwitz and, in particular, the more than 200,000 children who perished there and were denied the right to grow up and experience life. One image stuck in my mind from the moment I heard it described. It was of a 'procession' of empty baby carriages – property looted from the dead Jews – pushed out of Auschwitz in rows of five towards the railway station. The prisoner who witnessed the sight said they took an hour to pass by. The children who arrived at Auschwitz in those baby carriages, together with their mothers, fathers, brothers, sisters, uncles, and aunts – all those who died there – are the ones we should always remember.

From *AUSCHWITZ* by Laurence Rees
Published by Woodland Books

Reprinted by permission of The Random House Group Ltd.

Sponsored by Giffnock & Newlands Hebrew Congregation
in memory of Rev Ernest Levy a"h, a survivor whose
story and spirit inspired and continues to inspire.

Rabbi Dov Lipman

Abraham – Our Founding Father

The great Jewish medieval scholar and philosopher, Maimonides,
relates:

"No sooner was Abraham weaned, and he was but small, that his
mind began to seek and wonder: How do the heavenly bodies
orbit without a moving force? Who moves them? They cannot
move themselves...his heart sought, and came to know that
there is one God...Who created all and that in all existence
there is none other than Him. He came to know that the entire world erred...At the age of 40, Abraham recognised his
Creator...He continued to call in a great voice to the world,
teaching them that there is one God for the entire universe,
and that He alone is fitting to serve. He carried his call from
city to city and from kingdom to kingdom...Many gathered
to ask about his words and he would explain to each according to his understanding until he had shown him the path of
truth. Thousands and tens of thousands joined him...and he
implanted this great principle in their heart and wrote many
books on it." (*Yad Hachazakah* – Laws of *Avodah Zarah* 1:1)

Abraham is known for his compassion, kindness, gracious hosting of guests, and other remarkable traits between man and man.
But we cannot forget that which underpinned it all, his contribution in the realm between man and God – the very concept of man
relating to an omniscient, infinite Divine Being. That contribution
changed the entire world and served as the basis for Judaism.

This world-changing discovery of his came as a result of his
intellectual curiosity and honesty. He would not simply accept
what everyone around him taught and searched until he found the

truth. It is interesting to note that Maimonides describes a process which began when Abraham was a young boy and lasted until he was 40! He knew something was off when he was younger and continued to search and understand for decades before coming to his final conclusion and teaching it to the world.

Abraham's search for the truth and willingness to question continued well after his discovery of God. When God tells him that he plans to destroy the city of Sodom, Abraham challenges God, Himself – "will you kill righteous people with the wicked?" He continues to press and question until he is satisfied.

This teaches us a critical lesson that is also a core Jewish value: having the courage to ask questions and challenge that which surrounds us. The most important night of the year for the Jewish family, Passover night when we experience the Seder, is supposed to be run in question-and-answer format. The Talmud, the rich source of Jewish law written and compiled 1,500 years ago in Babylonia, is presented in question-and-answer format. The message from both is clear. We must be willing to ask questions and search for answers. We won't always be successful in gaining complete understanding, especially when dealing with the Divine, but this trait and process are critical for our development as human beings and in our worship of God.

There is one question which Abraham accepted that he could never fully comprehend – how God dealt with him. God instructs Abraham to leave his homeland and all will be good for him, and he does so and is met with a terrible famine in his new land. He flees to find food in Egypt and his wife, Sarah, is taken by the king. He and his wife cannot conceive a child together so he has no choice but to marry her maidservant through whom a son is born. Despite his love for this son, when he is finally blessed with a child with Sarah, at the age of 100, his first son, Ishmael, is a negative influence on his new son, Isaac, and he must send Ishmael away from home. He trusts God who commands him to kill his son, Isaac, and when he returns from that experience without actually having to kill his son, he finds out that his wife Sarah has suddenly passed away. Throughout these and other challenges, numbering ten in all, Abraham continues with his steadfast faith and trust in God. He does not understand the ways of God, but accepts that he, as a limited physical human being, can never fully comprehend the ways of an infinite, omniscient God. The Talmud relates that Moses, himself asked God to explain His ways and God responded that man cannot fully understand the ways of God.

Questioning, searching, exploring, challenging, growing, the internal strength to stand up for the truth, the courage to teach the masses, and accepting that we cannot understand it all. This is the legacy of Abraham, our father, and should be the basis of the spiritual journey which all of us should experience throughout our lives.

Sponsored anonymously in recognition of Chief Rabbi Goldstein's
leadership and vision of The Shabbos Project worldwide.

Chief Rabbi Dr Warren Goldstein

Shabbat – the Power of Creativity

The seven day week cycle is universally accepted. But there were
times in history (even as recently as the 20th century), when society proposed other units of time – such as ten days – for the week.
This is not surprising, because seven days is the only unit of time
in the year that is unconnected to a cycle within nature: the day is
linked to the rotation of the earth; the month to the moon's cycle;
and the year to that of the sun. The week, however, has no reason to
be seven days long, and it is noteworthy and significant, therefore,
that the Torah's cycle for a week is the one adhered to worldwide.

The Torah gave us a seven day cycle to teach us to emulate God's
creation of the world, to become creators like Him, as we move
through the same time-cycle with which He originally formed the
world. The first six days of the "work" week, correspond to the
first six units (days) when God was involved in active creation;
whereas the seventh day – Shabbat – parallels God's cessation of
activity on that seventh day. Rabbi Tzadok HaKohen of Lublin
adds that the seven day week symbolises an actual partnership with
God which explains the statement in the Talmud (Shabbat 119b)
that when a person makes Kiddush on Friday night, they start by
reciting Vaychulu (the last verses of the creation story) because it
is as if they are now paralleling God, being a partner with God in
Creation. Saying these words in Kiddush, therefore, is a declaration
that Shabbat is being observed as a holy day, not only because of
the commandment to do so, but following on from the concept
of God creating the world in six days and resting on the seventh.

Rabbi Tzadok says that the way we fulfil the mandate of
being God's partners in Creation is through the mitzvot. All of
the 613 commandments constitute our call to action to be God's

co-creators. The more *mitzvot* and good deeds that we do in this world, the more we elevate ourselves and the world around us, thereby fulfilling our mission as co-creators with God Himself.

Rabbi Joseph B Soloveitchik applies this idea of a partnership with God more broadly. We know that the Torah is not merely a history book but an instruction manual for life. Given this, asks Rabbi Soloveitchik, "Why is the first chapter in Genesis seemingly devoid of any *mitzvot* or ethical guidelines?" The beginning of Genesis appears to be merely a history of the creation of the world. If, as the term "Torah" implies, it is a book of *hora'ah* (a book of instruction and practical guidelines) what instructions are contained in the chronicle of Creation?

Rabbi Soloveitchik answers that inherent in this chapter is the *mitzvah* to emulate God. He mentions the specific commandment of "*vehalachta be-derachav*" (you shall walk in His ways) which the Gemara (*Sotah* 14a) interprets primarily in the context of *chesed* (loving-kindness): "Just as He is compassionate, so too shall you be compassionate...just as He visits the sick and comforts the mourners, so too shall you." Rabbi Soloveitchik applies this talmudic principle to the area of creativity as well: God is a Creator and, therefore, each of us should be a creator like Him. God said, "Let there be light," and so we have the *mitzvah* to bring light where there is darkness; He created a world, so too should we summon all our powers of creativity to advance civilisation – whether in medicine, engineering, technology or any other human endeavour. Our task in life is to emulate God, to be His active partner in creation, using our creativity and ingenuity to improve the world for the benefit of all humankind.

This accords with an idea of Rabbi Samson Raphael Hirsch, regarding the common denominator shared by all of the 39 prohibited categories of work on *Shabbat*. He explains that they are all not actually acts of labour per se (some require almost no physical input at all). Rather, they are all acts of creativity that impose human will on the physical world – which is why they are termed *melachah* rather than *avodah* (the normal world for labour). For six days we do *melachah,* and on the seventh day we rest. For six days, we are creative, as God was, thereby advancing civilisation, developing society and doing whatever is necessary to improve society. But on *Shabbat* we cease and, like God, we dedicate the seventh day to rest.

But what did God achieve by creating a day of rest? What in fact is the role of *Shabbat*, when it appears to be an empty day – given that conventional wisdom measures productivity as rising only from tangible activity such as making money or creating things that we can touch and feel. The remarkable answer is that *Shabbat* teaches us that creativity is not only about what we produce physically, but is also an internal, intangible process. On each day of the week, God completed physical phenomena (the land, sea, animals, stars), whereas on the seventh day, He created *Shabbat*. Thus, Creation was completed on the seventh day even though nothing physical was brought into existence.

Unfortunately, in today's materialistic society, many of us measure ourselves only by concrete productivity. We think that unless we are producing something that can be touched, measured or priced, we are not being constructive or using our time effectively. But there are two kinds of creativity: external and internal, and both are important. The internal, emotional, intellectual and spiritual elements of our development assist us in becoming better human beings, rather than simply becoming more efficient machines.

Shabbat gives us space and time free from the distractions, demands and pressures of daily life, so that we can develop who we are internally – and this is no less a creative process than our productivity during the week. When we desist from all physical creativity on *Shabbat*, we are free to create a renewed spiritual and emotional identity that imbues us with the inspiration and peace of mind that comes with living a life of purpose. When we take time out on *Shabbat* to sit, sing and talk together as a family, our most precious relationships are created and nurtured, and we draw the comfort and emotional well-being which comes from these loving bonds. When we learn Torah and pray on *Shabbat*, we connect to *Hashem* and to our awesome spiritual heritage, and are thereby enriched and inspired. All of these non-physical experiences are amongst the greatest acts of creation of which we are capable. *Shabbat* affords us the opportunity to engage a different facet of our creative selves – a creativity that enables us each week to transform and uplift every dimension of our lives in the most profound and exciting way.

The compelling message and creative energy of *Shabbat* has created a social movement transforming Jewish communities around the world: The Shabbos Project – an international Jewish unity initiative that brings together millions of Jews of every stripe and level of observance, and in cities across the globe to keep one *Shabbat* together. *Shabbat*, a model for human creativity, is itself becoming the catalyst to create a spirit of renewed inspiration and unity for the Jewish people today, guiding us to a brighter future.

Rabbi Ari Kahn

The Rabbi and the Professor

Many years ago, when I was a young yeshivah student, I had the opportunity to study with one of the great rabbis of the previous generation. His name was Rabbi Yisroel Zeev Gustman and he was one of the rabbinic sages of the 20th century. He was certainly the greatest "unknown" rabbi, as he fastidiously avoided the limelight.

His meteoric rise to the exalted position of religious judge in the Rabbinical Court of Vilna at the age of 20 was the stuff of legend – but, nonetheless, fact. Many years later, I heard Rav Gustman's own modest version of the events leading to this appointment: a singular (brilliant) insight which he shared with his fellow students was later repeated to the visiting Rabbi Chaim Ozer, who invited the young student to repeat this same insight the following day in his office in Vilna. Unbeknownst to Rav Gustman, the insight clinched an argument in a complex case that had been debated among the judges in Rabbi Chaim Ozer's court – and allowed a woman to remarry.

One of the judges adjudicating the case in question, Rabbi Meir Bassin, made inquiries about this young man, and soon a marriage was arranged with his daughter Sarah. When Rabbi Bassin passed away before the wedding, Rabbi Gustman was tapped to take his place as rabbi of Shnipishok and to take his seat on the court. Rav Gustman claimed that he was simply "in the right place at the right time."

During the war, Vilna was obliterated but Rav Gustman escaped. He hid among corpses, in forests and in caves for many long months. According to his own account he faced death over 100 times, but somehow he survived.

For me, Rav Gustman was the living link to the Jewish world destroyed by the Nazis. I never had to wonder what a rav in Vilna before the war looked like, for I had seen Rav Gustman, 35 years after the war. He headed a small yeshivah in the Rehavia section of Jerusalem, where he taught every day. But on Thursdays at noon, the study hall would fill to capacity: rabbis, intellectuals, religious court judges, a Supreme Court justice, and various professors would join – all who sought a high level Talmud *shiur* that offered a taste of what had once been. When Rav Gustman gave a *shiur*, Vilna was once again alive and vibrant.

One of the regular participants was a professor at the Hebrew University, Robert J (Yisrael) Aumann. Once a promising yeshivah student, he had decided to pursue a career in academia, but made his weekly participation in Rav Gustman's *shiur* part of his schedule.

In 1982, Israel was at war. Among those called to duty was a re-serve soldier, who made his living as a high school teacher: Shlomo Aumann, Professor Aumann's son. On the eve of the 19th of Sivan, in particularly fierce combat, Shlomo fell in battle.

Rav Gustman mobilised his yeshivah: all of his students joined him in performing the *mitzvah* of burying the dead. At the cemetery, Rav Gustman was agitated. He surveyed the rows of graves of the young men, soldiers who died defending the Land. On the way back from the cemetery, Rav Gustman turned to a passenger in the car and said, "They are all holy. Every single one of them." He then turned to the driver and said, "Take me to Professor Aumann's home."

The family had just returned from the cemetery and would now begin the week of *shiva* – mourning. (Shlomo was married and had one child. His widow, Shlomit, gave birth to their second daughter shortly after he was killed.)

Rav Gustman entered and sat next to Professor Aumann, who said: "Rabbi, I so appreciate your coming to the cemetery, but now is time for you to return to your yeshivah." Rav Gustman responded and said, "I am sure that you don't know this, but I had a son named Meir. He was a beautiful child. He was taken from my arms and executed in front of me by the Nazis. I later bartered my child's shoes so that we would have food, but I was never able to eat the food – I gave it away to others. My Meir is a *kadosh* – he is holy – he and all the six million who perished are holy."

Rav Gustman then added, "I will tell you what is transpiring now in the World of Truth – in Heaven. My Meir is welcoming your

Shlomo into the *minyan* and is saying to him, "I died because I am a Jew – but I wasn't able to save anyone. But you – Shlomo, you died defending the Jewish people and the Land of Israel." My Meir is a *kadosh*, he is holy – but your Shlomo is a *shaliach tzibur* – in that holy, heavenly *minyan*."

Rav Gustman continued, "I never had the opportunity to sit *shiva* for my Meir; let me sit here with you just a little longer."

Professor Aumann replied, "I thought I could never be comforted, but Rabbi, you have comforted me."

Rav Gustman did not allow his painful memories to control his life. And when a student implored Rav Gustman to share his memories of the ghetto and the war, the Rav replied, "I can't, but I think about those shoes every day of my life. I see them every night before I go to sleep."

He found solace in his students, his daughter, his grandchildren, and in every Jewish child. He and his wife would attend an annual parade (on *Yom Yerushalayim*) where children would march in song and dance. A rabbi asked Rav Gustman why he spent his valuable time on such a frivolous activity. Rav Gustman explained, "We who saw a generation of children die take pleasure in a generation of children who sing and dance in these streets."

On the 28th of Sivan 5751 (1991), Rav Gustman passed away. Thousands marched through the streets of Jerusalem accompanying Rav Gustman on his final journey. As night fell, nine years after Shlomo Aumann fell in battle, Rav Gustman was buried on the Mount of Olives. I am sure that upon entering Heaven, he was reunited with his wife, his teachers and his son Meir. I am also sure that Shlomo Aumann and all the other holy soldiers who died defending the People and the Land of Israel were there to greet this extraordinary Rabbi.

On 10th December 2005, Professor Robert J Aumann was awarded the Nobel Prize in Economics. He took with him to Stockholm memories of his late wife Esther, and his son Shlomo. I suspect he also took memories of his rabbi, Rav Gustman.

POSTSCRIPT:

The last time I saw Rav Gustman, I was walking in Jerusalem with my wife and oldest son who was in a stroller. We saw the *Rosh*

Yeshivah and greeted him. Then I did something I rarely do: I asked him to bless my son. Rav Gustman looked at the toddler, smiled and said, "May he be a boy like all the other boys." At first, my wife and I were stunned; what kind of blessing was this? We expected a blessing that the boy grow to be a *tzadik* – a righteous man – or a *talmid chacham* – a Torah scholar. But he blessed him that he should be "like all the boys."

It took many years for this beautiful blessing to make sense to us. The blessing was that he should have a normal childhood, that he have a normal life. Looking back, I realise what a tremendous blessing Rav Gustman gave, and why.

Today, our sons are soldiers in combat units in the Israeli Defense Forces and I pray that they return home safely along with all their comrades, and live normal lives – "just like all the boys."

Rabbi Malcolm Herman

8 Worlds within Words – The Mishnah and the Talmud (the Oral Law)

My first face to screen encounter with the personal computer was some 20 years ago. I was at least a decade behind colleagues and friends. I purchased a copy of *Windows for Dummies* and studied it conscientiously. I gradually learnt how to cut and paste, save information on floppy disks, and much more.

A few weeks later, I was visiting my sister and saw my seven-year-old nephew on the computer. I walked over to him and offered to dazzle him with my expertise. He politely moved to one side and I proceeded. He sat silently with a baffled expression on his face.

Without saying a word, he gently recovered the mouse. Suddenly the screen was alive with variation and animation. To compound my idiocy I said to him, "That's amazing! Which books do you read?"

He avoided me for several years.

How is it possible that a seven-year-old was more adept than a 30-year-old post grad? Quite simply, he had grown up with computers as part of his life – he was a *citizen* in the world of technology and I was a foreigner.

This anecdote provides a very important element to our discussion of the Oral Law.

Let's begin at the beginning. The Oral Law was given by God to Moses at the same time as the Written Law. It is the verbal elaboration of the written text. It dwarfs the written text in volume, such that Rabbi Samson Raphael Hirsch (1808–1888) famously compares the written text to the lecture *notes* and the Oral Law to the actual lecture. Despite the complication of 613 commandments and thousands of attendant details and, notwithstanding many challenges *en route*, it was maintained as an oral tradition for 1,500 years. So, here is the key question, "Is it really conceivable that the Jewish people maintained the integrity of the Oral Law with all of its intricacies, for 15 centuries?"

Enter computer-whiz-nephew. This anecdote demonstrates that irrespective of complexity, even a child can absorb complicated information, if that is the world that they inhabit. It becomes second nature to them.

This holds true for the custodians of the Oral Law. They lived it and breathed it. It regulated life at home and in the marketplace, in the synagogue and on street corners. They were *citizens* of the Oral Law.

The oral *nature* of the Oral Law was vital for a number of reasons. First of all, it gave Judaism exclusivity to the Torah itself. Whilst the written text was accessible to others, its wisdom could only really be unlocked via the Oral Law and that was the private domain of the Jewish people. Secondly, it created a dynamic and a vitality born out of the interaction between people that cannot be paralleled by the written word alone. The process of study is interpersonal and energetic.

However, by the end of the second century, the Jewish world had changed dramatically. The Second Temple had been destroyed more than 100 years earlier and Jews had migrated to far-flung corners of the earth. Roman oppression had fragmented the nation. Israel was no longer the home of Jewish life. Babylon had become a centre of Jewish scholarship and Jewish civilisation. One man, Rabbi Yehudah Ha-Nasi, recognised the cataclysmic implications of this change. Until the messianic era, Judaism would have to survive scattered throughout the Diaspora. Communities were in danger of losing touch with each other and Judaism was in danger of losing touch with its Oral Law tradition. It had preserved them and they had preserved it. It was clear that they would no longer be able to *live* it as they had done in the past, and now faced the challenge of continuity in exile.

Rabbi Yehudah Ha-Nasi made the momentous decision that the basics of the Oral Law had to be recorded. Utilising his personal friendship with the Roman Emperor, Marcus Aurelius Antoninus, and a temporary lull in Roman repression, he was able to convene the Torah scholars of his day to collate the teachings and transcribe them.

The Oral Law was divided into six sections. Each of these was composed of books and each book was split into chapters. The chapters contain short paragraphs called *mishnayot* in the plural and *mishnah* in the singular, which literally means "teaching." The six sections are: *Zerayim* (agriculture), *Moed* (festive times), *Nashim* (marriage and family), *Nezikin* (damages – civil and criminal law), *Kodshim* (sacred items and sacrifices) and *Taharot* (ritual purity). By around 180 CE, all of these were documented.

The style of the written Mishnah is minimalist. Single words communicate worlds, and every nuance is vital. It was a format which retained its oral nature, necessitating dialogue in the process of study.

Rabbi Yehudah himself was the *Nasi* (literally, the prince), the term applied to the leader of the Supreme Court of Israel, the Sanhedrin, hence the epithet that accompanies his name. He is also known as *Rabbenu Ha-Kadosh* (our holy teacher) and sometimes simply as *Rebbi* (our teacher). This is the ultimate testimony that he remains for all time the teacher of the Jewish people.

Over the next 250 years, both in Babylon and in Israel, this text became the curriculum of the great academies. The lines and the words were debated, analysed and dissected and these subsequent discussions – the expansion of the teachings of the Mishnah – were then recorded and became known as the Gemara (learning). Both parts together make up the Talmud (study).

The Talmud compiled in Israel is called the *Talmud Yerushalmi* (Jerusalem) and was written in the face of a renewed Roman tyranny. The Empire had become Christian at the beginning of the fourth century and embarked on a campaign to eradicate Torah study.

In Babylon, the Jews enjoyed greater freedom and two great personalities, Ravina and Rav Ashi, collated these discussions on the Mishnah into a vast compendium, over a 30 year period. The task was completed around 450 CE. It is known as the *Talmud Bavli* (Babylonian). The *Bavli* is larger than the *Yerushalmi* and the focal point of all Torah study. All discussions, whether halachic (legal) or philosophical, lead to the Talmud, and all decisions emerge from it.

To open a single page of its 2,700 folios is to tiptoe into a house of study that dates back 1,700 years. The discussion rages through the pages with a determination for accuracy and rigorous integrity. Sometimes, the discussion is interrupted for an appropriate anecdote or philosophical diversion, but the objective is always a single-minded pursuit of the truth. The goal is to deepen our relationship with God, through ever greater understanding of His communication to mankind.

The Talmud is structured around the doctrine of precedent. Torah scholars of the talmudic era cannot contradict those of the mishnaic era. They were after all generations closer to the Temple, the prophets, and Mount Sinai, and thus better qualified both in scholarship and piety. In the world of secular academia, fame is often attributed to those who discover that which *was not* known before. In the arena of Torah scholarship, respect is accredited to those who clarify that which *was* once known before.

From the 13th century right through to the 20th century, the Talmud was the target of attack by the Church. At times it was censored, at times it was banned and at times it was burned. Their venom was primarily targeted at segments that highlighted the singularity of the Jewish people, but the Church also understood that the Talmud is the soul of the Torah, and the Torah is the soul of our people.

Today, throughout the Jewish world, study of the Talmud remains central. The eight-year-old boy and the 80-year-old man can study the same page; the little boy with fresh eyes, darting from line to line; the 80-year-old man with experienced eyes that yet see fresh thoughts in well-worn lines. The little boy feels that he has conquered worlds and the old man knows that in those very words, there are worlds yet to conquer.

Rabbi Gil Student

A Peace of Torah

We live in a deeply unstable time in terms of political and social upheaval that only Torah can save. The world structure is crumbling before our eyes and our communities are following suit. The rapid change in technology of the modern era has finally reached a global turning point. It has toppled dictatorships, sparked chaotic, deadly civil wars and destroyed the once-powerful media of television and newspapers. Locally, we no longer have the same need for our parents, teachers, and rabbis to educate us about who we are, what we believe and how we behave. Technology often allows us to learn that on our own. "Ask your father and he will tell you, your elders and they will say to you" (Deut. 32:7) has been replaced by Google and Wikipedia.

I turned off my phone's buzzer when e-mails started arriving so frequently that my pocket was buzzing more often than not. Social media has increased that inflow of information to an overwhelming tidal wave. This marvellous tool, the smartphone without which I can no longer remember how I lived, is now drowning me in information. Too much of anything, no matter how good, is still overwhelming.

The confusion this causes has overtaken the social climate. The sadness and loneliness that are enveloping the Western world stem in part from an uncertainty of who we are. We are presented with a smorgasbord of identities, an overwhelming array of possibilities, so many choices that we are paralysed and confused. We can be whoever we want, but we have no way of knowing what to want. We are blessed to have access to a plethora of competing opinions, but how do we evaluate and decide between them?

Yet human beings are blessed with a powerful ability to adapt.

We can establish new governments or live with what others create; we can interact in person or virtually; we can obtain our news from wherever it comes. Even if our world collapses, we will continue living our lives. Change does not defeat the human spirit, even when that change is radical. But being in a state of transition is confusing, destabilising. The adaptation process takes time as we relearn some of our basic ways of thinking and acting. Today, change is so frequent that adaptation is part of our routine. We always look for what is new and incorporate it into our thought process. Torah is an unchanging constant in a constantly changing world.

What we actually lack most of all are the tools and the time to reach conclusions. Instead, we are bombarded with opinions, arguments and perspectives that seek to convince us one way or another. Our world is in a state of constant re-evaluation. The answer to all this lies in the Torah.

The Talmud (*Berachot* 64a) makes a remarkable statement that has puzzled students over the centuries. It states, "Torah scholars increase peace in the world," homiletically reading this idea into a biblical verse. The difficulty is simple: like any group of academics, rabbis interact with each other in ways that often include heated disagreements. The talmudic claim is, therefore, puzzling. Certainly, human nature hasn't changed so much since the time of the Talmud that infighting was invented in the interim. Some would even suggest that this is talmudic humour, said tongue-in-cheek to the reader.

The deeper answer lies in the personal nature of Torah study. For thousands of years, Jews have studied Scripture and Talmud as a religious and intellectual act of identity building. When everything changes, we avoid the confusion by anchoring ourselves in the ideas that spawned civilisation. Torah is our living heritage.

Torah is not an historical relic that we look at with nostalgia. Torah is a conversation that spans the ages, that brings ancient wisdom to contemporary problems. We engage with the texts, argue with them and each other, inhale their wisdom and incorporate their ideas into our worldviews. Torah is a way of looking at the world.

A remarkable facet of the standard page of the Talmud or Torah is that it is timeless. The original text is adorned with commentaries and marginal notes from throughout the ages. The sages of the Midrash and Talmud offer explanations from the early centuries. Rashi, who often combines those earlier thoughts with his own, provides an 11th century vantage, and Ramban, from the 13th. *Tosafot* is a fluid text that grew over three centuries. Later commentaries continue into the modern era through this day. Torah grows, lives, adapts. But, paradoxically, it remains fixed, anchoring us to values and ideas that have guided humanity throughout the ages.

Torah scholars may sometimes be discordant. They may argue vehemently about the ideas they hold so dear. However, the Torah they teach makes the individuals whole. It gives them a sense of being and purpose; it provides them with values that serve as a basis to evaluate the immense information available today. Thus, scholars increase peace by creating wholeness within the students. A person at peace with himself will not be overwhelmed by the immense choices and information available. He will evaluate them within a framework and with the assuredness of identity, which he has inherited from generations of devoted Jews.

If you want to know who you are, who you are destined to become, then find yourself a Torah teacher or study partner. Put away your phones and tablets for a time and open a text. Focus, learn, debate, internalise. You will find not only wisdom but meaning, purpose and a renewed spirit. Torah study will enable you to discover who you are, which will allow you to navigate the complexities of life today with a confident sense of self. About Torah teachings it is said, "For these are our lives and the lengths of our days" (Evening Prayers). This applies today more than ever.

Rabbi Davey Blackman

Hoshanah Rabbah – Education over Legislation

Hoshanah Rabbah is the last day of Succot. Throughout the Jewish world we circle round the *bimah* (the replacement of the *mizbeach* – Temple altar) in our synagogues, seven times, calling out to God repeatedly: "*Hosha na*" (Help us, please!). The word *na* has a numerical value through its Hebrew letters of 51, which parallels the 51 days of repentance from the beginning of the month of Elul (preceding Rosh Hashanah) through to Hoshanah Rabbah, the climax of the process of heavenly judgement – the last chance.

Judgement was made on Rosh Hashanah and sealed on Yom Kippur, but on Hoshanah Rabbah, the *Zohar* teaches us, judgement is delivered to be carried out. That is why the traditional greeting on this day is "*pitkah tovah*" (a favourable bill of judgement – for the entire year to come).

But in what way can we describe Hoshanah Rabbah as the climax for judgement, when *Ne'ilah* on Yom Kippur saw the gates of judgement close? The time that we declared, with our souls on fire, *Shema Yisrael, Hashem Hu ha-Elokim*, (Hear O Israel, *Hashem* is the Lord) when we blew the final blast of the *shofar* for the year. Surely that was the end of it? We've already made our last appeal!

The answer lies with a well-known idea embedded in the *mitzvah* of the Four Species. Our tradition teaches that each species represents a different component of the Jewish nation. Each of the four species has its own character: the *etrog*, as a fruit, has both taste and fragrance; the *lulav*, hailing from the date palm, has taste but no fragrance; whereas the *hadas* (myrtle) has fragrance to it, but no taste; and finally, there is the lowly *aravah* (the willow) which has neither taste nor fragrance.

These four represent the spectrum of the Jewish nation. There are those Jews who possess both *ta'am* and *rei'ach* (taste and smell). They have Torah learning and *mitzvot*: they are Etrog Jews. Then there are those who are well versed in Torah, yet poor in actions and good character: Lulav Jews. Equally, there are Jews who are rich in good deeds and character, but poor in Torah knowledge: Hadas Jews. And finally, many Jews of our time are the Aravah Jew, neither involved in the study of Torah nor really of its practice, yet aware that they are Jews.

"What shall I do with the Aravah Jew?" asks *Hashem*. "Shall I abandon him because he has no fragrance and no taste? But surely he's part of My people? Therefore," says God, "I give the commandment of taking the four species. My children will come together, and bind themselves together in one group, so that those Jews who are in possession of the ideal dimensions, will rub off on those who are lacking them. Through their concern for their fellow Jews, they will unite the people, including the less educated and non-practising Aravah Jew. The judgement of Succot is the dimension where we are judged on our sense of responsibility for others. This responsibility actually works both ways; the Etrog Jew needs to come together with the Aravah Jew, but equally the Aravah Jew needs to seek out the company of the Etrog Jew.

Yet interestingly, at one stage on Hoshanah Rabbah itself, we put aside the four species which have accompanied us all through *yom tov* and pick up a little bundle made only of Aravah. This is the focus on Hoshanah Rabbah: the Aravah Jew. Furthermore, although we make a blessing every day over the four species, the *mitzvah* of Aravah performed on Hoshanah Rabbah has no blessing attached to it.

The understanding of this custom lies in the history of the Jewish nation. Upon return from the 70 year exile in Babylonia and Persia, the last of the prophets of the Jewish people – Chaggai, Zechariah, and Malachi – looked to understand how best to motivate this new generation of Jews.

In the Temple, there was a *mitzvah* of *Aravah*, for which every day throughout the week of Succot, giant *aravot* were cut and brought from just outside Jerusalem, and the branches placed upright on the side of the altar. To give Jews who were outside the Temple, an opportunity to fulfil this *mitzvah* of *Aravah,* the prophets instituted the custom of having all Jews take the willow on Hoshanah Rabbah. This became what we call *minhag nevi'im* (the custom of the Prophets). Intriguingly, however, it is actually the only *minhag nevi'im* we have – the first and only custom they introduced into Judaism – and it served to unite Jews worldwide as they all began to carry it out, even though it was not mandated by legislation.

This ties into the concept of making a blessing. A blessing over a *mitzvah* carries the statement that there is a commandment, obligating me to carry out a particular action, whereas *minhag* (custom) is not legislature, and intentionally so. The idea of *minhag* is a subtle suggestion; it is motivation through education, to allow people to identify with a particular idea (in this case the *Beit HaMikdash*). *Minhag* has no imperative.

Perhaps Hoshanah Rabbah, the day of the Aravah Jew, with the "custom of the prophets" at its centre, is teaching us how to reach the Aravah Jew, namely through *minhag,* rather than legislation. You can't necessarily legislate for an Aravah Jew; you have to inspire them – to the point where the Aravah Jew willingly wants to be part of the four species experience. And custom often has a greater appeal to people than commandment in communicating the beauty of Judaism.

Ruth Ellen Gruber

Jewish Life in Europe after the Holocaust

Recently, over glasses of white wine in a trendy Budapest bistro, a friend of mine, whom I will call Rozsa, told me a story from her childhood that I had never heard before. In the early 1960s, when she was five or six years old, she visited her grandfather, a Holocaust survivor, in the small Hungarian town where he lived. He took her to the Jewish cemetery and stood with her in front of the entrance.

"See those beautiful letters?" he asked, pointing to the Hebrew. "At one point I could read them. But then I decided not to. Now I can't, and I regret it."

The anecdote typifies the experience of many Jews during the post-Holocaust Communist era, when established Jewish communities were organisationally weak, and study or even discussion of Jewish topics was discouraged, if not outright taboo.

Many of those who stayed in Europe through the Communist period hid, denied, or outright rejected their Jewishness – or at least lived it in a very low-key way. For some this was out of fear for others out of expediency. It was seen as a way to protect their children and their children's children from poisonous after-effects of the murderous past.

This didn't, of course, always work and, indeed, it could produce painful consequences of its own.

Rozsa grew up without any relatives outside of her immediate family. This, she said, resulted in a sense of loneliness and profound isolation that she feels even now, in her late 50s, a successful and accomplished woman with two grown children. Not long ago, she told me, she travelled to North America for the wedding of the grandchild of a distant cousin who had emigrated from Hungary before the Holocaust. "It felt so natural and normal," she told me. "Different generations being Jewish without any complexes. Family. It felt comfortable. Everything I did not have in my own experience growing up."

My own contact with Jewish life and heritage in Eastern and Central Europe dates back to the late 1970s and early 1980s when I was a journalist based in Communist Europe. I travelled widely throughout what we then called the East Bloc, and in the course of covering political, economic, and social developments, I made contact with many Jewish communities and individuals. Sometimes, this was for purely professional reasons, to interview people for articles. Other times it was personal. At other times still, I simply made contact as a Jew.

In Bulgaria, I drank tea with the elderly president of the Jewish community in Sofia and peeked into the city's Great Synagogue, at the time disused, its sanctuary choked with scaffolding, as part of a failed state plan to turn it into a concert hall. In Hungary, I attended Yom Kippur services in the vast Dohany Street Synagogue, the biggest synagogue in Europe. It was in such bad repair that its ceiling sagged dangerously above the congregation, wrapped in plastic sheeting and held up somehow by metal bars.

In Poland, when I covered the birth of the Solidarity movement, I had perhaps my most moving encounters. Here I met young Jews my own age who had joined with non-Jewish friends to form a semi-clandestine study group, dubbed the Jewish Flying University. To them, I was a "real Jew." Despite the fact that I did not speak Hebrew, did not keep kosher, and rarely went to synagogue, I had known all my life I was Jewish. They were just learning, mostly on their own. In addition to the rituals and customs, they were teaching themselves the Jewish intangibles, the collective memories, the quirks of language, and even sometimes physical or facial expressions that had been stolen by war, Shoah, fear, and Communist suppression.

These then-young people, my generation, became the anchors of what was to become, in the 1990s, the post-Communist Jewish revival in Poland. Today they are, more than two decades beyond that, its old guard.

I recall so vividly the distrust manifested by members of the

Holocaust survivor generation toward these newly emerging, questioning Jews, the Jews claiming or reclaiming long hidden or suppressed identity. Many survivors simply did not recognise them as Jews. "You guys are a fraud, a literary fiction," Marek Edelman, one of the leaders of the Warsaw Ghetto Uprising, told Jewish Flying University member Kostek Gebert, who is now a distinguished writer and journalist – and religiously observant. "The Jewish people is dead, and you have simply thought yourselves up, looking for originality and exoticism."[1]

Indeed, for some of those older people, their own fervent identity was "the last Jews of Poland." Their passing, they believed, would be the final chapter in a 1,000 year history. For some of them, thus, the emergence of "new Jews" shook the roots of their own self-definition; in effect, it challenged who and what they felt themselves and their role to be – and their Jewishness to represent.

Today, it is the generation of the children and even grandchildren of people my own and Gebert's age who are setting the parameters of Jewish definitions and practice – in Poland, in Hungary and also other countries. Much has changed: there are rabbis and schools and synagogues and JCCs and Jewish culture festivals and more. But for many, it is still not all that easy.

In Budapest, Linda Vero Ban, the wife of a rabbi, recently published a book entitled, *What Does It Mean to Be Jewish?* The text tackles questions such as the difference between religious and secular Jews; having people of various religions in one family; whether you can tell someone is Jewish by looking at them; and whether you have to believe in God to be Jewish. The brightly illustrated book is ostensibly aimed at children. But, says Vero Ban, its "hidden" target is actually those parents and other older generations who, even a full quarter century since the fall of Communism and 70 years since the Shoah, still struggle with these issues and don't know how either to answer the questions, or, like the fourth son in the *Haggadah*, even to ask them.[2]

1. Gerbert, Konstanty. "Jewish Identities in Poland: New, Old and Imaginary," in *Jewish Identities in the New Europe,* ed. Jonathan Webber. (London: Littman Library of Jewish Civilization, 1994) 165.
2. Vero-Ban, *What Does It Mean To Be Jewish?* (Budapest: Zsidongo Books, 2011).

Rabbi Dr Shlomo Riskin

What Made Moses the Greatest Prophet?

Moses did not rise to leadership because he came from a prominent Hebrew family – indeed, the Bible introduces him merely as a child of "a man from the house of Levi who took a Levite woman as a wife" (Exodus 2:1–2), and his adoptive mother, with whom he lived in the palace of Pharaoh, was a gentile Egyptian princess.

However, in the lead up to Moses' appointment as a prophet, the Bible relates three incidents in which Moses fought against acts of injustice: his slaying of an Egyptian taskmaster who was beating a Hebrew, his berating of a Hebrew raising his hand against another Hebrew, and his protecting a Midianite shepherdess from unfair treatment by Midianite shepherds. Apparently, Moses was chosen by God to lead the Israelites not because of his ancestral pedigree, but rather because of his compassionate righteousness and sense of moral justice. Prophetic leadership depends not on who your parents and grandparents are, but rather on who you are.

From the very beginning, Moses was reluctant to accept his leadership position. His argument is stated very clearly: "I beg of You, my Lord, I am not a man of words, not from yesterday, not from the day before…heavy of speech and heavy of tongue am I"(Exodus 4:10). Beyond the obvious understanding, Moses is not simply saying that he stammers, especially given that he repeats the same argument even after God promised to deal with his impediment. So what is Moses really saying?

The biblical text itself states that "[the Israelites] did not listen to Moses because of impatience and hard work" (Exodus 6:9) – usually taken to mean that the impatience and backbreaking work of an enslaved and downtrodden people made it difficult, if not impossible, for them to believe that their situation could ever change. But the medieval commentator Ralbag has a far-reaching interpretation of this biblical passage.

When Moses called himself "heavy of speech," he wasn't referring simply to a speech defect; he was rather referring to his personality. He understood that transforming the Hebrews from embittered and small-minded slaves into an inspired nation committed to becoming a holy people and a kingdom of priest-teachers, would require nurturing small talk. Moses would have to listen to paltry concerns and petty complaints until – step by step – his people would become elevated into a "God enthused" nation. "This is not for me," he is telling the Almighty. "I am a man of heavy speech, not of small talk; is it not too much to expect that the one who speaks to God, whose intellect has been developed to such an extent that it divines God's active intellect, should, at the same time, deal with the self-centred resentments and rebellions of a nation-in-progress?"

THE ROLE OF AARON, THE *KOHEN*

Aaron, the High Priest (*Kohen Gadol*), is of very different typology. First, the priesthood is all about genealogy – priesthood comes exclusively from being born into a family of priests. Hence, the task of setting up the *menorah* is given to "Aaron and his sons" (Exodus 27:21). The Bible even lists them by name, stating that they are to be brought forward to serve as priests. Aaron and his sons form a unit of familial inheritance from father to son, a phenomenon completely absent in the case of Moses.

The *kohanim* have special vestments that they must wear while performing the Temple service: four specific garments for the regular *kohanim,* and eight specific garments for the high priest. Indeed, if a priest is without his unique garb, he must vacate the Temple Mount – which leads the Talmud to declare that the sanctity of the *kohen* seems to reside in his garb. However, Moses the prophet has no distinguishing garment whatsoever.

Apparently, the prophet is a charismatic leader inflamed with the fiery passion of the spirit of the Lord; whereas the *kohen* inherits his position, which relies on priestly vestments to bestow "honour and glory" and inspire the masses with prideful religious fervour.

In order to understand the different and complementary roles

Moses and Aaron – these officiates – must play in the drama of Israelite leadership, we must first understand the essence of our Jewish mission.

Religion provides a stable and unchanging constancy in a world of frightening flux, it enables people to participate in rituals that existed before they were born and that will continue after they die. This allows transient mortals to grasp eternity, and to feel that they are in the presence of God. Herein lies the power and the noble task of the priest, the guardian of our ancient religious traditions. The verse which most defines him is: "Remember the days of old, understand the years of past generations. Ask your father and he will tell you, your grandfather and he will say to you" (Deuteronomy 32:7). His primary function is to safeguard the rituals; he must hand over the exact structure of the ritual, the precise text of the prayer or legal passage, from generation to generation. His expertise lies in his mastery of the external form – and preserving it at all costs.

But the root of Judaism is the sense of awe at being in the presence of God, the passionate commitment to divine command in the here and now! What happens when people get so caught up in the form that they lose the essence, so involved in the precise structure of the divine service that they forget that the real divine service lies in their human sensitivity? Then it is the prophet who must come forth, speaking as the mouthpiece of the Living God, reminding us that ritual is of no value if we forget the poor, the orphan, the widow and the other, the stranger and the proselyte knocking at our door. The prophet's message must insist that God would despise our rituals (Isaiah 1:11–17), unless: "moral justice rolls forth like the waters and compassionate righteousness like a mighty stream" (Amos 5:24) – so that our rituals lack elements of holiness if they do not ultimately inspire us to display greater human sensitivity. Moses exemplified these ideas through his prophecy and his constant search for justice.

Moses is the greatest of our prophets because his passion for God and his prophetic wisdom was combined with a love and compassion for his people that enabled him to inspire them to become God's Chosen People. Working together with Aaron, he overcame any "impediment" to be the exemplar of the sensitive religious leader and prophet.

Rabbi Shaul Robinson

How Can People Outside the Traditional Family Model Find a Home in Judaism?

Why are synagogues so noisy? For a long time, I struggled against what I saw as an unfortunate fact. Lately, I have begun to understand how it can be a blessing.

It is often said "shul is not the real centre of Judaism, the home is." Although there is much truth to this, Judaism has never been confined to family or to the traditional family structure. Shuls have an increasingly important role to play, because synagogue is the place that Jewish individuals – regardless of background or family unit – become part of the Jewish people.

As a rabbi on the Upper West Side of Manhattan, I meet a range of congregants who live outside the typical family unit. Singles, divorcees, widows/ers, single parents by choice, and many more, are increasingly part of the Jewish landscape. You can rue it, or embrace it, but it is not likely that this is something that is going to change any time soon. And these individuals play their part in strengthening the Jewish people. The community, at its peril, risks alienating and pushing away some of its best, brightest and most giving members, if we insist that the only model we know how to embrace is the traditional family unit.

I once had a conversation with a single man in his 40s that shook me to the core. He explained to me that, although *Shabbat* observant all his life, he no longer was. Nothing had changed in his belief system. But he was lonely. Deeply lonely. "For you, Rabbi," he said, "*Shabbat* is never a problem. You know where you will be – with your family. Maybe you will have guests, maybe you will not, but you know that come *Shabbat,* you will have a place. But not me. *Shabbat* is an effort every week: will I be invited? will I not? And after years of *Shabbat* becoming not something to look forward to, but something I dread, I just can't do it anymore." He was not rejecting *Shabbat,* his situation simply turned *Shabbat* into a trial rather than a celebration. Another individual tearfully told me that every *Shabbat* afternoon, she turns the television on at home "for company."

But I think the most devastating conversation along these lines was when I asked an elderly lady, a widow, if she was "looking forward to *yom tov*" and she answered, "Rabbi, I dread the *chagim*. All week long I keep busy with all sorts of volunteering activities, but when the holidays come, there is nothing to fill my day."

They have to be addressed and the sense of exclusion alleviated, and it is here that the synagogue comes into its own. In the design of the new Lincoln Square Synagogue, there were very few decisions that I got to make. But one I did claim for myself, and it's the thing about our beautiful new building that I love the most. Above the *Aron Kodesh*, there is, in common with most other synagogues, a verse from the Bible. But our verse is unique. I haven't seen it in any other synagogue. "*Shalom shalom la-rachok ve-la-karov amar Hashem*" (Peace, peace, to the far away and to the close, says *Hashem*).

I had many reasons to choose this verse. A shul has to be at peace. We extend a welcome both to those close to Judaism and those who feel far away. But they were secondary. The most important reason for choosing this verse was that I want everyone who enters the doors of our community to be welcomed. To have someone say "Shalom" (hello) to them.

Which brings us back to talking in shul. Nowadays, we frown on it and clearly we all should make an effort to contribute to a decorous, uplifting synagogue service to enable prayer to connect us to God. But shul is more than simply a place for prayer; it is a place to meet. Observably, people do talk in shul; it's just that we talk at the wrong times and to people we already know. And the latter is really the tragedy.

We have all had the experience of being new in a place – hoping to be welcomed, recognised. We feel awkward, out of place, ill at ease. Whether we will ever come back depends on whether we are made to feel welcomed. And too often, at least in synagogues and other Jewish places, we are not.

Interestingly, there is a source for allowing people to extend greetings to each other, even in the middle of prayer, based on the famous story of Abraham interrupting his conversation with God, in order to extend a hand to three strangers who appeared at his tent. "It is more important to take care of newcomers than to talk to the Divine Presence" concluded the Sages. And all who enter our synagogue – looking for what we are all looking for – welcome, companionship, belonging, community: all are considered "*orechim*" (newcomers). The late Rabbi Soloveitchik put it as follows: "To recognise a person means to affirm that he is irreplaceable."

The American sociologist Robert Putnam identified the way in which contemporary Western societies contribute to greater isolation and a disintegration of civic and communal belonging. But in his book, *American Grace: How Religion Divides and Unites Us*, he shows how people who participate in religious groups are more communally involved, more altruistic, more generous than their secular counterparts.

But it is participation, not religious observance *per se* that is critical here, as Putnam writes, "Devout people who sit alone in the pews are not much more neighbourly than people who don't go to church at all. The real impact of religiosity on niceness or good neighbourliness, it seems, comes through chatting with friends after service or joining a Bible study group, not from listening to the sermon or fervently believing in God. In fact, the statistics suggest that even an atheist who happened to become involved in the social life of a congregation (perhaps through a spouse) is much more likely to volunteer in a soup kitchen than the most fervent believer who prays alone. It is religious belonging that matters for neighbourliness."

Synagogues need to become places of welcome, of community, of outreach, of acceptance. That is their job. They need to cater for people of diverse family backgrounds because certain groups in a community can otherwise become invisible. Many synagogues, Lincoln Square included, hold regular *shabbatonim*, where the aim is that every single member of the community is either a guest or a host of fellow synagogue members.

Communities should consider the assumptions they make when setting the calendar for their weekly activities and programmes. Not running classes during the summer on the assumption that "everyone is away" overlooks huge numbers of today's Jewish community. Offering classes and, indeed, social activities on the long *Shabbat* afternoon or over two and three days of *yom tov* can be, almost literally, a lifeline to people who would otherwise be overwhelmed with loneliness.

But the most important thing of all that we can all do is to talk in shul – to make it a point, a personal mission for all of us, to make sure our synagogues are places of warm, genuine, sincere welcome.

In memory of Salek Orenstein zt"l, whose unyielding faith in God helped him survive the horrors of the Holocaust. His exceptional contribution to Jewish life is his enduring legacy. Dedicated by Josy and Sara Oresenstein and family.

Dayan Yonason Abraham

A Tale of Three Torahs

"Everything depends on *mazel*, even a *Sefer Torah* in the Ark." (*Zohar*)

More than 70 years ago, one of the jewels in European Jewry's crown was the community of Poznan – Posen. Poznan's rabbinic leaders included the famous 18th century genius, Rabbi Akiva Eiger, and it was a thriving vibrant centre with a Jewish population of several thousand, until the advent of Hitler.

Its geographical proximity to Germany meant that by the end of the first week of September 1939, Nazi terror had engulfed the Jewish community. It was then progressively persecuted, enslaved, and ultimately "liquidated" by the barbaric Nazi killing machine.

In the small shtetel of Zagorow, some 60 km from Poznan, lived the Jedwab family, who would have a significant impact on the Melbourne Jewish community, half a world away. Reb Yehuda Chaim Jedwab, the father of four boys and a girl, left Poland before the outbreak of the war with his two eldest sons, Mordechai (Max) and Avrohom (Abe), arriving in Australia in January 1939. He planned to establish a base there for his wife, Shaina Rajzel, daughter, Rivele, and sons Eliezer (Leon) and Moishe to emigrate to.

Tragically that wasn't to happen. After being trapped in the Nazi net, on Tuesday 23rd September 1941, the second day of Rosh Hashanah, Shaina Rajzel, Rivele and Moishe were murdered in gas trucks, the crude precursors to the sophisticated and efficient killing machines, the gas chambers.

Leon, was imprisoned in the labour camps around Poznan in September 1940 and sent to Auschwitz in 1943. After surviving extreme conditions, including the death march to Buchenwald, Leon was liberated on 11th April 1945.

47

In November 1946, Leon, the sole European survivor, was tearfully reunited with his father and brothers in Melbourne. Yehuda Chaim meanwhile had established a successful garment business, and went on to serve as the President of the Caulfield Hebrew Congregation.

Fast forward to Poznan 1998: No community, no organised Jewish life, even the magnificent shul no longer existed. The building still stood, but the accursed Nazis ensured that the soul of the once proud Poznan Jewish community was converted into a swimming pool.

Enter Leon and Tosha Jedwab.

On their first trip back to the region, some 50 years after leaving Poland, Leon and his wife Tosha, herself a native of Poznan, explored, discovered and reminisced about their youth. On their last day there, they visited the state-run Jewish museum, which contains artefacts and memorabilia of an extinct community.

And then Leon noticed it. A fragment of a *Sefer Torah*, pockmarked and burnt around the edges, displayed on the wall. Upon further examination, he discovered something that sent shivers down his spine. The surviving fragment was from *Parashat VaEtchanan*, beginning with the portion: *Ki tolid banim*... (when you bear children and establish yourself in the land and become corrupt and make idols... you will be lost from the land... for you will be destroyed...): the Torah portion which we read on Tisha Be-Av, the saddest day of the year, foretelling doom and destruction.

The burnt Torah fragment continued with the text of the Ten Commandments and *Shema*, the declaration of our faith in God, followed by "*vehaya ki yevi'acha*" (the portion of *VaEtchanan* that foretells the eventual homecoming to our land). This full *parashah* is read on *Shabbat Nachamu*, the *shabbat* after Tisha Be-Av, serving each year as a message of comfort and consolation, that despite suffering and dispersal, we would recover and return.

Leon was transfixed. In his mind, it was precisely these columns in the *Sefer Torah* that represented the message of catastrophe, of faith and observance, of the indestructible divine code of conduct, and of the nation's return to *Eretz Yisrael*, that he had lived through.

Being so moved by what he had discovered, Leon begged

the Polish curator to allow him to buy the Torah fragment. The curator was very sympathetic and did his utmost to persuade the authorities to permit Leon to buy it for the Jewish community in Melbourne. However, despite extensive efforts including an extremely generous cash offer, the government forbade the export of any "historic religious artefacts."

Disappointed, but appreciative of the curator's efforts, Leon and Tosha left Poznan promising to sew a special "mantel" (cover for the *Sefer Torah*) and send it to Poznan. They were true to their word. Within a few weeks of their return, Leon mailed off a beautiful, specially designed mantel in honour of that precious piece of testimony to Jewish survival, the Poznan Torah fragment.

A short few weeks later, Leon received a letter from Poznan. He excitedly opened it to read a message of thanks from the curator. It ended with an interesting question, "I know how interested you were in the Torah scroll. I've managed to locate the fragment of a different Torah through my contacts. Provided it is being sent to some museum or public interest centre, I think I could arrange for it to be sent. Are you interested?"

Leon considered the offer. True it wasn't the same as the amazing fragment he had seen in Poznan and, therefore, obviously not as meaningful. But it was still a *Sefer Torah*, still holy and still had to be respectfully preserved and treated. Besides, what would it sound like to the gentile curator if he turned down the offer?

Accepting the offer, Leon hastily established the Leon Jedwab Judaica Museum. Sure enough, a few weeks later, a long cardboard tube arrived. Nervous with anticipation, Leon opened it and carefully removed the fragile piece of parchment. A very different style of writing, just over three columns of writing....and then it hit him. In front of him, pockmarked and burnt, was the same *parashah* beginning with "*Ki tolid banim*," followed by the Ten Commandments and the *Shema*. The very same piece that had survived in the amazing Poznan Torah fragment had miraculously survived in another *Sefer Torah*, been kept by a Polish gentile, discovered by his new friend the curator and sent to him here in Australia.

I was contacted by Leon on *chol ha-moed* of Pesach 5760 and two weeks later he came to see me, armed with pictures of the Poznan fragments and a package with the second Torah's fragment.

It was really an amazing coincidence and I was both humbled and amazed by Leon's enthusiasm and excitement.

Some six weeks later, I was honoured to be invited to affix a *mezuzah* on the front door of the new Holocaust Memorial Centre extension in Melbourne. It was a moving experience, in that the senior members of our shul had faithfully volunteered for years as guides, inspiring tens of thousands of Australian visitors to the centre, both by relating their personal harrowing Holocaust experiences and tales of survival, as well as by personal example. The Centre thus serves as a remarkable synthesis: it is at once a memorial to the millions of *kedoshim* and their suffering, as well as a source of hope and optimism for a more tolerant future.

Arriving with my wife, half an hour early, we used the time to tour the centre. To the left of the entrance is the main display hall, crammed with pictures, documents and other surviving exhibits and Holocaust mementos.

There, on the wall, was a third *Sefer Torah*. Behind a glass display case was a Torah fragment, brought from Kovno Lithuania by Mr Saul Spigler and presented to the Holocaust Centre. It was faded, burnt around the edges with a bullet hole through the writing and, unbelievably it was the same portion from *Parashat Va-etchanan*: "*Ki tolid banim*," foretelling destruction, which we read on Tisha Be-Av, continuing with the Ten Commandments, and *Shema* until the end of the Torah.

Three *Sifrei Torah*, one message! "We survived with, through and for our Torah."

Hear O Israel, *Hashem*, our God, *Hashem* is one!

Dedicated to Lily Ebert, an Auschwitz survivor, who has inspired
thousands with her message of courage, faith and tolerance.

Elana Chesler

The Crusades and Ashkenazic Jewry

During Roman times Jews had moved north of the Alps establishing small settlements. In the ninth century, Charlemagne
expanded his empire and granted various freedoms to the Jews
which triggered a further shift into Northern Europe. However, a
substantial Jewish population and culture only developed there a
century later, when, at the invitation of local Christian rulers and
in response to new economic opportunities along the Rhine, Jews
settled in northern France and Germany. The term Ashkenazic[11]
evolved to describe the ethnic origins of Jews descending from
these communities based in medieval France and Germany.

These communities produced some outstanding scholars
whose works include enduring and significant commentaries on
the Talmud. A key rabbinic figuree was the 10th century leader
called Rabbenu Gershom – often referred to as "the Light of the
Diaspora" – *Meor Ha-Golah* who lived in Mainz (Mayence), which
became a centre of Torah and Jewish study. He is known for important rulings that he issued including instituting a ban on polygamy.

The most famous of the Ashkenazic medieval rabbis and com-
mentators though was unquestionably Rabbi Shlomo ben Yitz-
cha, known by the acronym of Rashi, who was born in France in
1040 and studied in Germany under the leading talmudists of the
generation. He returned to his hometown of Troyes at the age of
25 to teach Torah and earned a living from growing and tending
vineyards.

Rashi's commentary on the Torah drew on the writings of his

1. Ashkenaz literally means Germany but in the Middle Ages refers initially
to Jews who lived in northern France and Germany, and subsequently to
the Jews of Austria, Bohemia, Switzerland, and Hungary as well.

teachers and on his breadth of knowledge of Midrash, Talmud and grammar, and to this day is by far the most widely read Jewish Bible commentator. Rashi is acclaimed for his ability to present the meaning of the text in a concise and clear fashion, such that he appeals to both learned scholars and beginners. His Bible commentaries also influenced non-Jewish who studied them.

Rashi's commentary on the Talmud, which covers nearly all of the Babylonian Talmud, has been included in every edition since the first printing by Daniel Bomberg in the 1520s and remains an indispensable aid to navigating the Talmud.

Rashi did not have any sons, but his daughters – whom he educated comprehensively in Torah – all married talmudic sages and fathered great scholars. His sons-in-law, grandsons, and students, formed part of a group of scholars known as the *Ba'alei HaTosafot* (Masters of Addition), who lived in Ashkenaz during the 12th and 13th centuries. Their writings are known collectively as '*Tosafot*' and are printed as a commentary in most editions of the Talmud, opposite Rashi's own commentary. The best known amongst them was Rabbenu Tam (1100–1171), one of Rashi's grandsons and to this day, the two types of tefillin that people wear are known as Rashi and Rabbeinu Tam tefillin.

Rashi lived until 1105 surviving the horror of the first Crusade in 1096, which saw the slaughter of thousands of Jews in Western Europe, and about which he wrote several *selichot* (penitential poems) mourning the destruction. Jews were massacred or forced to convert and entire communities were annihilated.

The first Crusade was launched by Pope Urban II in 1095 against the backdrop of the political and social situation in Asia Minor. Despite the schism of 1054 between the Roman Catholic and Eastern Christian churches, the Byzantine Emperor appealed to Rome for help against the Muslim Seljuk Turks who had conquered a large region, including Constantinople and Palestine.

The stated goal of this Crusade was the recapture of the Holy Land and the Church of the Holy Sepulchre in Jerusalem and the Pope promised those who signed up that their sins would be forgiven by God. However, for many it was the perfect opportunity to make a fortune in looting and ransom.

Although the knights were ostensibly men of honour who had pledged themselves to serve a holy cause, the reality was vastly different. Whilst a certain pageantry accompanied them, the knights were trained for war and the Crusades offered a perfect outlet for the ambitions of land-hungry knights and noblemen. The arrival of the Crusaders into a village usually triggered a local mob-like violent outbreak under the guise of legitimacy.

Initially, the Jews were not the primary focus of the Crusades; it was rather the Muslims and their lands. However, as the army of peasants and knights marched through Europe, it occurred to them that there were many other infidels in their midst, beyond those in the Holy Land, namely the Jews – who had in fact committed the far greater crime of deicide. The Crusades then turned into a campaign of terror and destruction against the Jews in Europe, during which at least one quarter of Ashkenazic Jewry was wiped out.

In certain places, the Jews were offered local protection. The Bishop of Worms attempted to shelter the Jews of his town, but the crusaders broke in to his episcopal palace and killed at least 800 Jews there when they refused to accept the Christian faith. At Regensburg, Metz, Prague, and throughout Bohemia, one massacre followed another.

It is estimated that over 60,000 obeyed the Pope's calling and fixed crosses to their outer garments (giving rise to the name, "crusaders"), although only 15,000 reached Jerusalem, where they put the city under siege. After breaching the walls, they entered the city and killed the Jews of Jerusalem, burning their synagogue down. In the words of Raymond D'Aguilers, one of the contemporary Christian chroniclers:

> Let it suffice to say this much at least, that in the temple and portico of Solomon, men rode in blood up to their knees and bridle reins.

The first Crusade foreshadowed even greater disaster, marking a turning point in the relationship between the Jews and their Christian neighbours and created the first broad movement against Jews since the seventh century's mass expulsions and forced conversions. The Jews of Europe endured a total of eight Crusades during the 12th and 13th centuries,[2] with the Second (1147) *and* Third (1188) being particularly ferocious (especially against the Jews of England during the reign of Richard the Lion-Heart).The ritual murder charge and the blood libel charge levied against British Jewish communities were developed at this time. These fiendish accusations were based on creative fiction but effectively tarred the Jewish community with inescapable fury delivered by the hands of their Christian neighbours.

The social position of the Jews in Western Europe went into terminal decline, and was followed by centuries of persecution and restrictions, which included forcible conversions, anti-Jewish rioting, further blood libels and the ghettos. Legal restrictions became more frequent, which prepared the way for the anti-Jewish legislation of Innocent III, and ultimately culminated in the expulsion of the Jews from most Western European countries including upper Bavaria (1276) and England (1290) and France (1394). The Crusades thus formed the turning-point in medieval European Jewish history.

2. In his online series on Jewish History, Rabbi Ken Spiro notes that following the Crusades, successive Muslim dynasties left much of the coastal plain of Israel (between Jaffa and Haifa) desolate out of a lingering fear that the Crusaders might one day return. This facilitated the purchase of large areas of land by the early Zionist movement in the late 19th and 20th centuries. The coastal plain includes cities such as Tel Aviv, Petach Tikva, Herzliya, Ra'anana, Netanya and Hadera.

Sponsored by Clayhall United Synagogue, in memory of Baruch Obuchowski, one of our most cherished members, a kind and gentle man.

Rabbi David Aaron

The ABC of Kabbalah

Many years ago, when I first began the study of the Kabbalah, the ancient mystical interpretation of Judaism, I stumbled upon the learning centre of a great kabbalistic master. The place was crowded, so I figured there must be some kind of public event going on, and went in. The great kabbalist was speaking, but suddenly he stopped. I realised that he had noticed me come in and was staring in my direction. Trying to be as unobtrusive as possible, I made my way to a seat on the sidelines, but his eyes followed me across the room. I got a very uncomfortable feeling, which only intensified when he pointed at me and motioned me to come forward.

The entire room was looking at me now. My heart was pounding. I had heard that these masters have the ability to look right through you, to your soul. I didn't know what to expect as I approached him, and I was scared. He was quite old and had a long white beard and bright blue, penetrating eyes. He spoke in a soft voice with a thick accent, but he only asked me a few innocuous questions about my family and myself. Then he held out an apple in his hand and dramatically raised it before me, dangling it by its stem.

This great man wanted to give me an apple? I had no idea what this was all about. I reached to take the apple. But the crowd shouted, "No!" I became flustered and withdrew my hand. He offered the apple again and again I tried to take it. Again the crowd said, "No!" Then I saw that people were motioning for me to cup my hand and hold it beneath the apple. I did so. The great kabbalist smiled and dropped the apple into my hand. He then bent over and, in a tone that seemed to admonish me, whispered in my ear, "What have you been learning?" Before I could answer, he turned and walked away.

As simplistic as the message seems, it took years before I realised what it really meant. "Kabbalah" literally means "receptivity" – indeed, it is the art of learning to receive. The master was trying to show me that I had not yet learned the real meaning of the Kabbalah. The lesson was: when you are offered a gift, do not take it; instead, make of yourself a space that can receive it.

Kabbalah is not only about getting more out of life; it is about receiving life as a gift. It is about the art of receiving life's gifts of love, spiritual growth, awareness, creativity, freedom, happiness, and holiness. Mastering the art of receiving is not merely a private matter for each of us. The Kabbalah specifically and the Torah generally both teach that our individual lives reflect a universal process. Human psychology is really a particular manifestation of cosmology. All of reality shares in our struggles, feels our pain, celebrates our joy and cheers us on to live fully. Conversely, all of reality hurts when we inflict pain upon others and ourselves. We are all connected to one another – individually and collectively, to the universe and to all that is. We are not alone. Knowing this gives us strength, hope, courage and energy.

WANT A LIGHT?

A story is told about three men who were imprisoned in a dark dungeon. Two of them were intelligent, but the third was not. Every day, when their food was lowered into the dark dungeon, the third fellow would fumble with the utensils and cut himself. One of the others would help him by practising a routine with him to handle the darkness, but because the food was presented in a different way each day, it always confused him. The other prisoner then said, "Let's bore a hole in the wall and let a ray of light in, and then he will be able to see and eat without help."

The Kabbalah is all about light. Its main message to us is that we have the power to increase the spiritual light in the world or decrease it. All our actions, words and thoughts control the dimmer switch that turns the light up or down. What is the power of light? When you turn the light on in your room, it lets you see what is there. Otherwise you grope in the dark, knock things over, bang your knee and walk into walls. This is also true with spiritual light. Without it, your spiritual world is dark. Without spiritual light you can't see love even when it is right in front of you. You knock over people who love you. You step on souls. You walk right past meaningful moments. And you have no sense of direction.

According to the Kabbalah, a person who only has access to physical light lives in the World of Shells or Peels – called *Olam Ha-Kelipot*. Such a person only sees physical things, those which are external and superficial. The shell or the peel is only the outside of the fruit and is, therefore, secondary to the fruit. If you can only see the shell or peel, you confuse the wrapping with the true contents. You are impressed with the packaging and miss the true gift inside.

Kabbalah teaches us the secrets of how to access the spiritual light that lets us see what's inside. Given that what you see is what you get, when you want to receive the eternal spiritual gift wrapped in this world, you need to increase the spiritual light to see and get inside. This physical world is only the packaging, but what is the gift inside?

What is the greatest gift you could ever give or get? Presence. Not presents, but Presence. When I think of my childhood, my most precious memory is of my mother sitting by my bed and reading to me *Winnie the Pooh*. What is so great about that? My parents gave me lots of gifts. I got a terrific train set and lots of other toys. But they didn't last and they mean very little to me today. What I still treasure and continue to enjoy are those precious moments when I knew my mother was there for me. She wasn't interested in Pooh Bear or Piglet. She never read those stories at any time for herself. My mother concentrated her entire being into those moments and was completely there for me. She gave me the greatest gift you could ask for – her Presence.

What is Presence? Presence is like chocolate cake. I can't tell you what chocolate cake tastes like; you will only know how delicious it is when you taste it yourself. I could tell you what the ingredients are, but the cake is greater than the sum of the ingredients. Presence is like the colour green. I can't describe it, but when you see it, you will know. So I can't tell you what Presence is. I can tell you that its ingredients are love, care, respect, honesty, meaning, beauty, wisdom, and much more. To know Presence you have to experience it.

According to the Kabbalah, God created you and me and put

us into this world to give us the greatest gift imaginable. Divine Presence. Kabbalah calls this "*Shechinah*." Divine Presence or the "*Shechinah*" fills everything.

But how do we turn on the light that lets the eyes of our soul see it? How do we become receptive to the ultimate gift of God's loving Presence? By giving our loving presence to each other so that we become receptive to the Divine Presence. And the more you give, the more you receive.

Rabbi Dr Jonathan Rosenblatt

Poking the Lion: The Strange Jewish Path to Happiness

Happiness, the universal human goal, is surprisingly difficult to define and very elusive to pursue. In contemporary Western culture, it is often sought through acquisition, diversion, and consumption – experiences that transport man beyond his awareness of existential fragility. However, these pursuits of happiness – actually a retreat from unhappiness – ultimately disappoint and fail. The greyhounds end up endlessly chasing the mechanical rabbit, drawn by the promise of a destination called "happy" – the Shangri-La, the Paradise on earth – but the frantic journey never produces an arrival at all. Instead, it provides a desperate, doomed attempt to stay on the track a little longer, before age, illness, and ultimately death flick the exhausted runner away – only to have his space on the track taken over by someone else, who is likewise entranced by the mechanical rabbit's promise.

In Jewish tradition, happiness – reflective joy – is the result of a cycle of duties and actions. The festival of Succot, which is the quintessential "Time of our Rejoicing," is the annual climax of two different cycles, both of which are paradoxically the greatest anxieties of human experience. And precisely because we have dared to poke the lion of our fears, we are treated to a festival of joy,[1] which concludes with Simchat Torah, the ultimate day of joy. To understand this correctly, we need to first define the cycles that meet in Succot.

Succot is the third and concluding Pilgrimage Festival, and

---

1. In a similar way, two of the most joyful events of a Jew's personal life – the feasts marking circumcision and marriage – contain the twin elements of high anxiety and ebullient joy.

follows from Pesach and Shavuot, which all together form the festive days linked to the agriculture of the Land of Israel. It marks the time of the ingathering of the crops. The human drama – especially in ancient times – played itself out against the blade of hunger. The laws governing labourers in the Bible and the Talmud assume an economy which, for many, had each day's food directly dependent upon that same day's work. Famine, drought, and plagues were realities of life and death. When the crop was safely harvested there was respite and thanksgiving, and the Jew was bidden to celebrate, even as he prayed for rain for the coming year and contemplated anxiety for the future. To pray was in some way to imagine the worst, to engage in the possibility of disaster, yet to be comforted by the faith in a Heavenly Father who seeks His children's good.

The companions of these seasons are the poor and the vulnerable for whom even the season of plenty brings no relief, other than in the generosity of those more fortunate. They are reminders of the tenuousness of prosperity. There is temptation to keep them out of sight, to forget the transient nature of satiety, but Maimonides cautions that without the poor, our experience of joy is rendered inauthentic – "the joy of the belly." Joy can only be real if there is a true sense of rejoicing, which is a collective experience.

Succot is also the final element in another series of three festivals: the Days of Judgment. Within the agricultural cycle, the fear of hunger, and by extension, all economic distress, is ever-present. However, in the Judgment cycle, the focus is even more terrifying: Life and Death. Rosh Hashanah demands attention to the power of the Divine King and to the ensuing judgment. There is hardly a mention in the prayers of personal failing and sin; there is no need. We find ourselves under the dazzling light of God's strict justice. We sing of His Majesty, even as we are aware that we are singing a hymn to our own unworthiness. Some traditions even fasted on Rosh Hashanah. Not a fast like that of Yom Kippur when man is likened to an angel and is freed from the need to eat. The fast of Rosh Hashanah is the fast of the hopelessly ashamed, the incontrovertibly guilty. Even the dominant tradition of honey and rich foods rises from a determination to affect confidence in God's ultimate mercy – all the while recognising that without that mercy we stand at the brink of the abyss.

Then on Yom Kippur we shout our transgressions and beat our breasts, stoking the fire of our faith in a divine love so powerful that no failing will eradicate the warmth of its forgiveness. Our unworthiness, our profound dependency on God, paradoxically, produces a nearly buoyant sense of well-being. It is in the wake of this process that the Jew enters "*zeman simchatenu* – the season of our rejoicing." And how is this joy expressed? By entering a fragile structure – the *succah* – constructed of agricultural detritus, that exposes the Jew to the vagaries of the elements. In this homage to transience, we are commanded to dwell with God *as if* we were residing in the luxury of our secure homes. And in the synagogue, a festive bouquet is waved in celebration during *Hallel*, as we recount occasions in history of miraculous divine intervention. Yet on Hoshanah Rabbah, the climax of it all, we pray against a litany of possible natural disasters. Tradition bids us to sing our dreads.

The final day of the season is Simchat Torah, where rejoicing is transformed into a highly refined form. The botanical totems are replaced by the scrolls of the Torah. Throughout the festival, a representative scroll stands in the synagogue's centre, silent and mysterious. On Simchat Torah the centre is empty, perhaps symbolising a people with no Temple to anchor existence. Now there is only the circuit. All of the scrolls leave the Holy Ark to join in. And they do not only march in solemn resignation, the circle dances! The scrolls dance! – the joyous respite earned by survival of the cycles of anxiety. It is a transformative joy because it is in the company of the Torah. Simchat Torah presides over the transition from reflection to action, from the festive toward the prosaic, and ushers us back to the working world, now armed with the lessons of joy-inflected living, knowing that Torah leads man *into* and through life, with all its threats and terrors.

The lesson of Succot and its legacy, as emblematised by Simchat Torah, is that the path to joy leads through the valley of trembling. There is no hope for happiness if we retreat from what we fear, no matter how beguiling the respite. Only if we taunt the lion of our fears, do we emerge – with God as our companion – into happiness.

Avraham Duvdevani

Opportunity within Crisis

We are currently in the 66th year of Israel's independence, following a 2,000 year exile. But the amount of time that has elapsed since 1948 and the routine of day-to-day life causes us to forget how amazing that event was. We grow accustomed to things, even including independence, which presents the danger of cutting ourselves off from our past – a past filled with suffering yet magnificence – and equally losing a vision for the future.

In the first years following the establishment of the State, "Jewish identity" and "affiliation with Israel" in both Israel and the Diaspora were fuelled by two of the most dramatic events to take place in the 20th century: the Holocaust, in which so many of our people were murdered and the danger of extinction hovered over our people; and the Homecoming, three years after the Holocaust, when the State of Israel was established, stimulating the ingathering of many of the exiles.

Yet, despite these two watershed events, we find ourselves nowadays at a crossroads. The Diaspora Jew no longer accepts the view of the transience and instability of the Jewish Diaspora, albeit that for many in the Diaspora, Israel occupies the position of being a fundamental basis of Jewish identity.

Times have changed and a new generation has entered the community and is assuming leadership roles, a generation of individuals born after the country's establishment who were not part of that collective experience.

The excitement of the State has given way to routine and to judging Israel by common and occasionally severe criteria. Amid such a process, Israel has lost much of its attractiveness. Furthermore, the other components of Jewish identity are also in the process of erosion. On a number of levels, the Jewish community framework in the Diaspora fights for its existence.

The liberalism that has breached the walls of the community has created a two-way movement – of Jewish sons and daughters leaving the community and assimilating into general society, and the inrushing wind of Western world culture and secularism into Jewish society.

One characteristic, in particular, stands out in marked contradiction to the foundations of Judaism. In recent decades, the climate within Western culture has pushed the idea of personal gratification and self-fulfilment. The ideology of individualism, of "every man for himself" has taken over in society and culture. It has become a world of "me" and of "here and now," and it is no wonder that the Jewish national experience and the Jewish community experience are losing ground in favour of individualistic experiences that promise personal reward and are based on the indulgence of the individual.

Yet before succumbing to despair, we need only recall Soviet Jewry during the Communist period and its Jewish-Zionist awakening. From a situation of despair, when no one gave it any chance of awakening due to being cut off from the mainstream for 70 years, a transformation took place. Their renaissance should prove to us that despite everything, our nation possesses a tremendous hidden strength, which is seen through the nation's historical experiences, often veiled, almost invisible, but in existence nonetheless.

This internal spring is the connection that each Jew, simply by being a Jew, has with the rest of Jewry – *Kelal Yisrael*.

When we say *"Kelal Yisrael,"* what do we mean? In a nutshell, *Kelal Yisrael* is not the total number of Jews in the world today. It is not any particular Jewish organisation, nor even the whole set of Jewish organisations. It is much more than that.

Kelal Yisrael is a "non-organised" and "non-represented" organic body. A body with an internal common language understood only by itself, with a shared sense of awareness and of the future. *Kelal Yisrael* is me and you and any Jew who, by virtue of being Jewish, wants to be a Jew.

In any place where the soul of the individual aspires to connect with the collective, that is where *Kelal Yisrael* is found. It lives in the heart and soul as a type of international "code" that an outsider would not readily understand but that a Jew feels in every fibre of his being.

For Jews, who throughout the year connect with the Jewish people in some sort of way (community, synagogue, club, Jewish movement, etc.), the *Kelal Yisrael* within them is visible. For others who lack this association, the connection is nonetheless present, although very concealed and the processes of assimilation push them further and further outward. Such that often, it is only as a result of momentous events such as those which spark fear of existential danger to the Jewish people and its communities, or to the State of Israel, that this connection to *Kelal Yisrael* becomes aroused. Then, what was hidden can begin to speak and the hidden ember is able to become a flame.

In order, therefore, to fight the processes of disengagement from Jewry and Judaism without crisis, we must do this: deepen within our consciousness the idea of *Kelal Yisrael*. We must educate our children into the ideals of solidarity, a love of humankind, of giving to others and of volunteering.

In sum, we must firstly make apparent in the eyes of all Jews, a recognition that we are in a time of persistent Jewish national danger, a danger no less existential than the danger of annihilation during the Six Day War or of destruction during the Communist Soviet regime. Assimilation lies in wait, alienation spreads, and the link to Israel weakens to the point of disappearance. And secondly, we need a sober vision of activism; from this will come our ultimate salvation. These forces will strengthen our link to the *Kelal* – the Jewish community and to Israel itself.

Rebbetzin Holly Pavlov

19 Miriam: Tapping Life's Potential

There are times in our lives when things look so bad, so hopeless
that we would despair of any possibility of change. Yet, as a wheel
turns downward, so does it turn upward, and if we hold on long
enough, and if we trust in God enough, what looks like a desperate
situation could be transformed into redemption.

This is a message we learn from our ancestors, and no one lived
this more than Miriam.

She was born at the darkest time of the exile in Egypt, a time
when Pharaoh's soldiers were throwing babies into the Nile River,
when the exile was so bitter that she was named Miriam from
the Hebrew word "*mar*" (bitter). Yet Miriam always believed in
redemption. She always knew the time would come when the Jews
would be saved. The question was how and when, but never if!

MIRIAM AND WATER

Pharaoh decreed that all baby boys should be thrown into the Nile.
As a result of this decree, Miriam's father, Amram, concluded: "We
are toiling for nothing." He separated from his wife so they would
have no more children. Following his lead, all the Jewish men
divorced their wives (*Sotah* 12a).

Miriam told him, "Father, your decree is harsher than Pharaoh.
Pharaoh only decreed on the males and you decreed on the males
and the females. Pharaoh only decreed for this world and you for
this world and the world to come. Pharaoh is a wicked person, so
it is questionable if his decree will be carried out, but you are a
righteous person, so your decree will definitely be fulfilled." Amram
listened to her and remarried his wife, and all the Jewish men did
the same (*Sotah* 12a).

Miriam's argument was: you are not in charge of the world. All a person can do in this life is to try to reach up to *Hashem*. You must try to bring life into this world, but whether you succeed or not, is up to *Hashem*. And whether the evil decree is nullified or upheld is also in *Hashem's* hands.

When Jewish babies were born, frantic mothers tried to hide them, and when Moses' mother could no longer conceal him, she made a basket for him, pitched it with tar, and told her daughter Miriam to take him to the river.

Miriam did as she was told. But she did more as well. After she put the basket in the water, she watched and she waited for the potential miracle. She waited for salvation. Indeed, the daughter of Pharaoh discovered the child, took him home and raised him.

Eighty years later, the Jews left Egypt and crossed the sea, led by the very same Moses. Salvation had arrived! With the sea split, the Jews sang and rejoiced in their salvation. Miriam, too, sang – for she had believed in salvation from the beginning. Miriam and the women not only sang, they played instruments. Where did they get them? When the Jews left Egypt, the righteous women brought them because they were confident that *Hashem* would perform miracles for them (Rashi, Exodus 16:20). The timbrels were an expression of their trust in God.

We, therefore, see Miriam by the water twice: once when she put baby Moses in the basket on the Nile and the second time, as she led the women in song when they crossed the sea and moved from slavery to redemption. Our rabbis tell us that she was rewarded for believing in redemption when things seemed lost and for celebrating that redemption as she sang at the sea.

Her reward was a well of water, a travelling well that accompanied the Jewish people in the desert for 40 years. Besides the obvious connection between Miriam and water, wells are a metaphor for spirituality and Torah. What is a well? A place that is discovered only when we dig deep into the earth and find water that is hidden from view. The water was always there, but we must find it. The same is true with spirituality. When we dig deep into this physical world, we discover spirituality. This spirituality is only uncovered through the process of digging and working hard. The "water" is there, but one has to discover it.

The well is a metaphor of finding *Hashem* in hidden places. It is not a simple thing to do. One does not find *Hashem* easily – only through very real endeavour.

There is a kabbalistic idea that everything in the world has either masculine or feminine energy. Masculine energy is potential, whereas feminine energy is the actualisation of potential. The masculine requires the feminine to actualise his potential. Without the feminine, he remains mere potential. Masculine is giving, from above to below. Feminine receives from below to above. In the relationship between *Hashem* and Israel, Israel is feminine, receiving divine abundance from above. *Hashem* is masculine, bestowing abundance upon us. *Hashem* is, in a metaphorical sense, potential waiting to be actualised in this world. The Jewish people "actualise" *Hashem's* potential by bringing Him into the world through human endeavour, *mitzvot* and learning Torah.

In Kabbalah, a well is feminine. It is the expression of human ability to actualise, dig, and bring potential (water) into reality.

Miriam was given a well because she saved Moses and believed in the redemption. The potential for redemption exists but isn't actualised without human endeavour. *Hashem* brings redemption only after human actions. We dig and *Hashem* brings forth water.

And whilst it is true that Miriam's name means "bitter," yet Miriam's life was not bitter. It was full of song. She had the faith that life is good. If it is bitter now, hard now, there will be salvation. "*Mar*" might mean bitter, but the second part of Miriam's name, "*yam*," means "sea." In the depths there is a well and there is water. Out of the bitter, comes a sea full of water.

Rabbi Micah Greenland

Getting to Know My Uncle Lou: Making Prayer Invigorating

Doesn't God already know what I want or need? Why do I need to ask?

Why do I have to daven so frequently? Three times a day is a little much, don't you think? I just told God what I needed during *Minchah*; does He really need to hear it again at *Ma'ariv*?"

Why does a perfect God need to be "buttered up" with our praises and our thanks? How does that benefit Him? Is He somehow lacking if we just cut to the chase and ask for what we need?

Why pray in Hebrew? The words honestly don't mean anything to me.

The questions above are just a small sample of the questions and frustrations I have heard over the years from teens about Jewish prayer. Indeed, these are challenging questions. Too often though, they are discussed strictly within the context of a teen "Q&A" or youth group session. But, in reality, it's not just teenagers who struggle with a true understanding of *tefillah*; almost everyone has at one time or another. Ultimately, it is quite common to find ourselves, even during moments of prayer itself, wondering how to find meaning and resolution from an experience that feels foreign and distant.

Before I propose some way to make prayer more palatable and meaningful, let me share with you a story, albeit a fictional one, about my Uncle Lou. Growing up, my parents always insisted I schmooze and spend time with Uncle Lou. At weddings, bar mitzvahs, and nearly every opportunity they had, I found my parents nagging me, "Micah, go speak to your Uncle Lou." But, to be quite frank, I did not enjoy talking to Uncle Lou. He was not a gifted conversationalist, and I always struggled to find mutual areas of interest to discuss with him. (It seems appropriate to emphasise that this story is entirely fictional – I love my uncles!) After years of strategically avoiding my parents' supplications that I engage with my incurably awkward uncle, I finally discovered what the fuss was all about.

One day, my parents sat me down and explained that all the major avenues of accomplishment in my life and things that I enjoyed – camp, school, extra-curricular activities, even the house we lived in and the clothes I was wearing – were all funded by the generosity of my Uncle Lou. I always knew that there must be someone else helping my parents, who were not financially comfortable, but I was simply shocked that it was my Uncle Lou.

For many teens, sadly, but honestly, their relationship with prayer and God is just like the one I described with Uncle Lou. They are encouraged by parents or others to speak to this mysterious "Uncle" in their lives, but they know not how to cultivate conversation or appreciate the role their aloof Uncle has in their life. If prayer is to be successful, teens and adults alike need to realise that we owe our entire existence to God's generosity and goodness.[1]

At its core, prayer is really about initiating, improving, and deepening one's relationship with God. It has absolutely nothing to do with meeting God's needs; He has none. Rather, prayer is an opportunity to connect to the Divine and reflect on our needs, recognising that every single need and desire that we have – indeed, everything that we have ever received or will ever receive – comes from one source: God Himself. The more we come to acknowledge that, the closer we will feel to Him and the more genuinely we will appreciate the degree and magnitude of God's relationship with us as individuals, on an intensely personal level.

Viewed in that light, prayer is clearly not about identifying for

1. I owe a debt of gratitude for this essay to Rabbi Yehoshua Karsh, who has been a mentor of mine in improving my own davening. It was he who first introduced me to the "Uncle Lou" metaphor for relating to God. More of Rabbi Karsh's wisdom on *tefillah* can be found at: http://torahlearningcenter.com/index.php/library-home/essays-by-y-karsh/88-essay-26.

God's benefit what we need or want, or about "buttering" Him up, so to speak, so that He's more likely to say "yes." Rather it is about helping us to recognise the critical and central role that God plays in our lives – that He is responsible for our successes and helps us overcome challenges or obstacles. When we praise or thank Him, it is for *our* benefit, to heighten our awareness of God as the true Master of the Universe and to be cognisant of God's capacity to provide.

Like most people, I often struggle in remaining mindful of God as truly present during my davening, but I once heard a very helpful approach in the name of Rebbetzin Feige Twerski. Before beginning the *Amidah*, after taking three steps back, imagine standing before a towering pair of oak doors. Each door is magnificently etched with beautiful carvings and right behind the door sits the King. Before taking the three steps forward, to begin the *Amidah*, imagine from behind the oak doors, you suddenly hear your name being announced, summoning you to an audience before the King. "Micah Greenland, the King is ready to see you." As you take those three steps forward, with the right imagery, it will be more than three small steps, it will be a giant leap to stand in front of the King of Kings through whom all your needs are decided and provided.

Whether it's your Uncle Lou or the oak doors, we need to start thinking about prayer differently. Imageries and analogies are both means to the same end: developing a relationship with our Creator. Granted it may take a lifetime, but much like the revelation of my Uncle Lou, once you realise the role God plays in your life, the conversation will never be the same.

Rabbi Yaakov Asher Sinclair

21
Hovering Above the Pit: Zeide's Coat Tails

It was a dark, cold night in the Janowska concentration camp. Suddenly, a shout pierced the air: "Everyone out of the barracks immediately. Anyone remaining inside will be shot on the spot!"

Pandemonium broke out. People pushed their way to the doors while screaming the names of friends and relatives. In a panic-stricken stampede, the prisoners ran in the direction of the big open field. In the middle, they saw two huge pits.

Once more, the cold voice roared in the night:

"You Jews need some exercise! You pitiful specimens! One by one you will jump across these pits. If you make it, you can go back to your beds, but if you fall into the crater, you will be machine-gunned to death before you can crawl out. I'm sure you'll agree that this should make for an interesting evening's entertainment…"

Imitating the sound of a machine gun, the voice trailed off into the night followed by wild, coarse laughter.

It was clear to the inmates that they would all end up in the pits. Even at the best of times it would have been impossible to jump over them, all the more so on that cold night in Janowska. The prisoners standing at the edge of the pits were skeletons, feverish from disease and starvation, exhausted from slave labour and sleepless nights.

The stillness of the night became punctuated with the rattle of machine-gun fire and the last cries of a holy Jew taking his leave of this world. In that silent queue of destiny, stood a giant of the soul – the Bluzhever Rebbe *zt"l*. The Rebbe had lost his wife, his children and his grandchildren to the Nazi murderers, but he never lost his faith in God.

Next to him stood an irreligious Jew. The two had met in the camp and a deep friendship had developed between them. He said to the rabbi, "To jump over this pit is impossible. Why should we perform for these sadist pigs? When it's my turn, I'm not going to jump. Let them shoot me where I stand. I'm not going to jump through hoops for them like a dog."

Quietly, the Bluzhever Rebbe replied: "My friend. The Creator has given us a most wonderful gift – the gift of life. However, He has given it to us with a … condition … that we shouldn't return it to Him before he takes it back from us. Every second of our life is precious. While it is still in our power to live, we must hold on to life with all our might. If we jump and we make it to the other side, we will have honoured the gift that He gave us. And if we jump and we fail, we will arrive in the next world a few short seconds later than if we had refused to jump."

The decisive moment had arrived. The Bluzhever Rebbe stood at the mouth of the abyss. He closed his eyes and it seemed to the young man that a smile came over the Bluzhever Rebbe's angelic face – as though he had recognised an old long-lost friend. Summoning what little strength was left in his frail body, the 53-year-old Rabbi took a few steps back and then leapt into the darkness.

The Bluzhever Rebbe opened his eyes. He had landed on the other side. And seconds later, his friend landed next to him.

"We are here, we are alive." He said. "How did you possibly have the strength to make it across?"

"Just before I jumped," said the Bluzhever Rebbe "I saw a vision of my *zeide*. And in front of him was his *zeide* and all the holy Jews back through the ages to Abraham; all those Jews who kept our holy Torah even when it cost them their lives. I saw my *zeide*, jumping across the crater in front of me. So I stretched out my hands and grabbed onto his coat tails. And he pulled me across."

The two remained in silence for some moments. Finally, the Bluzhever Rebbe said, "I understand how I made it across, but how did *you* manage to jump so far?"

"Rebbe. I was hanging on to *your* coat tails," he said.

Rabbi Berel Wein

Spanish Jewry in the Middle Ages

The greatness of the Jewish community in Spain (which translates
as "Sefarad" in Hebrew) during the Golden Age of the Jews in
Spain is reflected in the lives of a number of great people. In general,
history is really extended biography. It is a narrative of the lives and
events of people and often, by knowing the biography of certain
individuals, we are able to glimpse the society and times that they
lived in, and gain a more complete understanding of the historic
process that they helped further. In this vein, let us discuss one of
the greatest Jews who lived during the Golden Age of Spain: Rabbi
Judah HaLevi (1075–1141).

We do not have a detailed biography of his life, but we know
that, as a very young man, he studied in the academy of the Rabbi
Isaac Alfasi (the Rif) with Rabbi Joseph ibn Migash. We also
know that he was a physician and that Jews were already famous
in Spain for medicine.

His entire life he longed to live in the Land of Israel and when
he was in his sixties, he finally embarked upon that fateful journey.
Travel back then, of course, was not like today and it took many
weeks during which he made many stops. He went to Egypt, Damascus, and various Jewish communities throughout the Middle
East until he arrived in the Land of Israel.

His end is shrouded in legend, which says that when he finally
arrived at the gates of Jerusalem and bowed down to kiss the earth
of the holy city, he was killed by a Bedouin Arab bandit who took
him by surprise. The fact that he died in the Land of Israel is known
although his burial place is not.

Rabbi Judah HaLevi was a prolific poet; indeed, he became the
poet laureate of the Jewish people and his poetry has been adapted for the synagogue and home. One of his most famous pieces

is *Yonah Matzah Bo Manoach* – The Dove Found Rest, which is sung in Jewish homes on *Shabbat* (and was originally written for a bride and groom). Equally well known are his stirring poems about returning to Zion which are said on Tisha Be-Av, the day in the Jewish calendar that commemorates the destruction of the two Temples.

The fact that he used his poetry to express the longing of his People to return to Zion is noteworthy because the assumption is that at the height of the Golden Age of Spain the Jews were happy and settled there. Yet the truth is, that even in the midst of the Golden Age, Jews were discriminated against and pogroms occurred. No matter how well integrated and successful, they did not see themselves as Spanish in the way American Jews today feel American, even though there was a degree of assimilation into Muslim-Moorish life. Rabbi Judah HaLevi's poems were meant as a declaration that the Jews of Spain had no intention of viewing Spain as their permanent homeland.

He also authored a famous series of poems that he called *The Poems of the Sea*, which were written on board ship whilst he was on the way to *Eretz Yisrael*.

His poetry remains baked within the heart of the Jewish people and penetrates their core, but as great as that accomplishment was, he was much more than that.

Rabbi Judah HaLevi was also a great philosopher. His famous book *The Kuzari* was written in Arabic and later translated into Hebrew by the Ibn Tibbon family, renowned translators in their own right. It is based on the story of the Khazars, the kingdom in central Asiatic Russia who converted to Judaism. Rabbi Judah HaLevi took that incident and wrote about it as if the King of the Khazars had invited scholars from the three main monotheistic religions to present their ideas and ultimately determine whether the kingdom would convert to Islam, Christianity or Judaism. Through the words of the Jewish sage, Rabbi Judah HaLevi portrays the ideas of Judaism to the world. Today, it would be called a case study of comparative religion.

Aside from expressing the philosophy of the Jewish people, he expresses the case against Christianity and Islam. There are certain ideas presented in the book that, since his time, have remained the basic philosophy of the people of Israel, one of which is *consensus omnium* (everyone agrees). He points out that all three religions agree on various fundamental matters such as the divinity of the Torah, the existence of Moses and Mount Sinai, and that the Jewish people were at one time the Chosen People. The dispute between the three religions only comes later. The *consensus omnium* is therefore that the origins of the Torah and the Jewish people are true. In effect, Rabbi Judah HaLevi puts the burden of proof on those trying to change the original claims of Judaism. (This is a talmudic idea: the burden of proof is on those trying to extract the money from the person holding it.) And, furthermore, if each of the monotheistic religions agree with these basic ideas, then it would appear logical to believe in it.

A second major underpinning of Jewish belief that Rabbi Judah HaLevi expresses in *The Kuzari*, reflects the reality that there is no people as sceptical as the Jews. Even miraculous events do not shake us. We are great believers, but also great doubters. Rabbi Judah HaLevi says that an event such as the revelation at Mount Sinai could not have been "sold" to the Jewish people if it did not happen as described, occurring as it did before millions of people. The Jewish people refused to accept paganism, Christianity and Islam due to that very great collective sceptical nature. Therefore, he writes, the fact that we all have this common tradition and that this common tradition has been accepted for so many thousands of years, is itself proof of the correctness of the Tradition.

A third major philosophic point he makes is that the Jewish people are special. Special is not better, but different. He points out that civilisation is tied up with the lot of the Jewish people, and that advances and reverses in civilisation somehow are either Jewish in origin or they impinge upon the Jewish people. In a prediction regarding European and world history, Rabbi Judah HaLevi says that the relationship of governments and empires to the Jewish people is the barometer by which civilisation will be measured. If the Jewish people come to redemption in their own land and the world accepts it, then that will be the messianic era for the rest of the world. However, as long as the Jewish people have not found rest there, then the remainder of the world will be troubled.

The life of Rabbi Judah HaLevi and his contributions give us a clearer picture of what the Golden Age of Spain was like at its zenith. From this time on, the situation of the Jews there would change due mainly to three factors – all of which are present today in the general world. Firstly, Muslim fanaticism would return. Secondly, the Christians embarked on re-conquering Spain which would also radically alter the Christian attitude toward the Jews. And thirdly, the combination of assimilation and the worsening of their economic situation would cause Spanish Jews to rethink their preoccupation with poetry, philosophy, language, etc. There would arise within Spanish Jewry a reaction that warned (200 years before the Spanish expulsion was decreed) that the eventual outcome of this situation would be the forsaking of the Torah and embracing matters which were not intrinsically Jewish. In turn, this would culminate in the destruction of the Spanish communities if there was no return to Jewish heritage and roots.

This essay is dedicated in memory of Rosa Meth who rebuilt despite losing her family in the Shoah. Remembered by her daughter, grandchildren and great-grandchildren.

Rabbi Shraga Feivel Zimmerman

23 Jewish Eternity

A few years ago, a Scotsman came to my house and told me he felt he had sinned against the Jewish nation and that he had been directed to my address to seek guidance. What had he done? On a visit to Auschwitz, whilst he stood at the site of the gas chambers and crematoria, he had picked up a small pebble from the ground and brought it home as a souvenir.

Subsequently, however, his conscience pricked him day and night, because he felt this stone was sacred to the Jewish people, as part of the site of their suffering, and he had removed it from its place. I told him that I would take it and deal with it in the correct way and he should no longer worry.

Aware that this pebble had no requirement of burial, I wondered nevertheless what should be done. On a visit to my *Rosh Yeshivah*, Rabbi Dovid Soloveitchik of Brisk, Jerusalem, I sought his advice on the matter. Not known for approaching things with undue sentimentality, he sat deep in thought for several minutes. Then, with a voice full of feeling, he stated the following:

> It is written in the Talmud that in the future time of Judgement, the beams and stones of a person's house will testify as to what has gone on inside that home. We see from here that even the inanimate materials of a building have a task in this world, to act as a constant witness. This stone forms part of the site of suffering of the Jewish people. Put it back and let it fulfil its purpose of being God's witness to the atrocities perpetrated there.

Yet in spite of all the persecution and near-destruction our nation has suffered, the Jewish nation continues to exist; Torah is studied; *mitzvot* are observed; Jewish children are raised and educated within Judaism and Torah. Dr Moshe Rothschild, the founder of the Ma'aynei HaYeshua Hospital in Bnei Brak, related a wonderful story which highlights this sense of eternity.

When he was studying medicine in Rome, he received a call late one evening. On the other end of the line was none other than Rabbi Yosef Shlomo Kahaneman, the Ponovezher *Rav*. The *rav* called to him and said, "Moshe'le come with me somewhere now."

The doctor was quite surprised and said "Must we go now? Its pouring outside and driving conditions are treacherous. What's so urgent and can't wait till morning?"

But the rabbi was persistent and said "I have just arrived in Rome and I feel that I can't go to sleep before we do this."

Dr Moshe went to the *rav's* residence and was asked to drive him to the Arch of Titus. This arch is probably the greatest symbol of the Roman conquest of Israel 2,000 years ago. Its detailed features and pompous inscriptions symbolise Roman triumphalism over the Jews and the destruction of our Temple.

When they arrived there, the Rabbi got out of the car, and in the pouring rain raised his voice in triumph and said "We are here! And where are you Titus? We are *Kelal Yisrael*, the nation that you butchered and murdered. You captured the Temple and then destroyed it. You pillaged the Temple vessels and brought them here. But we have survived despite your conquest. I stand before you as the Ponovezher Rabbi, as the head of Ponovezh Yeshivah, which was built right after the Holocaust, to replace the one destroyed in Ponovezh, Lithuania. We have built up an empire of Torah!

And where are you today, Titus? What remains of the mighty Roman Empire? What became of Rome? Empires that shook the world have been reduced to history. You have been condemned to the past. What became of your glory? All that remains is this arch. An arch and nothing else." And with this he got back into the car.

Indeed, following the destruction of the Jewish communities of Europe, an intense period of rebuilding took place and continues to our own time. Incredibly enough, this was true even in the Warsaw Ghetto. The Jewish Council kept a chronicle in which each day's events and statistics were recorded, including that day's deaths and deportations. After each day's account there was a cryptic four-letter entry in Hebrew: *"Nili"* (*nun, yud, lamed, yud*). Those who studied the chronicle after the war struggled to uncover the meaning of this codeword, until they realised that it was an acronym of *Netzach Yisrael Lo Yeshaker* (the eternity of the Jewish people will not be a lie).

Similarly, the Jewish historian, Sir Martin Gilbert, tells the story of a flight back to London from Israel. On board he made the acquaintance of an elderly chassidic man from North London. Some time later the historian received a phone call from the man, inviting him to come immediately to his Stamford Hill home. Despite the late hour and inclement weather, Sir Martin Gilbert made the journey from Highgate.

There sat the old man with another man whom he introduced as his brother. "My brother and I lost 86 members of our family during the war," he said. "Just tonight one of my granddaughters gave birth to what is now the 87th member of our family to be born since the war. I wanted you, as a historian, to be here to celebrate our victory over Hitler."

Around 30 years ago, I attended a *simchah* at which a religious Jew from Europe, the father of a family of outstanding Jews, related his own personal story:

After surviving the War, he found that he had lost everything, his entire family, his community. He was consumed by questions to which he had no answers. Why should he of all people have survived? He felt certain that he was no greater than any of his contemporaries. In short, he felt that there was clearly no reason behind his survival – all was random. He lost his faith, and for some time lived a life far removed from Judaism.

However, he soon married and the couple were blessed with a son. After a few years, the most orthodox *Talmud Torah* of the city where he had settled was surprised to receive a visit from this man, who had come to enrol his son in the school. The heads of the institution could not understand why he, a lapsed Jew, should be interested in providing his son with a Torah education.

"I have long been bothered by the question of my survival," said the man, "but I have reached the following conclusion: what I may have done to deserve to live, I cannot know. But the fact that I *did* survive obliges me to educate my own son in the path of Torah."

Our survival may not be based on any logical formula, but one thing is for sure – we who remain, have an obligation to give the next generation the best possible opportunities in Torah and Judaism.

Truly, "*Netzach Yisrael Lo Yeshaker.*"

Proudly dedicated in loving memory of Rev. Abraham and Lena Chait,
Dr Ronald and Golda Steinberg and Mrs Hannah Feldman a"h by
Cantor Rev. Henry and Helena Chait and Shragi and Shifra Feldman.

Cantor Albert Chait

Chanukah – Embracing Our Identity

In the well-known Chanukah story that we recall every year, the Syrian-Greek Emperor, Antiochus IV, turned Jewish religious observance into a capital offence. He focused specifically on *brit milah*, *Shabbat*, *Rosh Chodesh,* and Torah study, as they are the foundations of our observance. *Rosh Chodesh* was the first commandment to be given to the Jewish nation, just as *brit milah* was commanded to the first Jew. *Shabbat* is the *ot* (the manifestation) of our covenant with God, and study of Torah is the everlasting undertaking we made as a nation at Mount Sinai.

The Greeks believed that curtailing the practice of these four would destroy our unique identity, by breaking down the spiritual being of the Jew.

However, Antiochus's attempt to impose Hellenistic idealism foundered, and we Jews today celebrate the festival of Chanukah, declaring our religious authenticity to be very much alive and well. We light the menorah each night in festivity and in tribute to the victory of the Maccabees in rededicating our priorities and our Holy Temple – aided by the Hand of God.

Every year, during those eight days, we discover the potential and the opportunity to practise precisely those *mitzvot* that were threatened by the Greeks. The days of *Shabbat* and *Rosh Chodesh* always occur during the festival of Chanukah; *brit milah* is echoed both in the occurrence of in the only eight day festival observed in the Land of Israel, and the very affirmation of every male Jew's covenant with God; and the study of Torah is customary as the lights of the menorah are kindled.

Yet Chanukah is one of the only *mitzvot* that is publicised to the outside world; we position our Chanukah lights in the front window of our homes, for all to see, because the festival contains two distinct elements: on the one hand, it is vital for those in the Diaspora to show gratitude and appreciation for being able to practise and observe their religion in peace – a situation that the Greeks wished to outlaw; on the other hand, as a Jew, it is important at this time of year to reflect on our identity.

As the contemporary American Jewish author, Rabbi Benjamin Blech, observes, "oil is likely to be the most politically incorrect liquid of all, in its complete refusal to compromise on its uniqueness. It chooses to remain separate and distinct. Mix it with water and notice how immiscible oil remains, preserving its own identity. No matter how hard you try, oil stays true to itself and rejects the possibility of assimilation."

Perhaps this is why it became the ultimate symbol of the Chanukah miracle. It takes immense courage, even in a very accepting and tolerant 21st century Western society, to stand up for one's beliefs and ideals, to be a minority within a majority culture.

Ancient Greece was obsessed with aesthetics and held beauty above all else. And, whereas there is harmony in physical beauty, ultimate beauty in this world – as Judaism has always taught – is the union of the spiritual and physical worlds, the fusion of all the elements into one complete whole. Maintaining identity means harvesting all the goodness around us whilst still embracing the ultimate values that God and His Torah have given us.

Equally, Chanukah underscores our faith and identity at a time when it is threatened by oppression rather than assimilation. Yosef Begun, a refusenik in the dark days of the Russian winter, wrote:

In 1976, I was arrested and sent to jail in Moscow. At my trial I was accused of not doing "social, useful work." But the real issue was that I had been teaching Hebrew privately to a few dozen students. The sentence for "parasitism" was two years of internal exile. I was sent to a remote area 10,000 kilometres away, on the north-eastern edge of Siberia.

It took two and a half months on deplorable prison trains and being lodged in 11 transit prisons along the way, to arrive at the destination: the infamous Kolima region of the Gulag where, during Stalin's reign of terror, millions were sent to do hard labour. From that grisly time, only one thing remained: the intense cold. The Pole of Cold, the coldest spot on earth, was 200 kilometres from where I was sent. The temperature reached minus 72. The joke among the locals was, "In our area, 12 months of the year are winter; the rest is summer."

In a small town, populated by gold miners, I was the only Jew. My spirit was nourished by letters from friends and many supporters from abroad. But Chanukah once again had a very special meaning for me. Lighting Chanukah candles in that dark, desolate place would disperse the gloom around me. I took a piece of wood and a saw and fashioned a *chanukiah*. I made eight indentations and hammered a nail into each, onto which I could stick a candle.

On a particularly dark, cold night, as I lit the candles that serve to remind us of the Maccabees' victory over their enemies, Jewish victory gleamed in that isolated world of snow and ice. Reciting the *Shehecheyanu* blessing and singing *"Al ha-Nisim,"* I experienced a profoundly warm feeling. And I dreamed of the miracle which we all awaited: freedom and *aliyah*. The next morning I wrote a letter to a friend, saying that on the eve of Chanukah, I felt that I was together with all my friends and with all our people. I also had the privilege of lighting the most north-eastern light of Chanukah.

The flame of our faith shines brightest when the danger of assimilation or extinction is defeated. And it is this glowing light of the festival of Chanukah that we take with us to the four corners of the world. At this time of year, it is important to align our festival away from simply rivalling 25th December as a "Jewish equivalent," and instead to fly our unique Jewish flag: to preserve our Jewish heritage and rise up against the threat of assimilation. To see our environment as a spiritual one, cloaked in a material exterior.

> *Dedicated to Father Desbois in acknowledgement of the*
> *incredible work he has undertaken to preserve and perpetuate*
> *the memory of the murdered Jews of eastern Europe.*

Father Patrick Desbois

Shoah by Bullets

Long before German bureaucrats met in 1942 at Wannsee to plan for the deportation and mechanised murder of European Jewry in extermination camps, before Birkenau, Treblinka, Sobibor or Belzec were built, hundreds of thousands of Jews had already been murdered by the Nazis and their local collaborators in the towns and villages of Ukraine, Lithuania, and Belarus.

These first mass victims of the Holocaust were not transported in crowded cattle cars to secluded industrialised killing centres that define the term "Holocaust" for most of us. These victims – mostly women, children and old people – were taken from their homes, on foot or by truck, to locations just outside the towns and villages where they lived. There they were shot at close range, one human being killing another, and all in the presence of local residents, non-Jewish neighbours, even friends. The murders were co-ordinated by German special killing squads – the *Einsatzkommandos* – but the shooters included units from the surrounding area, as well as willing local nationals or volunteers. These killing sites are now all but invisible. They offer up none of the architectural design that shape the iconic imagery of the Holocaust such as the *"Arbeit Macht Frei"* encased in ironwork, or the chimney of a crematorium. Even the place names: Bogdanivka (where more Jews were murdered than Babi Yar), Busk, Novo Zlatopol – and hundreds of others, fail to register or resonate with most students of the Shoah.

These people were largely forgotten in the post–World War II era. Their stories and the fates of their communities were obscured by clouds of Soviet secrecy and antisemitism, which was just as the Nazis and their collaborators wanted. It has taken 15 years of research, enquiry, and persistence to bring this picture back into the open, primarily by speaking to thousands of witnesses to the Shoah who are not Jewish: neither perpetrators nor victims, but witnesses to the murder.

UKRAINE, SPRING 2007

We finally reached our destination: Senkivishvka, a small village with a church, a town hall, and one shop that has not changed since the Soviet era. We approached an old lady on the street and asked her if she lived here during World War II. Her directions led us to Luba, who 61 years earlier had witnessed a murder she would never forget, that of the village Jews. Early in the morning the farmers had been forced to dig a ditch, "over there" she said pointing with her left hand. A truck then unloaded 50 Jews at a time from the village, mainly women and children; her neighbours, friends and classmates.

At the edge of the ditch the earth had been packed into a makeshift ladder. The Jews undressed, and then family after family walked down the steps where a man called Humpel – a German policeman, with pistol in hand, murdered them. Less than ten metres away, Luba and her sister saw everything. At regular intervals, he stopped shooting, climbed out of the pit, took a break, drank a small glass of liquor, and went back into the ditch. The massacre lasted one full day. After the interview, I got back into the van, having just recorded the testimony of the 460th witness to the murder of Jews in the Ukraine.

In the village of Khativ, we met Olena. She was a young bride on the day of the Jews' execution and was bringing in the harvest with a friend. In the distance they caught sight of two German military trucks, filled with Jewish women, standing up. The trucks approached until they passed them. In one of the trucks she suddenly recognised a friend of her mother's who began shouting "Olena, Olena save me!" The more she shouted, the more Olena hid herself in the wheat. "I was young, and I was afraid that the Germans would kill us too. That woman shouted until they took her to the pit. Right until the last moment I heard her shouting: "Olena, Olena save me."

We sat there on the blue wooden bench for a long time, in

silence. After having seen her talking to us, several neighbours came to reproach her. She replied, "You know at my age I am not frightened of anything anymore, not even death!"

Initially, during my first searches, I was convinced that all the mass graves were hidden in the forests. I had always been told that the Jews had been murdered in secret, far from view. The first witness who took us to a mass grave located at the centre of a village was a man named Vassil Protski. A short man, wearing a blue cap, he led us to the edge of a wide lawn. "This is where they were killed," he said. "I was watching from down there, at the side of the road." Whilst we were speaking, the owners of several neighbouring houses came running out – apparently they had understood what the recorded interview was about. One of them interrupted the witness: "My vegetable allotment patch. That's my vegetable patch! Leave our gardens alone." Without realising it, with their protestations, they were only confirming what everyone in the area knew: the bodies of shot Jews were under the tomato plants.

Thus I discovered that the Jews had not all been killed in forests. The Nazis feared the forests because often they concealed groups of resistance fighters – Soviet partisans – so the Germans assassinated the Jews in the middle of towns, in full view and with the knowledge of everyone.

A woman of 91, Anna Tchouprina began crying during a very long testimony given from her bed. As she remembered the deaths of Jewish children, she repeated over and over, "It's not possible, it's not possible…" They had killed more than 8,000 people in view of her house. We found out that the Germans had had *carte blanche* regarding how to kill the Jews. A legal framework was in place that required them to assassinate the Jews, but the methods used were left to their initiative, even their sadism.

All this happened from 1941–1944, in the very heart of Europe, one of the oldest civilisations in the world that had been shaped by centuries of Christian thinking and by the Enlightenment – yet human beings had stopped recognising their own fellows! This enigma, this non-recognition of human by human, has always preoccupied me.

In Ukraine, there were no extermination camps, no barbed wire to separate the condemned from their assassins. The former suffered in agony, while the latter asked for more food. The Germans would eat chicken less than ten metres away from the gaping mass grave.

It is difficult to hear that a German gunman asked for meat and vodka, while Jews were about to be murdered nearby. It is difficult to hear about the everyday life of the assassins of the Reich while their victims waited for death, weeping, with their family. Yet that was the Shoah. Human beings who killed other human beings, believing they were superior and that they were killing sub-humans.

From the book, *The Holocaust by Bullets* (Palgrave Macmillan)

Sponsored by www.gatheringthevoices.com, a unique website of online oral testimony from refugees who sought sanctuary in Scotland to escape the racism of Nazi-dominated Europe.

Rabbi Eli and Rebbetzin Lauren Levin

Ruth: For the Love of It

26

A wealthy nobleman, a popular aristocrat and a widowed, foreign, penniless convert. These three are all protagonists of the Book of Ruth and yet only one of them changes history – against the odds.

How is it that Ruth, who appears so vulnerable and pitiful, who is so disadvantaged in multiple ways, stands out as the heroine of the book?

Megillat Ruth begins by introducing us to one of the leaders of the Jewish community of that time, a philanthropist, Elimelech. The Midrash relates that he was capable of sustaining the entire generation.[1] However, when Israel is hit by famine, Elimelech relocates to the plains of Moab with his family. The wealthy leader would have been called on even more at this time of crisis, yet he shirks these responsibilities, leaving Israel and his nation behind.

Later on, we meet the aristocrat Boaz, who is described as "a mighty man of valour,"[2] denoting his aristocratic background and moral stature. Not only does he provide for the poor, but is clearly sensitive to who is needy, noticing Ruth as the newcomer collecting in the field. When Ruth asks him, "why have I found favour in your eyes to acquaint yourself with me, especially considering that I am a foreigner?"[3] the contrast between him and Elimelech is accentuated, as Elimelech had failed to maintain his support of even his own brethren.

However, it takes Ruth to activate Boaz's true leadership capabilities. When Boaz encounters Ruth collecting grain in his field he blesses her saying, "May God repay you for your work, and may

1. *Ruth Rabbah* 1
2. Ruth 2:1
3. *Ibid*, 2:10

87

your reward be complete from the Lord, the God of Israel, under *whose wings* you came to take refuge."[4] Whilst Ruth does acknowledge that Boaz has comforted her with his blessing, she responds with a request: "And [Ruth] said, "Let me find favour in your eyes, my master."[5] Why does she still need to ask for this? Perhaps Ruth is reminding Boaz that the "complete reward" from God that he has blessed her with may well need a human conduit. Indeed, she then reiterates this point more explicitly when she asks him to redeem her. She says: "spread *your wings* over your maidservant because you are the redeemer."[6] Here, she uses the same language from the blessing he had bestowed on her, but turns it around to him, questioning his own responsibility to help.

Thus, despite Elimelech and Boaz possessing the financial wherewithal, the social stature and highly regarded reputation, it is Ruth – a convert, widow and outsider – who reinstates the principles of unmeasured altruism and social responsibility. In this regard and with a punch of irony, the *megillah* reminds us that everyone can make a difference in the world, if only they are sincere and remain sensitive to the plight of others around them.

The sage Rabbi Zeira accordingly commented: "This scroll does not contain issues of purity or impurity, nor prohibitions or permissions. So why was it written? To teach us the magnitude of the reward for those who bestow loving-kindness."[7]

There is a second trait of Ruth's that stands out, and it is inextricably linked to her ancestry. Ruth is a Moabite, and the Moabite nation was born from an incestuous relationship between Lot and his daughter, who proudly named her son "Moab": "he is from my father." Lot was Abraham's nephew and, whilst in earlier years, the two shared a close relationship, he later separated from his uncle.[8] Ruth follows in the Abrahamic way, and carefully avoids becoming like her blood ancestor Lot.

Just as Abraham had been commanded to leave: "Go from your land, and from your heritage, and from your father's house, to the

4. *Ibid*, 2.12
5. 2.13
6. 3:9
7. *Ruth Rabbah* 2
8. Genesis 13

land that I will show you,"[9] Boaz admires Ruth for "leaving your father and mother and the land of your heritage, and you came to a people that you have previously not known."[10]

Abraham is known for his hospitality and kindness to strangers. Within his own family, he was also a uniting force. He never forsook his nephew Lot, despite the estrangement, and saved him when he was in danger.[11] During the narrative of the binding of Isaac, Abraham ensured that there was a unique synergy between him and his son Isaac, as is denoted by the repetition of the phrase "and both of them went together."[12] Similarly, Ruth acts as a uniting force. Following the death of her husband, the natural expectation is for her to leave Naomi and return to her people. Yet she embraces a different destiny: she cleaves to her mother-in-law, and the two destitute widows arrive in Bethlehem together. They go as a duo: "the two of them went,"[13] reminding us of Abraham and Isaac's synergy many moons before them.

In this way, Ruth redeems her own lineage. She actively chooses to accept social responsibility and familial camaraderie, unlike Lot's separatist and divisive behaviour years earlier. She emulates Abraham, and in so doing, becomes a future matriarch of the Jewish people, the great grandmother of Kind David, and the first woman to be called an "*eshet chayil.*"[14]

Every year on the festival of Shavuot, when we commemorate the giving of the Torah, we read the Book of Ruth. We remember the paramount importance of sensitivity and kindness to others. We received the Torah as a nation with one heart, and like Ruth, each one of us can be pivotal in achieving this unity and creating a just and compassionate society.

9. *Ibid*, 12:1
10. Ruth 2:11
11. Genesis 14
12. *Ibid*, 22:6–8, see Rashi's commentary
13. Ruth 1:19
14. *Ibid*, 3:11

*In loving memory of Meir ben Avraham and Sheena Bat
Ben Zion z"l. Dedicated by their grandchildren.*

Rabbi Hershel Becker

Building Blocks for a Jewish Home

Where does the Torah start? In the beginning – literally! The first word is *Bereshit*, which translates as "In the beginning." Yet, with further analysis, we discover an even earlier starting point to the Torah.

Every letter in the Hebrew alphabet has a name, numerical value, and shape, and each of these factors is significant. The first letter of the Torah is *bet* and its name is spelled with three letters: *bet-yud-tav*. Together, they spell the word *bayit* meaning "home." So that actually the first word found in the Torah is *bayit*. What is a *bayit*? And what is so important about it that it should serve as the Torah's beginning?

Our forefather, Jacob, was travelling to find a wife and establish a home. He stopped for the night and "he took from the stones of the area and placed it by his head."[1] He took three stones, but they were not simply stones. They symbolised the three Patriarchs.[2] Each signified a distinct element necessary to build the House of Israel: Abraham represented *chesed* (loving-kindness). He brought all passers-by into his tent and established his abode as a centre of hospitality. Isaac represented *avodah* (service). He devoted himself, body and soul, to the service of *Hashem* and was placed upon the altar as an offering. Jacob represented Torah. He earned the accolade, "the dweller of tents (of study)"[3] by his distinguished devotion to Torah learning.

Jacob did not intend merely to build a house. He was seeking to establish the Tribes of Israel. He took these stones and the

1. *Bereishit, Vayetze* 28:11
2. Rebbe Nechemiah in *Bereishit Rabbah* 68:11
3. *Bereishit Toledot* 25:27

characteristics they represented to serve as the foundation. In fact, the word for a stone in Hebrew is *even*, which is a contraction of the two words *av* (father) and *ben* (son), because the stones represented the use of a foundation to build the future.

Indeed, there is a kabbalistic teaching that each of the stones wanted the merit of having the righteous Jacob rest his head upon it. Miraculously, they were joined as one stone (that is why the verse regarding the stones mentions, "placed *it*," rather than "placed *them*").[4] Jacob then placed that stone as a monument that would be used to found a house that "…would be a *Beit Elokim* (a House of God).[5] And, when the *Beit HaMikdash* (the house that was the Holy Temple) was built, this stone became the foundation stone.

The merging of the stones indicates that it is insufficient to limit oneself to one element, *chesed, avodah,* or Torah. One should strive to blend all three components. A home can serve as one's private escape from the world; it is a sanctuary. Yet, it can be so much more. When its focus is to foster character of the highest quality, a home can become a centre that can have a positive impact on the world.

The world stands on three pillars: Torah, *avodah* and *chesed*.[6] These elements also form the essential ingredients for the foundation of the Jewish home.[7]

TORAH: Every establishment requires a system of values and laws. The teachings of the Torah nurture our souls and serve as our guide. When books of Torah are on shelves in our home, they positively reflect their value in our lives. When they are found on our tables and nightstand, they indicate a closer bond with Torah study. Scheduled learning among the family members and friends, as well as hosting Torah study in the home, emphasise our essence as People of the Book.

AVODAH: *Avodah* transforms our association with God from awareness to action. It is not limited to a synagogue; rather, it is a vital component in each Jewish home. A woman whom I met shared with me her concerns regarding her children's futures. I introduced

4. *Chullin* 91b; *Bereishit Rabbah* 68:11
5. *Bereishit Vayetze* 28:22
6. *Pirkei Avot* 1:2
7. Rabbi Meir Shapiro in *Chayim Sheyeih Bahem Nisuim*, pp 528–529

her to the prayer which is recited after lighting the *Shabbat* candles. It incorporates a mother's heartfelt plea that her children and descendants follow the path of righteousness. When we met again years later, she thanked me for sharing with her what had become a weekly ritual, linking her to future generations.

CHESED: In caring for others, we indicate our inherent connection to each other and to God. There was a recorded practice observed in France over 600 years ago. When a person died, his coffin would be fashioned from the wood of his dining room table. At that table, those who had been in need had found sustenance and comfort. The table in one's home is considered like an altar and providing for others is viewed as a great offering. These personal merits of *chesed* combine with the merits of others and support the world.

If we take a second look at the letter *bet*, we can see that even its shape offers information that is essential to the establishment of a home. The character *bet* in the Torah has a crown that protrudes from the top and points upward and at the base of the letter is a stem that points to the right. The Talmud[8] states that the letter *bet* is asked, "Who created you?" In response, it points upward. Then it is asked, "What is His Name?" In response, it points to the letter *alef* that precedes it. Alef, which means "master" (*aluf*) and has a numerical value of one, refers to God, *u-Shemo Echad* (Whose Name is One). What we do in our houses does not stay passively in our house. Rather, it shapes and forms our home so that it points to what we value. The attributes of a Jewish home and the actions of its household members indicate the recognition of our Creator and our purpose.

By using the word *bayit* (home) as the starting point, the Torah reveals that the home is where *the principles that form* the pillars of the world must be studied and practised on a constant basis. Once this foundation is firmly in place and the directional signposts pointing towards God are in view, we can learn about the design of creation as a whole and fulfil its purpose, by establishing each Jewish home as a *Beit Elokim* (a House of *Hashem*).

---

8. Jerusalem Talmud, *Chagigah*, chapter 2, *halachah* 1

Dedicated in memory of Mordechei Zev Ben Ezriel Yitschak
Tennenbaum by his family as a supporter of Jewish continuity.

Rabbi Mordechai Ginsbury

The Symbol and the Sign

Reverend Leslie Hardman *a"h* was Minister of Hendon United
Synagogue from 1946 until 1979. In those years, through his passion and zest for Jewish living, his commitment, enthusiasm and
inspirational leadership, Reverend Hardman, together with his
wonderful wife, Josi *a"h*, "grew" the community into one of the
largest and most influential of Anglo-Jewry. A significant part of
Reverend Hardman's formidable personality was undoubtedly
shaped by his experiences as a British Army Chaplain during the
course of the Second World War and, in particular, by his personal
involvement in supporting and reviving the shattered spirits of his
fellow Jews who had been incarcerated in the infamous Bergen
Belsen concentration camp.

After Reverend Hardman's passing in 2008, some of us in the
Hendon community, galvanised by one of his grandsons, Daniel
Verbov, joined with him to produce a commemorative book – *My
Dear Friend* – which is filled with Reverend Hardman's teachings,
sayings and stories. Amongst them is one of the most poignant
illustrations of the holiness of the Jewish spirit that I have thus
far encountered.[1]

Reverend Hardman related how one Friday morning, a mid-
dle-aged man, a survivor of the unimaginable horrors of Bergen
Belsen, knocked hesitantly on his office door and asked to be given
something to eat. Reverend Hardman was somewhat surprised
for he knew that the British authorities were doing whatever they
could to provide for the material needs of the survivors. The man
explained that he was looking for something a little special with
which to honour the Sabbath day. Rev Hardman produced a can of

1. The story is adapted, with publisher's permission, Vallentine Mitchell, 2009

93

sardines from a stock of tinned items which he kept in his cupboard, which was accepted with "pathetic eagerness."

As he was about to close the cupboard Reverend Hardman felt a restraining hand on his arm and a voice saying, "Rabbi, wait, please, please."

"What is it?" he asked.

"I saw the *tefillin*!"

The man spoke with awe in his voice, gazing at the bag containing Reverend Hardman's *tefillin* which lay on the bottom shelf of his cupboard.

"It's four years since I wore them last," he said, his eyes fixed on the well-remembered shapes outlined in the velvet bag. As Reverend Hardman brought his *tefillin* to the table, the man put down his sardines and picked up the *tefillin* with shaking hands. Sobs clutched at his throat and tears ran unheeded down his puffy cheeks.

"Rabbi, please...please may I use them?" he asked.

With still shaking hands the man took the *tefillin* out of the bag. Reverently he kissed them and, having undone the leather strap and taken the cover off the box, he placed it on his upper left arm reciting the blessing. He then removed the second box from the bag, kissed it too, and then placed it on his head, reciting the second blessing. He wound the remainder of the strap around his middle finger and back on to the palm of his hand reciting the verses from Hosea (2:21–22): "And I will betroth You to me forever; I will betroth You to me in righteousness, and in loving kindness, and in mercy; I will betroth You to me in faithfulness and You shall know the Lord."

For over 3,000 years the Jewish people have donned *tefillin* daily, other than festivals and *shabbatot*. The man had loyally done this as well himself, presumably from his bar mitzvah until the time when the evil Nazis snatched him, together with millions of his brethren, from all that was familiar, warm and secure – just because he was a Jew! Through four long years of a living "hell on earth" he had been denied this and all other precious *mitzvot* – all he could have done was pray. How he must have prayed for freedom, for mercy, for strength...he must have asked God to spare him beatings, typhus or worse...to save his family, restore his people...or maybe just for a morsel of food or a drop of water. Or, perhaps, he had simply called to his God: "Lord where are You?"

Some of his prayers had been answered. Once more, he knew what it was to eat and drink, to wash oneself, to put on clothes, and to sleep securely. As a Jew, he had begun to reconnect with the laws and customs of his religion that had come down to him through the generations over thousands of years. In the act of putting on *tefillin*, he was renewing the bond of connection between himself and his Maker.

The man became calm, his hands ceased to shake, the lines smoothed around his eyes and mouth and his whole body relaxed. He began to pray and it was as though a warmth was rising from the *siddur* he was clutching, permeating his very being.

Reverend Hardman gave the man some space, moving away from him until he had finished. The man removed the *tefillin* as lovingly as he had donned them, carefully replacing them in their bag.

He told Reverend Hardman: "I felt that God was pushing me away from Him. With every bad thing that was done to me it seemed that He was pushing me further and further away; but I clung to Him, I would not lose Him, I wanted him always." And then he quoted from Psalms (42:2): "As the hart longs for streams of water, so does my soul long after You, O God." "Rabbi," the man said, "I thought God no longer wanted me but when you put these *tefillin* in my hands it was a sign ... He has allowed me to come back to Him!"

The man straightened up and wiped tears from his eyes. Reverend Hardman, also unable to control his emotions, took the *tefillin* bag and put it into the man's hands.

"Take these," he said. "Keep them. May God bless you."

As Reverend Hardman turned back to his desk the first thing he saw was the can of sardines. The man had gone!

Rabbi Aubrey Hersh

Books, Ghettoes and the Reformation – A Century of Turmoil

Europe's geographical vistas expanded in the 1500s, with the circumnavigation of the globe and the discovery of lands in the Far East. But for the Jews, the map had been severely redrawn and the borders narrowed, following their mass expulsion from Western and Central Europe as the Middle Ages drew to a close.

Jewish settlements existed in very few of the cities in which the great medieval communities had lived. In many ways the 16th century would begin a new phase in Jewish history and would bring about a century of change and of contrasts.

Starting from the Fourth Lateran Council in 1215, antisemitism had escalated within society and the Jew became a pariah. So that, despite the Renaissance period strongly affecting intellectual life in Christian Europe, it conspicuously failed to create any change in attitude toward its Jewish neighbours. By 1500, there was no country which had not carried out severe discrimination against the Jews, in most cases ultimately expelling them.

The exiles from Spain and Portugal travelled to the Ottoman Empire, especially Turkey, whereas most of Ashkenazic Jewry went east to Poland and Lithuania. Both groups brought their own language with them: Ladino in the south and Yiddish in the north.

Surprisingly, having recently endured so many expulsions, the new sanctuaries offered to the Jews were open invitations. The Ottoman Empire was unquestionably the most powerful of its time, but the Sephardic immigrants brought with them valuable trading skills and knowledge of European languages and conditions. In consequence, they soon became active in politics and diplomacy.[1]

Turkey became a remarkable haven for thousands of Jews fleeing Christianity, the Sultan going so far as to write to Pope Paul IV in 1556 to demand that he end his persecution of the Jews of Ancona, Italy, a request that the Pope was obliged to carry out.

In Poland, too, Jews were granted royal protection, as well as a great degree of self-government. Sigismund II allowed the Jews to elect rabbis who would be answerable only to the king, a policy that eventually expanded into the Council of Four Lands, an institution that served as the central body of Jewish authority in Poland, until the 18th century.

Jews were seen as an economic requirement, to administer the estates of the nobility and serve as middle-men between them and the peasantry, although certain cities – including Warsaw – invoked their right of *non tolerandis Judaeis*, which excluded any Jewish presence. Further east, towns such as Lublin and Brisk established thriving Jewish communities, particularly after 1569, when Poland unified with Lithuania.

Yet despite the new freedoms extended to Jews in certain European countries, the century introduced a new and forbidding word into its vocabulary: the Ghetto.

In 1179, the Church had forbidden Jews and Christians to dwell together, but this had not been strictly enforced. However, following a military defeat for the Venetian Republic in 1516, for which the Jews were blamed, the Jews were segregated into one area of the city, the site of an old iron foundry.

A gated entrance was created to the Ghetto, which was guarded by Christian gate-keepers, paid for by the Jews. Curfew started at nightfall, after which it was forbidden for any Jew to be found outside the Ghetto, or any Christian within it. The Ghetto also gave rise to terrible living conditions – indescribably overcrowded, with little daylight and even less privacy. Outbreaks of fire were particularly dangerous; the whole area was sometimes reduced to ashes before help could be brought from outside.

The Ghetto model spread rapidly throughout Europe and

1. Cecil Roth: *A Short History of the Jewish people*, p 276.

crowned other types of humiliation that the Jews had to endure, such as the wearing of a Jewish badge of shame and the discriminatory and offensive oaths they were made to swear.

The Christian Church itself did not escape religious conflict in the 1500s. The flames of the Reformation and counter-Reformation engulfed its offices and officers, ultimately leading to the Thirty Years War in 1618. However, rather than ameliorating the fate of the Jews, it added to their misery. The Catholics placed a great degree of blame for the Reformation on the Jews, since the movement emphasised great reliance on the biblical text, and several of the Reformers had studied Hebrew with prominent rabbis of the day.[2]

This, despite the fact that Martin Luther – the head of the Protestant movement – was strongly antisemitic. Having authored an apparently sympathetic work, his tone changed when he saw the Jews were as opposed to Protestant Christianity as they had been to Catholicism. In his subsequent writings, such as *Concerning the Jews and Their Lies*, he describes them as, "...a base whoring people, full of the devil's faeces," and advises that "...their synagogues and schools be set on fire." A chilling prediction for Germany.

The 16th century did, however, bring some light to the darkness with the development of the printing press. The Jews were reliant on text for all aspects of their lives and made early use of the new art of printing even before its arrival in Venice, where Daniel Bomberg produced the first *Tanach* with rabbinic commentaries in 1517 and the first printed Talmud in 1523.

It was of particular benefit to two authors who were writing a halachic treatise – each initially unaware of the other but subsequently in conjunction. Rabbi Joseph Karo in Safed and Rabbi Moses Isserles in Krakow produced the *Shulchan Aruch* (Code of Jewish Law), which was printed during their lifetimes and remains the most important halachic work ever issued. It was significant, not only because it codified the law clearly and concisely, but also because it incorporated the views of both Ashkenazim and Sephardim, allowing it to become the default halachic book of the Jewish people.

Printing was important enough to the Jews that, in the 1500s,

2. *Ibid*, pp 267/299

Hebrew books were produced in Antwerp, Prague, Krakow, Salonica, Constantinople, and beyond. Even the small town of Safed in Israel had its own press, when a comparatively small group of Jews settled in the Holy Land and revived Jewish life and scholarship there.

Safed became central to the dissemination of Kabbalah, due to the concentration of great scholars in its city, especially Rabbi Moses Cordevero (Ramak) and Rabbi Yitzchak Luria (Ari). Their teachings, alongside those of the Maharal in Prague, brought about an expansion of the teaching of mysticism, aided by the printing of the *Zohar* in 1558.

However, the advent of printing did not pass without adverse input from the Church. War was often waged on Jewish books, which were either confiscated or disfigured by the censors. In an orgy of pious vandalism, the Pope declared, in 1553, that the Talmud was blasphemous and ordered the confiscation of every volume in Italy.

On Rosh Hashanah of that year, hundreds of volumes were publicly consigned to the flames in the Campo Dei Fiori in Rome, and others were burned in Venice and Florence. This was followed by a papal ban on the subsequent printing of the Talmud and other Hebrew books. As a result, printing was expanded in Poland and the Ottoman Empire.

For the Jews at the beginning of the 16th century, with the geography of five centuries lost to them and the effects of the persecutions of the Middle Ages still apparent, the century appeared to predict a decline of Jewish learning, religion, and life. Yet the shift of Jewish life into the East, and a greater prevalence of Jewish literature, breathed new life into the nation and allowed them to both recover and rebuild.

Rabbi Shaya Karlinsky

The Definitions of Self

Western society places a premium on the acquisition of wisdom, strength, and wealth and it is a fundamental goal of the individual. Judaism too, values those who possess these attributes. Yet there appears to be a world of difference between Judaism and the West in terms of definitions, as is clear from the principles taught in Mishnah, in *Pirkei Avot* (Ethics of the Fathers).

In Chapter 4:1, Ben Zoma says: "Who is considered wise? One who learns from everyone. Who is mighty? One who controls their (evil) inclinations. Who is rich? One who is happy with their portion." Each of these answers is accompanied by a verse which serves to illustrate the point.

The Maharal raises a number of questions regarding the answers given by the Mishnah. Firstly, why don't we define wisdom more simply, namely as a person who possesses significant amounts of knowledge, especially of Torah? Secondly, whilst a person who is happy with their lot can be considered rich (given that they are satisfied with how much they have), the Mishnah implies that only this type of individual is considered rich, to the exclusion of any others. This is difficult, both intuitively, and in light of the Gemara (*Shabbat* 25b), which teaches that one who has 100 wheat fields, vineyards, and servants (diversified assets and a qualified supply of labour) is considered a rich person, seemingly linking assets to the definition of wealth. Finally, the Maharal questions, what is the underlying connection between these three attributes – beyond the fact that they are much sought after?

He explains that the revolutionary aspect of the statement by the Sages lies in the fact that wisdom, might, and wealth are being defined only insofar as they reside within man. They are real, but only if they actually describe the individual. Which is why the

Mishnah phrases the question as: "Who is wealthy," rather than "Who has wealth"; and similarly, "Who is wise," rather than "Who possesses wisdom." In other words, those who integrate what they have into what they are, as opposed to external accomplishments. An individual may well live in a house, but that is almost peripheral to knowing who he or she is.

As such, the quantity of information that people acquire is not an accurate description of who they are, since the knowledge exists almost independently. It does not emanate from within, nor does it necessarily impact on the decisions they make in life; it is theoretical and external. What *is* integral to the individuals is their desire and search for knowledge, which propel them to learn from everyone, in an attempt to satisfy that longing. Only they can accurately be described as wise, for their wisdom is not coincidental, but the result of personal effort. Moreover, since knowledge of life does not reside purely in academic texts, only those who learn from everyone – from those who are deemed great and those deemed simple – using every interaction as another opportunity to fulfil that longing for knowledge, can be considered truly "wise."

The same principle carries over to the idea of who is mighty. If we would define a mighty person as one who is able to overpower others, his or her might becomes relative to the one who was defeated, and is neither absolute nor exclusive. The dictionary definition of "might" falls short, therefore, since conquering cities or defeating opponents is subject to the strength of the vanquished. It is dependent on them.

Only those who are able to exert self-control over their (evil) inclinations and instinctive drives, and who are successful in that battle, are actually mighty, because their strength emanates completely from within – fighting against an internal enemy – and is dependent on no one else. It is human beings' control over their drives, resulting from their choices, that makes them worthy of the title *gibor* (mighty). Moreover, if physical strength were the criterion for determining might, there would be many animals that are significantly stronger than human beings, such that physical strength is clearly not a unique trait in defining man or humanity.

As for the concept of wealth, to describe a person as *ashir* (wealthy) based purely on the amount of assets he or she has is flawed, since this money is not an intrinsic part of the individual. Furthermore, one is only wealthy relative to someone with less money and, therefore, as much as one has, one is always poor in comparison to the one who has even more. It remains a relative definition rather than an absolute one. Whereas the individual's *perception of* and *attitude towards* his or her resources and assets are aspects of wealth that are truly objective and internalised, if people are content with their situations, they actually own what they have.

The secret behind this perspective lies in viewing resources as a gift from God, to be used in accomplishing transcendent goals. Since the motivation for additional assets is based on the desire to make spiritual use of them, if greater wealth is not forthcoming, the individual is able to accept their present status. This *ashir* is thus self-sufficient in utilising what he or she has –possessing true wealth.

At the same time, it is important to understand that such people are not fooling themselves by living in a fantasy world, with the impression that they lack nothing materially. Certainly a person has real needs. But they acknowledge that resources are provided by God for people to accomplish individually the goals with which God has tasked them. This underlying perspective generates fulfilment and is able to manifest itself, irrespective of a person's actual assets.

The Mishnah links these three ideas together specifically, because wisdom, wealth, and strength help create a person's position and perspective. We need to use them to develop our humanity by internalising what they offer: striving to acquire wisdom, winning the inner war over instincts and inclinations, and seeing wealth for what it is and equally for what it is not.

Rabbi Gideon Sylvester

Tikkun Olam

31

Three years ago, I spent the summer in a small fishing village in Ghana volunteering with young children who had been rescued from slavery. Many of them suffered from malaria, and they lived in mud huts with little food, no running water, and no sanitation. The idea of taking an Orthodox rabbi to help children in Africa was the brainchild of the American Jewish World Service as a magnificent example of *Tikkun Olam* (Mending the World).

Although the term *Tikkun Olam* has its origins in the ancient books of the Mishnah and mysticism, today the term is used for any activity in which Jewish people promote social justice, loving kindness, and ethical living, from work with the poor to environmental projects.

These activities have deep roots in Jewish tradition. At the beginning of our history, God charges Adam and Eve to take care of their world and they are placed in the Garden of Eden "to work it and take care of it."[1] Abraham, the first Jew, makes an impact on the world around him.

Although it would be no mean achievement for Jews to take responsibility for the religious observance and the welfare of the 14 million or so other Jews in the world, Judaism is interested in more than only our private, devotional relationship with God or even the building up of a Jewish state. These are crucial, but Judaism is also concerned with universal values and with the world around us. It wants us to make our mark on the planet and bring it to harmony, tranquillity and spirituality.

The biblical prophet Isaiah, living in First Temple times,

1. Genesis 2:15

exquisitely describes the role of the Jewish people in making the world a more just and happier place.

> I the Lord have called you in righteousness and will hold your hand and keep you and give you a covenant of the people for a light to the nations, to open blind eyes, to bring out prisoners from the prison and those that sit in the darkness of the prison house.[2]

This work, together with our study of Torah, ritual commandments, and prayers draws us closer to messianic times, ushering in an era of peace for the whole world when:

> They will beat their swords into ploughshares and their spears into pruning hooks. Nation will not take up sword against nation, neither shall they learn war anymore.[3]

Our history of persecution and assimilation has led many Jewish communities to turn inwards, downgrading these activities. Still, our religion includes obligations to our environment and obligations to non-Jews. A *mishnah* rules that we allow them access to the charitable produce set aside for the Jewish poor;[4] the Talmud extends these responsibilities to healing the non-Jewish sick, burying their dead and ensuring their welfare.[5]

In a fascinating contemporary interpretation of the *mishnah*, Emeritus Chief Rabbi Lord Sacks defines these laws as the earliest recorded code for promoting good community relations and social cohesion amongst people of different backgrounds, even where they profoundly disagree about their fundamental beliefs.[6]

So the principles of *Tikkun Olam* help us to build a happier, safer world, but what sort of Jew do they produce and what effect do they have on our spiritual lives?

Rabbi Yaakov Yechiel Weinberg (1884–1966) was one of the leading rabbis of the 20th century. In one of his letters, he beautifully explains the spiritual effects of mending our world.

2. Isaiah 42:6–7
3. Isaiah 2:4
4. *Mishnah Gittin* 5:8
5. *Gittin* 61a
6. Rabbi Lord Jonathan Sacks, *The Home We Build Together*, pp 177–9.

Opening with what seems like quite a technical question, he asks why we do not make blessings before performing interpersonal commandments, such as honouring parents and giving money to charity, whereas the performance of ritual commandments such as lighting *Shabbat* candles or laying *tefillin* is always preceded by a blessing. Rabbi Weinberg suggests that this is because these commandments should concentrate our minds and our hearts on our relationship with other people.

If we were to precede our charitable acts with a blessing, we might become so focused on God that we would forget the human being standing before us. So for a moment, we are instructed to put God on the "back burner" and to focus on the people around us. When we do so, we not only help to mend our world, we actually create a *Kiddush Hashem* (a sanctification of God's name), helping others to relate to God. For few things create a more religious atmosphere than when we see acts of loving kindness.

During one of Poland's freezing winters, the great leader and Chief Rabbi of Lodz, Rabbi Eliyahu Chaim Meisels (1821–1912), went to the palatial home of Yisrael Poznanski, a wealthy factory owner. Still in his dressing gown, the man invited the rabbi in, but the sage remained in the doorway and launched into a lengthy talmudic discourse, seemingly unaware that his host was shivering from cold. The host's teeth were chattering and, before long, his lips turned blue. Each time the host invited him in, Rabbi Meisels demurred, saying that he would only be another few minutes.

Feeling that he was about to faint, he finally interrupted the rabbi and persuaded him to come in. As they warmed themselves by the stove, Rabbi Yisrael continued, "I am sure that you are wondering about my strange conduct. The people are freezing; we need the money for fuel. If I had asked you to help while you were warm, you would not have even begun to understand what it means to live and study in an unheated room in sub-zero weather. Now that you felt what they feel, I am sure that you will help me."

Tikkun Olam takes us out to the doorsteps and sensitises us to the fate of others. It invites us to take a hard look at our lifestyles and challenges us to mend the world so that God's universe will be healthy, happy, and safe for generations to come.

Dr Robert Rozett

Why Did the Nazis Murder the Jews?

There is no simple answer to why the Nazis murdered the Jews. Rather, there are a number of underlying reasons that led them to undertake their murderous crusade. Perhaps most salient are the Nazi's overarching goals, their racial antisemitic ideology, the long history of antisemitism, and the nature of the war.

A principal goal of Nazi Germany and its leaders was to turn Germany into a superpower. In fact, harbouring an idealised view of history, Nazi leaders actually sought to return Germany to what they believed was its rightful place in the world order. Germany should be strong, independent, and totally self-sufficient, allowing its leaders to pursue domestic and foreign policies without any consideration of resistance from other nations – particularly regarding its policy of enlarging its territory and dominating Europe. As a superpower, the Nazis aspired to create a new world order and to fashion a utopian civilisation based on the principles of Nazism. Nazism would become a sort of civil religion, replacing Christianity and Enlightenment principles, thereby rejecting both the ideas that man was created in God's image and that all men are created equal.

Nazi ideology was racist and maintained that race was the key to human endeavour and history. The Nazis did not invent this idea, but co-opted it from a number of sources that had emerged in the 19th century. Nazi racial ideology was far from scientific, even though it sought to cloak itself in science, and therefore contained contradictions in thought and deed. According to this ideology, the Germans and kindred people, referred to as the Nordic Aryans, constituted the so-called Master Race – the race with an innate right to rule over inferior races, and the race that created and continued to foster civilisation. Other Europeans were deemed inferior to the Nordic Aryans, even though some were still termed Aryans, and each group had its place on the rungs of the racial ladder. Concerned primarily with Europe, the Nazis devoted much less thought to people outside of the continent, although they did come to regard the Japanese as another kind of superior race and native Africans as sub-human. Jews were not seen as the most inferior race, but as an anti-race, with physical and behavioural characteristics diametrically opposed to those of the Nordic Aryans. As the anti-race, Jews were considered the arch-enemy.

The Nazis attributed to the Jews responsibility for all the world ills and for the rival ideologies of the age that Nazism abhorred. The Nazis called Bolshevism (Communism) Jewish, and believed all Jews to be Bolsheviks. Concomitantly, they also termed Plutocracy, a world run by the wealthiest capitalists, to be Jewish and maintained that Jews had invented both capitalism and communism in order to control the world. The Nazis despised Judaism and sought to replace these values with their own.

The racial view of mankind meant that since Jews were born with a cornucopia of evils they were immutably destructive and, thereby, posed a threat to all mankind. So the solution to the so-called "Jewish Problem" could not come from improving Jews. Since Jews could not change, the Nazis sought to rid Germany and, with time, the territories it later dominated, of Jews and all things they considered Jewish.

The long and deep seated antipathy to Jews in Western Civilisation, often abetted by the teachings of the different Christian churches, facilitated a wide acceptance of the Nazi version of Jew-hatred. Moreover, it fostered much agreement with, or at least acceptance of, Nazi persecution of Jews as it developed. Ultimately, many people both inside and outside of Germany became willing collaborators with the Nazis, intertwining their own local and personal agendas with that of the Nazi state. Central to this process across Europe was the idea that Jews were frequently considered foreign to the national fabric, and thus outside the circle of social responsibility.

During the first years after coming to power in Germany in 1933, the Nazis passed laws and decrees to isolate the Jews and remove them from society, essentially to convince them to leave. By 1938, they began forcefully taking away Jewish property and using or-chestrated violence to drive the Jews from their midst. When, in 1939, Germany invaded Poland with its large Jewish population, the Nazis still sought to isolate and rob the Jews, but from the start, used even more force and violence. Separation inspired the policy of concentrating Jews in ghettoes in Eastern Europe, where conditions were generally very bad, and marking Jews with special badges. The ensuing physical removal of the Jews did not translate to systematic mass murder until the second half of 1941. Rather, at first, it led to various schemes to remove the Jews to the Soviet Union, a reservation in Poland, or to the island of Madagascar. None of these stratagems proved viable.

The invasion of the Soviet Union on 22nd June 1941 was primar-ily motivated by two complementary ideas: the need for territory to make Germany fully self-sufficient and the desire to crush the Jewish-Bolshevik threat once and for all. The latter undoubtedly contributed considerably to the start of the mass systematic murder of Jews in the newly conquered areas. The highly ideological nature of the invasion translated into an intensified brutality, which in turn made the murder even more acceptable in Nazi eyes.

There is no single document that declares the adoption of the policy of the Final Solution, the murder of all Jews under Nazi domination. But we know from the course of events that by early 1942, at the latest, this was the policy. Different arguments have been put forth for the coalescence of the Final Solution: the eupho-ria of Nazi success on the battlefield that made the Nazis believe they could do anything; a growing understanding that they might not win the war on their own terms, which led them to emphasise solving the "Jewish Problem" once and for all; or a snowball effect after the first murder, actions that led to even more murder, and then to an overall policy. What remains clear, however, is that at the heart of all of these explanations lies the idea that definitively solving the "Jewish Problem" became the key for everything else the Nazis sought to achieve. The idea that a specific group of people, their culture and their values, must be eliminated for the sake of human civilisation was unprecedented in history and is a hallmark of the Holocaust.

> *My involvement in Holocaust education began in Tokyo with Righteous Gentile, Chiene Sugihara. This essay is for amazing people who risked their lives for our people. Scott Saunders, March of the Living UK.*

Dr Erica Brown

King David: Small but Mighty

Sometimes the underdog really does win. The person or team least likely to triumph has an unexpected victory, and it gives the rest of us hope. We, too, may be down and out on our luck, smaller or less powerful than our competition, but we, too, might be able to conquer or win, beat the odds or battle the giants.

This is the message of popular writer Malcolm Gladwell's last book, *David and Goliath*. He wants us to think differently about perceived obstacles and disadvantages and question assumptions. Going to a mediocre university may be better for you than a top tier institution. A disability may prove your greatest strength. Discrimination may actually work in your favour.

Gladwell begins his thesis with our very own King David. What was it about the early David that made him Israel's most popular king, a man to whom we still dedicate a children's song in school and camp, "David, king of Israel, lives forever"? What is it about David's tenacious spirit that still lives with us eternally?

To understand this, we turn first to I Samuel 16, where we meet David in unusual circumstances. Samuel the prophet was told that King Saul was to be replaced. He searched for a new king and identified a heroic-looking figure and asked God if this man was to be king: "Do not consider his appearance or his height, for I have rejected him. The Lord does not look at the things man looks at. Man looks at the outward appearance, but the Lord looks at the heart." Someone may look like a leader, but fail miserably at the task. God advised Samuel to seek leadership in unexpected places.

God advised Samuel to go to the home of Jesse of Bethlehem. Jesse showed Samuel seven of his sons, but Samuel felt that none fit the bill: "Are these all the sons you have?" "There is still the youngest," Jesse answered, "but he is tending the sheep." Samuel said, "Send for him; we will not sit down until he arrives." So he sent and had him brought in. He was ruddy, with a fine appearance and handsome features. Then the Lord said, "Rise and anoint him; he is the one" (1 Samuel 16:11–12). David was not an obvious leader. He was the youngest and had the least experience. He was handsome, but not tall.

In the next chapter, David demonstrates why he was a worthy choice. He was shepherding while his older brothers were at war against a brutal enemy: the Philistines. They had a champion warrior named Goliath who was more than nine feet tall and weighed down by costly armour. Goliath had a spear that few could lift and he challenged the Israelites outright: "Choose a man and have him come down to me...If he is able to fight and kill me, we will become your subjects; but if I overcome him and kill him, you will become our subjects and serve us" (1 Samuel 17:8–9).

The Israelite army was petrified. They had no one to champion their cause, no one, that is, until David appeared as a delivery boy, bringing food and friendship to his brothers on the field. David heard the challenge and did not cower from it. But King Saul was not supportive of the idea: "You are not able to go out against this Philistine and fight him; you are only a boy..." Many young men would have been offended and gone home. Not David. He told Saul of his physical strength as a shepherd who protected his flocks from lions and bears. He was not afraid. Finally Saul caved in: "Go, and the Lord be with you." Saul lent David his armour, but it did not work. It was too big for David, so David faced his enemy with only a staff in his hand and five smooth stones in his pouch. When Goliath saw the helpless, hapless David, unarmed and uncovered, he mocked him.

How in the world did David win?

David credits his winning to God's help. He fought a battle not only of strength but also of wit. David was incredibly intelligent, much cleverer than the animal-like Goliath, who may have had brawn, but was short on brain. The text takes us into the moment of stunning and unexpected victory: "As the Philistine moved closer to attack him, David ran quickly toward the battle line to meet him. Reaching into his bag and taking out a stone, he slung it and struck the Philistine on the forehead. The stone sank into his forehead, and he fell face-down on the ground."

Gladwell offers a theory. Ancient armies, he contends, had three kinds of warriors: cavalry, foot soldiers and projectile warriors. You could go to battle on a horse, on foot, or using artillery to stretch your reach beyond your physical limits. "Slinging took an extraordinary amount of skill and practice," Gladwell tells us. In the hands of a competent slinger, a rock becomes a devastating weapon. David was fast on his feet because he was not encumbered by heavy armour. He had speed and manoeuvrability. He also took his enemy by surprise. Goliath was expecting hand-to-hand combat. Instead, he was met by a projectile fighter from a greater distance who surprised him with an unexpected strategy. David could never have won fighting Goliath's type of battle. He won because Goliath was no match for David's type of battle.

Ordinary people face giants all of the time. We all do. Instead of feeling defeated before we even compete, David reminds us that it is not the mighty who win. We can and have won great historic battles by being smarter, more creative, more tenacious, more able to turn our disadvantages into advantages and more aware of what we have to lose. We also win when we realise that ultimately all of our victories come from our greatest source of strength: God.

Rabbi YY Rubinstein

Why Does Judaism Place So Much Emphasis on Marriage?

In the beginning, the very, very, beginning, *Hashem* created someone called Adam and he was the very first man...er...except that he wasn't.

The Talmud points to the wording in the Torah, "Male and female He created them," and drops quite a bombshell. The first man was actually the first woman too.

Confused?

The Talmud explains that Adam was originally made both male and female, a hermaphrodite.

The obvious question is: why did Hashem originally make us that way?

To compound the confusion, the Torah then says that having made Adam, Hashem "changes His mind." He declares, "It is not good, Man's state of being alone" and takes the female part from Adam leaving only the male, and creates two separate individuals.

You should know, there is only one word that does not occur in the vocabulary of the Almighty and that word is, "Oops!" He doesn't make mistakes.

But: "it's not good, man's state of being alone" and then having to "adjust" the original design, seems to suggest that He did.

The mystery is solved by Rabbi Ephraim Luntschitz (1550–1619) in his commentary called the *Keli Yakar*, where he writes: "Had Hashem created men and women as separate individuals at the very, very beginning, then they would not feel the need to come together except, as many in the animal kingdom, for the sole purpose of procreation. After that, they would separate and go their own way."

However, if the original and "natural" state was that they were one and the "artificial" state is that they are separated, then they would innately want to recapture the way they were…the way they were meant to be. Recreating it would become their task and their adventure. Maintaining it and growing it would become their challenge.

More interesting still is that completeness of a man or a woman is achieved intellectually, cognitively, and spiritually, when these two distinct and different parts come back together again.

The original separation meant that not only was their physical being split in two, so was their spiritual self, their soul. Judaism says that when you marry and find the other half of your soul, you in fact find the other half of yourself (the Talmud tells us of the heavenly assistance you are given to do so).

The incomplete elements of either half are completed by their reunification.

A 2013 brain connectivity study from Penn Medicine reported on the proceedings of the US National Academy of Sciences. It found striking differences in the wiring of men and women's brains. Dr Ragini Verma said, "These findings show us a stark difference and complementarity in the architecture of the human brain that helps provide a potential neural basis as to why men excel at certain tasks, and women at others."

Co-author, Dr Ruben C Gur, said, "It's quite striking how complementary, although different, the brains of women and men really are."

The key word here is of course "complementary."

I don't know if you enjoy music. I tend to like classical music, so allow me to use that as a vehicle for this discussion. The repertoire contains many solo pieces, particularly for the piano. I always felt personally that no matter how brilliant the composer – Bach, Mozart or Beethoven – the music becomes tedious eventually. Now add a violin; when a solo becomes a duo, so many more musical avenues open up. If you like Rock, think of the live concert where the lead guitarist takes off on his own. No matter how talented, there is always an extra feeling of exhilaration when the other band members join in. The music simply becomes richer and deeper.

The Torah says that richer, deeper and better occur when a

man and woman reunite, and each bring their different voices and harmonise.

That the old-fashioned model of marriage today, at least as it exists in the West, is broken is quite clear, but *our* model of marriage isn't.

Let me be clear here. In the order of the books of the Talmud, the one dealing with divorce, *Gittin* comes before the one on marriage, *Kiddushin*. You really do have to know how to get yourself out of a mess *before* you get yourself into it. Sometimes, a marriage just has to end for many varied reasons and often one party is left high and dry. This is a discussion way beyond the scope of these few words.

But Jewish communities that embraced the worldview that administered the coup de grace to marriage at large suffered the same fate.

Of course, there are many similarities between the two models, but it's the dissimilarities that are crucial; how we *see* marriage, how we *do* marriage, and what we *think* it is all about.

When we do marriage the way the West does marriage, then we undo marriage the same way too.

Which leads me back to the previously mentioned, procreation…and kids.

Research shows consistently that children find the divorce of a parent much harder to deal with than the death of a parent. No less than Barak Obama has publicly addressed the disaster within the black community of the absence of fathers in the rearing of children. Solo performances tend not to be as strong. Obviously there are cases, especially with the tragic loss of a spouse, where a parent has no choice but to be both father and mother, but the Torah presents the family unit as the ideal both for the children and the parents.

It is obvious that children from such a marriage are able to observe and learn from seeing the complementary state of a man and a woman together, intellectually, cognitively and spiritually. They can hear a duo where the music is richer and deeper.

There is nothing nicer than seeing a couple who have been married for sometimes 50 years, who are clearly as much in love with each other as they were when they married. In Judaism's model of marriage, one plus one equals one.

In admiration and honour of Solly Irving for his Emunah
and his commitment to Holocaust education, from
his grandchildren and great-grandchildren.

Rabbi Hanoch Teller

Not So Long Ago and Not So Far Away

This is the story of 13 years and a birth so unusual that, for a handful of people, every detail remains to this day vivid and unforgettable. The birth was unusual not in the clinical sense, but in the historical sense – unusual in that which preceded and followed it. It is the story of Menasheleh, growing up under what seemed to him to be perfectly normal conditions. For him, his entrance into the world and into our people's immortal Covenant remained more or less a mystery, over which he had never lost much sleep.

But mostly it is the story of the saintly Leah, Menasheleh's mother. After Menasheleh's birth she dedicated herself to the fulfilment of the secret vow she had made during some of the darkest days our People have ever known. Only after her death did her husband find a yellowed slip of paper containing a short note, written in Hebrew, which she had dated 12th Menachem Av, 5704 (1944): "I have been here for three weeks. My husband, father, family, and Ida are, I know not where, and I have heard nothing of them. Here in this camp, at 3 o'clock in the afternoon, I hereby make a vow that if God reunites me with my family and with the Jewish people I will bring up my children to be dedicated to Yiddishkeit, and l will help them and their father learn Your Torah all their days."

And she did.

Leah even found time to celebrate, and 13 years after Menasheleh was born it was time to make a *brit*. A *brit*?! Yes, my friends, a *brit*. For Menasheleh. But don't worry. It was not his first. Have you ever been to a bar mitzvah in Williamsburg? I mean old Williamsburg, ten or 15 short years after the liberation of Europe. Who better than the Jewish residents of Williamsburg, knew how few had returned from the European inferno. And who better understood the meaning of a *simchah*.

And there at the bar mitzvah, there is a guest. A bit shabbier than the rest, a bit more bent over. His sleeves are frayed, and his shiny trousers are a mite too short. He speaks to no one and hardly touches his food. His hands exhibit a slight tremor, but his eyes, his amazingly green eyes, shine like two emeralds. No one seems to recognise this strange figure.

The rav gives his speech and then it is young Menasheleh's turn to present his carefully prepared Torah lesson. As he stands up, so does another figure, one with green eyes. The stranger clears his throat and picks up a bottle of soda, tapping a spoon determinedly against its side. With little choice, Menasheleh's father allows him to speak. And in a voice of surprising strength and clarity, the uninvited eccentric calls out one word: "Menasheleh."

The boy looks up at the man who speaks again, but this time an octave or so higher, and he's singing: "Menasheleh, oy Menasheleh." The song continues: "*Rabbotai* (Dear Guests), you think this kugel is *geshmak* (tasty)? Have I got news for you! I once tasted kugel many times better! You think we're here to celebrate Menasheleh's bar mitzvah? Well. I've got even bigger news for you! We're actually here to celebrate Menasheleh's *brit*.

"A story, my friends, listen to a story. It happened not so long ago, and not so far away. It was already the summer of 1944 and the Nazis were in a hurry. Their enemies were closing in fast. But by this time, friends, half of Hungary's Jews were ashes. We did not know this, of course, but when they put us on that train, very few of us thought we'd ever come back.

"How many holy Jews died on that train? Don't ask. How many lost their minds? Who knows? But eventually we got there. Where? Believe it or not, we were in a work camp in Vienna not Auschwitz – four trains were routed there from Hungary. And with us was a woman who was pregnant. A woman? She was really no more than a girl. Where was her husband? She didn't know. Wasn't she afraid to give birth? No, she already had two daughters; giving birth didn't scare her, but something else did. What if it was a boy? How would she make a *brit*? But she brought one clean diaper with her, so that if it was a boy, he would have a nice, clean diaper for his *brit*.

"This woman, her name was Leah, got an "easy" job working in an office because she spoke so many languages. This was July, she was due in September, and she was trading rations for cigarettes. Why cigarettes? Well they were the currency of the camps. What would be when the baby was born, if she needed to buy something for him, if she needed some special favour? So all the time she was trading rations for cigarettes. Thank God, it was an easy pregnancy; at least she wasn't *shlepping* heavy loads and getting beaten every day.

"She was such a wonderful woman, always doing favours, always encouraging everyone, and a wonderful mother to her own little girls. They were too young to work. All day they were alone. "If the bombers come," she told them, "run into the woods. They don't drop bombs in the woods." But at night, when she came home to them, she sang to them, and told them stories to strengthen their faith. One of them got sick, unfortunately, and didn't recover.

"Anyway, everybody loved our Leah'leh. And all the time, she prayed for a girl and traded rations for cigarettes. But God played a trick: first He sent our Leah'leh to Vienna instead of Auschwitz, and then got her a "good" job in an office. What did He do then, *rabbotai*? Oy! He gave her a boy!

"'What will be?' she wondered. The day after the birth, she was already on her feet. She was talking to Dr Tuchman. Tuchman, even within a *Judenrat*-encased heart, still had a spark of a Jewish soul. Sometimes he was willing to help his fellow Jews. "Dr Tuchman," she told him, "I want you should get me permission from the *Lagerfuehrer* to make a *brit*."

"'Young woman,' he told her, 'what's the matter with you? Amalek (the arch-enemy of Jews) should give permission to have a *brit*? They're already asking when you'll be back at work. I don't even want to mention your name! Go hide and nurse your baby, and I'll try to get you as many days off as I can."

"'But Dr Tuchman,' she said, 'a boy must have a *brit* on his eighth day!'

"'But young woman...'

But Leah didn't understand the word "but."

"She said, "Dear Dr Tuchman, when God gave us the *mitzvah* of *brit milah* (circumcision), He didn't say that we're exempt in a concentration camp. If He decides that I can't make a *brit*, then I won't. But until I know otherwise, I have no choice but to try. So if you won't speak to the *Lagerfuehrer*, I'll do it myself."

"*Nu, rabbotai,* how do you say no to such a righteous person? Even Tuchman couldn't. And so the next day, he was there bright and early.

"'Young woman, I can't believe it. I spoke with Amalek himself, and he says you can make a *brit*!'

"But Leah'leh had another worry on her mind. "Who will carry out the *brit*? Who will be the *mohel*?" she asks.

"'Young woman. I'll see what I can do.'

"And the next day Tuchman was back, all smiles. "You're not going to believe this. A transport arrived yesterday, and there was a *mohel* on it!" But then suddenly he got very serious. "Young woman," he said, "I don't know what kind of merits you have, but somebody wants that boy of yours to have a *brit*. I met this man yesterday. He's not only a *mohel*; he's also a rav and a *shochet*.'

"'Anyway, I told him the story. He said he doesn't have his *mohel* knife here. Before he left, he managed to pack only his *chalef*, his slaughtering knife. After all, he thought, a Jew never knows where he might find himself. So he packed his chalef before he left, but not his knife for *brit milah*. So I said to him that we have surgical instruments at the hospital. And maybe he could... but before I could finish he opened up his bag to look, and nearly fainted: there was no *chalef*, only a *mohel* knife!'

"Leah didn't answer for a minute. And then she said, "Dr Tuchman?"

"'Yes, young woman?'

"'Would you be *sandek* and hold the baby during his brit?'

"And so that's how it was, *rabbotai*, not so long ago, and not so far away. Our Leah'leh, she named her son Menasheh, and she prayed that God should give her the strength to lead her pure little boy to Torah, to *chuppah*, and to good deeds. And when you cried, Menasheleh, when you cried at your first *brit*, do you know what your mother said to you? "Don't cry," she said. "When you turn

13, I'll make you a real *simchah*. Your father and I together. We'll make you a *brit* like nobody ever saw."

And then the stranger whispers, "And you know what, Menasheleh? You stopped crying."

"Oy, Menasheleh, my Menasheleh," he sings, choking now on his own tears. "Do you see, Menasheleh? Do you understand that this is not only your bar mitzvah, but the *simchah* of those who never made it? The celebration of those whose mothers didn't have the strength yours did, and those not blessed with your good fortune. And Menasheleh, it is also your second *brit*. Do you understand what had to happen so that you could have your first *brit* at the proper time? Can you fathom what tremendous self-sacrifice that was? Do you see what being a Jew means to your mother and to so many holy Jews who did not come back? Do you understand your great merit and your great obligations?"

Then, suddenly he stops, this strange man. He looks slowly around the room. He coughs twice and resumes talking. His voice becomes louder. His green eyes begin to sparkle. His right thumb begins tracing great arcs in the air, and the sing-song becomes even more pronounced.

"And the cigarettes, *rabbotai*, what ever happened to all of Leah'leh's cigarettes? What's a *brit* without a festive meal? She traded those cigarettes for enough bread that at least 10 men could eat a few morsels. I know, because I had a couple of crumbs myself. And she traded them for some wine, an onion, some half-rotten potatoes, a bit of salt, a couple of eggs – very expensive items, eggs – and who knows what else. And somehow, this day, I don't know where she baked it, she said it was her secret – she made a kugel. And believe me, *rabbotai*, if you think the kugels of Williamsburg are *geshmak*, that kugel that Leah'leh prepared for us there in that Nazi hell had the taste of Heaven."

Dayan Ivan Binstock

False Messiahs – Shabbetai Zvi

In 1667, the members of the Portuguese Synagogue in Amsterdam
found themselves in a terrible quandary. The previous year, along
with thousands of Jews in the Jewish world, they had been swept
up in the euphoria of messianic mania. The announcement that a
Jew from Turkey, Shabbetai Zvi, was the Messiah, had been greeted
with tremendous excitement across the Jewish world. Following
the rupture to Jewish civilisation in the wake of the expulsion
from Spain in 1492, the brutal massacres of Ukrainian and Polish
Jewry in the Chmielnicki uprisings of 1648, and the upheavals of
the Russian-Swedish war of 1655, the news of a Redeemer seemed
to be the answer to a centuries-old prayer.

That year, in Amsterdam and in many other communities, every
boy born had been called either Shabbetai or Nathan (after the
Messiah's prophet).

Then disaster had struck. The news that Shabbetai Zvi had
converted to Islam dealt a devastating blow to community morale
across the Jewish world. Yet there were practical ramifications that
remain with us to this day. For example, in Amsterdam, in anticipation of Shabbetai Zvi's coronation, the community had begun
to adopt the *Birkat Kohanim* (Priestly Blessing) every *Shabbat*, as
opposed to just on *yom tov*.

The question was posed to Rabbi Jacob Sasportas, who had
been an outspoken critic of Shabbetai Zvi well before the latter's
betrayal. Sasportas, in a responsum (*Ohel Yaakov* 68), was firmly
of the view that the practice must stop and the community must
revert to its former practice of *Birkat Kohanim* only on festivals.
He was appalled that there should be any practice that would set
a positive light on the period of Shabbetai Zvi. Yet community
records reveal that Sasportas was unsuccessful and the practice

of *Birkat Kohanim* on *Shabbat* continues in Amsterdam to this day, a permanent reminder of one of the most ignominious mass movements in the last two millennia.

There have been many false messiahs, both before and after Shabbetai Zvi. For example, in 1413, a Spanish scholar, Moses Botarel, claimed that Elijah had appeared to him and appointed him as the Messiah, and in the 18th century, in Poland, Jacob Frank (1726–1791) held attention briefly before he converted to Catholicism. None have had the impact, neither during their lifetimes nor subsequently, as was the case with Shabbetai Zvi.

Shabbetai Zvi was born in Smyrna in 1626, on the 9th Av, a day traditionally regarded as the day when the Messiah would be born. He was a gifted youth, blessed with a very pleasing appearance and singing voice. In his adolescent years, he began the study of Kabbalah, and soon gathered round him other contemporaries who studied with him.

In his later teens, he began to exhibit the behaviour we would now identify as manic depression. Periods of extreme euphoria oscillated with periods of profound depression, punctuated, occasionally, with episodes of normality.

In his euphoric state, Shabbetai Zvi felt impelled to commit acts contrary to *Halachah*. He would pronounce the Tetragrammaton (the Ineffable Name of God) as it is actually written, and undertake bizarre rituals. In his melancholy state, he would withdraw from society to wrestle with the demons that he felt were overwhelming him.

The news of the terrible massacres of Jews in the Ukraine 1648 prompted him to proclaim himself as the Messiah, but no one took him seriously.

He was expelled from Smyrna for his antinomian behaviour. For a number of years, he wandered with a band of followers around communities in Asia Minor only to be expelled repeatedly for his bizarre activities – at one stage he had performed a *chuppah* with a *Sefer Torah* and declared himself, the Bridegroom of the Torah!

In 1662, he came to Jerusalem where he enjoyed a period of relative stability and, in 1665, he visited Gaza where he had heard that there was a prophet who could diagnose a person's afflictions of the soul. Shabbetai Zvi, enjoying a rare period of insight into his condition, was looking for a way to rid himself of his torments.

Instead, Nathan of Gaza proclaimed Shabbetai Zvi as the Messiah. Nathan was a brilliant scholar, writer, and publicist. These skills combined to make him an outstanding and persuasive mouthpiece for his chosen candidate. Historians are still divided as to whether Nathan himself was a charlatan, or indeed genuinely believed Shabbetai Zvi to be the Messiah. Either way, Nathan was able to provide a kabbalistic justification for all of Shabbetai's bizarre excesses.

Boosted by Nathan's supreme confidence in him, Shabbetai proceeded back to his native Smyrna in September 1656 and then to Constantinople, where he announced he would be taking the crown from the Sultan. His arrest and detention in a fortress in Gallipoli didn't in any way deflect the growing momentum of the movement.

Nathan had issued a call for Jews to repent and prepare themselves for the Messiah's imminent return as king. It was heeded by communities worldwide. From Yemen to Amsterdam, from Kurdistan to Prague, Jews responded in their tens of thousands. The movement was boosted by rumours that the Ten Lost Tribes were returning. Gentiles looked on, askance, as their Jewish neighbours sold their homes and belongings in preparation for their return to the Holy Land. Samuel Pepys reported in his diary that a Jew in London was offering ten pieces of gold for a wager of 10:1 that a Jew in Smyrna would be crowned Messiah in the year 1666.

Shabbetai's increasingly grandiose claims of seizing the Sultan's crown eventually led to the latter giving Shabbetai an ultimatum: convert to Islam or be beheaded. Shabbetai chose the former, taking a number of followers with him.

There were individual rabbis who, at the time, challenged the validity of Shabbetai's claims. Yet they couldn't argue with the results. Tens of thousands of Jews were being motivated to become more observant. Attendance at synagogue, *mikveh*, acts of charity etc., all rocketed. After Shabbetai's apostasy, the agonising question remained: How to explain that this repentance had been based on falsehood?

This dilemma led some to continue to support Shabbetai even after his apostasy and his death in 1676 and the death of Nathan in

1680. They advocated an ideology of secret transgression, whilst at the same time being openly observant. Today, the only remnants of Sabbatianism remain in the members of the *Donmeh* sect in Turkey who are identified with the descendants of the original followers of Shabbetai Zvi into Islam.

The yearning for a messianic redeemer, which is a fundamental tenet of Jewish faith, is at least as urgent as it ever was, 70 years after World War II. There were rabbis who in the immediate lead-up to and during World War II saw the exterminations and horrendous outrages committed against our people in eschatological terms, and defined them as *chevlei mashiach* (the birth pangs of the Messiah). Alas, 70 years on, we still await that great happening. The many false candidates who have littered the pages of Jewish history, especially the infamous career of Shabbetai Zvi, only serve to sharpen our expectations for the right individual. May he come, speedily, in our days.

In loving memory of Michael Berman by his wife
Esther, children and grandchildren.

Anthony Julius

Jews and Good Citizenship

Can we learn how to be good citizens by studying canonical Jewish texts? In a tradition as rich and diverse as our own, something can always be found. But it may be that in its mainstream thinking, we will find very little. We must take that risk; we must be ready to acknowledge the possibility of a lack.

What do we mean by "good citizen"? Do we mean: A law-abiding person, paying his taxes, deferring to legitimate authority, not causing any trouble? Call this the "passive or minimal good citizen." Or do we mean: A person realising himself in his contribution to public affairs, and participating as one among equals in the governing of his society? Call this the "active or maximal good citizen." Each conception has its champions.

On the first, minimal conception of the good citizen, the Jewish tradition has much to say. How might the prudent Jewish subject best relate to the ruling powers? *Pirkei Avot* (Ethics of the Fathers) gives our tradition's most considered answer. In summary, he should pay his taxes and keep his distance. In the language of the tractate itself: "Love work and despise mastery; do not make yourself known to the government; if you cannot avoid contact with it, be cautious, because it is not your friend; but pray for its welfare, for it is only fear of it that stops men swallowing each other alive."

If the *Pirkei Avot* Jew has a favoured political form, it is hereditary monarchy. But he is in his heart apolitical, and he has his gaze fixed on messianic days. So far from regarding politics as a vocation, he regards political (and commercial) cares as burdens, which it is the merit of Torah study to ease.

What then of the maximal conception? Here we need to look not to the Jewish tradition, but to the Ancient Greek tradition. We find it stated in many places. In the philosopher Aristotle's work, for example, a citizen is a man who rules and is ruled in turn, and politics itself is a distinctively human excellence. We regard the man who takes no part in public affairs, not as one who minds his own business, but as good for nothing, declared Pericles, the great Greek statesman. Actually: *worse* than good for nothing, added the French revolutionary Robespierre, thinking in the same tradition, many centuries later. For him, passive citizenship was "an insidious and barbarous expression." We are all, by necessity, involved in the political life of our society. The choice is not between passivity and engagement, but between good will and enmity. You are either for, or you are against the state; you are among its rulers, or you are among its enemies.

To which the *Pirkei Avot* Jew says: Save us from the exertions of the Periclean, the terrors of the Robespierrean. We do not wish to be citizens, we wish only to be subjects. We do not wish to exercise power in partnership with our fellow citizens, pursuing the common good. We wish instead to be ruled by a wise and just king, whom we will then bless. But even if it is the case that normative Judaism defines itself partly in opposition to pagan political values, and reaches its maturity before the modern form of the state emerges, is it as simple as this, a passive Jewish tradition set against an active classical tradition, the two making a binary pair?

There are Jewish projects of the last 100 years that would suggest that this is *not* so – projects that come closer to the active, maximal conception of citizenship.

By a "Jewish project," I mean any religious, political or cultural programme pursued for the benefit of the Jewish people as a whole, advanced by self-identifying Jews, and informed by both a creative relation with the Jewish tradition and a sense of the integrity and value of the whole of *Kelal Yisrael*.

The pursuit of prayer, study, and good deeds is the most ancient of Jewish projects. It is not the only one. Chief among modern projects is Zionism. The Zionist Jew is consumed by politics. His project, an incontestably Jewish one, is the rebuilding of the Jewish State, and the achievement of sovereign self-rule for the Jewish people. In this, nothing can be taken for granted; everything must be worked for; it is as if the State has to be rebuilt afresh regularly, just to preserve it. The minimum thus asked of the Israeli is maximal citizenship. Despite almost every disadvantage, the project has been an immense success. But it is limited to citizenship in Israel alone. It seems counter-intuitive to imagine that Zionism might contribute to the development of a Jewish conception of active citizenship in the Diaspora.

What then of that other project, very familiar in Diaspora life, the engagement of communal leaders in politics on behalf of their community? Call this "confessional politics." It is not only a Jewish practice, but Jews may be said to have invented it, or at least been among its earliest practitioners. It has two aspects: lobbying the state for benefits and privileges, and seeking to steer the state closer to the community's own values. It is an opportunistic, self-interested group engagement, and it has its place. But a Jewish conception of good citizenship cannot be exhausted by a set of stratagems for protecting Jews and promoting Jewish values. It is not public spirited enough.

So, neither quite works for us in the Diaspora, and there are no other Jewish projects, complete in themselves, from which we might derive a specifically Jewish conception of active good citizenship. Assimilation cannot be such a project, even though it promotes a harmonisation of private Jewish life and public secular life, which is liberal democracy's creditable norm. The historic cause of political emancipation was not in itself a project, but rather the precondition of political projects. The historic and contemporary cause of fighting antisemitism is pursued in part to keep the possibility of all Jewish projects alive. We had once to fight for the right to participate as equals in the political process; in the face of antisemites, we find that we must continue to assert that right. Having won it, and now defending it against our enemies, the question presses: How should we best exercise it?

We might dispute the value of active citizenship; we cannot deny its origins. The provenance of the active conception is classical, then, through and through. The Jewish philosopher Emmanuel Levinas wrote, "We needed the Greeks to give us art." To which we might add, "We also needed the Greeks to give us politics." Levinas perhaps had in mind Ben Zoma's question: "Who is wise? One who learns from all men" (*Pirkei Avot*, IV.1).

Nevertheless, there are elements in the Jewish tradition, in our texts and history, that can enrich and inform this classical conception, and which many individual Jews among us honour: first, a regard for compromise, derived from the halachic obligation to follow the paths of peace (*mipnei darkei shalom*); second, a respect for dissent – which we might derive from the talmudic passage concerning the rival schools of Hillel and Shammai ("These and these are the words of the living God"), but which finds independent sanction in centuries of *kibbitzing*; third, a concern for the excluded – derived from the verse, "Do not mistreat the stranger; you were a stranger in Egypt" (Exodus 22:21); and fourth, a recognition of the legitimacy of resisting oppression (the story of Exodus).

The principle of respect for compromise allows consensus within the community to emerge, and encourages all to participate in reaching it. The principle of respect for dissent allows a voice to those of the community who are outside the consensus, and encourages the free circulation of ideas and opinions. The principle of respect for the stranger allows peace of mind to those outside the community but within its power. The principle of legitimate resistance allows the oppressed to imagine a more just social order, and then act on that imagining. Though we may need to go to the Greeks to learn about active citizenship, we do not need to go to them empty handed. We can go to them bearing these gifts.

Rabbi Dr Norman Lamm

Barter, Contract or Covenant

(From an address delivered on *Shabbat* 29th October 1960)

Brit is one of the most important words in the whole of the Jewish
religious vocabulary. It means in essence "religion" and implies a
relationship between God and man, a dialogue. So that for those for
whom God is only an ideal, or an abstraction, rather than a living
reality, it is absurd even to speak about *brit*, as it is valid only in the
context of God as *Elokim Chayim* (a living God), who engages the
heart and mind of men. Similarly, the word "religion" derives from
the old French and Latin *"relegare,"* which means "to bind, to hold
tight." Thus, both words mean to forge a close bond between God
and man. How an individual reacts to *brit*, how he conceives and
approaches it, tells us about the quality of his religious experience.

Regrettably, for some people, *brit* means a form of barter, a
religious bargain that one strikes, whereby man approaches God
on infrequent occasions and proposes a form of religious haggling
or spiritual commerce: "I will give charity, You take care of my
portfolio"; "I will fast on Yom Kippur, You will provide me with
health"; "I will recite the *Yizkor*, You take care of my family until
the next such occasion." This is akin to paganism and a distortion
of Judaism – no matter how prevalent it is.

For others, *brit* means not "barter," but "contract." Admittedly,
this interpretation does not limit meeting God to rare moments.
It understands that the dialogue between God and man must be
on-going – but it is still only a contract and shares many of the
same misunderstandings. Its underlying and unspoken presuppo-
sition is that man acts in certain decent ways only because in this
manner he will receive certain rewards. Now, while it is true that
we Jews believe in reward for virtue and ultimate punishment for

vice, we cannot base our religious experience squarely upon this concept. Our rabbis taught: "Do not be like servants who serve the Master only on condition of receiving reward." The "contract" interpretation, although more advanced than "barter," is still not enough of a relationship.

The true and highest interpretation of *brit* is that of "covenant." Covenant does not deny reward and punishment, they are terms and conditions of the covenant after all – but they are not its essence. The real nature of our covenant is two-fold – both originating with Abraham.

The first is the *brit bein ha-betarim* (the covenant between the pieces). God's covenant takes place at a point when four animals are separated into halves and a flame passes between the pieces. It is also then that God gives Abraham *havtachat ha-aretz* (the promise that He would give him and his descendants the Land of Israel).

Rabbi Joseph Albo, one of the great medieval philosophers, explains the symbolism of the *brit bein ha-betarim*. For just as one half of a body cannot live without the other, so too the two parties to the covenant are inextricably bound together, and existence is impossible and unthinkable without the other. Man cannot exist without God and, while God can certainly exist without man, He needs man to fulfil the purpose of creation. Without man, the whole drama of God's creation is, in the words of Shakespeare, "full of sound and fury signifying nothing." It is intensely personal and intimate and it is why at this covenant, God gives Abraham the Land. For God chose this Land for us, and when Israel chooses to settle and live in it, hope and dream for it, then the Land is a bridge uniting God and Israel. This *brit* teaches us that the dialogue between God and man, though it is one between subordinate and superior, must be of great intimacy.

Only with this covenant, can we survive in this lonely universe: when we recognise that God is not only in heaven, but that He is here and now, that our destinies are linked and our fates intertwined. Rabbi Samson Raphael Hirsch correctly pointed out that a difference between the Greek and the Hebrew conceptions of God is that only Israel was able to use *Elokenu* (our God) and *Keli* (my God). The possessive tense reflects a profound human closeness with the deity, the God of the *brit bein ha-betarim*.

The second aspect of *Brit* is the covenant of circumcision. God commands Abraham to circumcise himself and his children thereafter and at this occasion, gives Abraham *havtachat ha-zera*, the promise that he will be survived by descendants who will become a great nation. The quality revealed in *brit milah* is that the covenant must not only be one of closeness, it must also be eternally binding, and thus circumcision became the sign of the covenant. Just as *ot* (the sign) is cut into the human flesh and is permanent, indelible and irrevocable, so too the "covenant" is eternally binding. Abraham's descendants are forever committed to God and Torah – indelibly and irrevocably. That is why at this time, God gave the promise that Abraham would be survived through the ages by children. For if the covenant is eternal, there must be a Jewish people to continue.

These two elements define the Jewish conception of religion and it is these that separate Torah Judaism from others. We are unable to agree with the idea that every generation is free to choose from the covenant that which it wishes, or that people may accept truth as taking whatever form they please. The *brit* is indelible and unchangeable.

Only recently, the Prime Minister of Israel, David Ben Gurion, in opening the Knesset, complained of the lack of idealism among the new generation. "They lack," he said, "true patriotism for the Holy Land and a sense of historical continuity with their people."

Mr Ben Gurion has spoken well. But he has described the symptoms, not the cause. Our diagnosis is simple. A generation or two ago many Jews rebelled; they denied the *brit* and so the oneness of Israel with God began to fall apart. When we deny the oneness of the covenant, the *brit bein ha-betarim*, then we must expect that there should be a weakening of the loyalty of both God and Israel to the Land.

And when that generation subsequently rebelled against the second aspect of *brit* by denying the eternally binding character of Torah, they similarly rejected the principle of the continuation of the relationship of God and people. Therefore, they must expect that God is not bound to His *havtachat ha-zera*, to His commitment that our people will continue as a historical unit through the ages.

Naturally, there is one last aspect to *brit*. And that is that, as partners to the *brit*, we are bound, not just as individuals, but as a people. We are bound to each other as descendants of Abraham our father. It is our duty to recall not only the first two aspects, but also the third: our bond to our fellow Jews. We are the people of the covenant, a covenant which continues eternally, in a nation of our fellow Jews.

Elie Wiesel

A Prayer

39

Reprinted with permission from *The New York Times*, 2nd October 1997

Master of the Universe, let us make up. It is time. How long can we go on being angry?

More than 50 years have passed since the nightmare was lifted. Many things, good and less good, have since happened to those who survived it. They learned to build on ruins. Family life was re-created. Children were born, friendships struck. They learned to have faith in their surroundings, even in their fellow men and women. Gratitude has replaced bitterness in their hearts. No one is as capable of thankfulness as they are, thankful to anyone willing to hear their tales and become their ally in the battle against apathy and forgetfulness. For them every moment is grace.

Oh, they do not forgive the killers and their accomplices, nor should they. Nor should You, Master of the Universe. But they no longer look at every passer-by with suspicion, nor do they see a dagger in every hand. Does this mean that the wounds in their soul have healed?

They will never heal. As long as a spark of the flames of Auschwitz and Treblinka glows in their memory, so long will my joy be incomplete.

What about my faith in You, Master of the Universe? I now realise I never lost it, not even over there, during the darkest hours of my life. I don't know why I kept on whispering my daily prayers, and those reserved for the *Shabbat*, and for the holidays, but I did recite them, often with my father and on Rosh Hashanah eve, with hundreds of inmates at Auschwitz. Was it because the prayers remained a link to the vanished world of my childhood?

But my faith was no longer pure. How could it be? It was filled with anguish rather than fervour, with perplexity more than piety.

In the kingdom of eternal night, on the Days of Awe, which are the Days of Judgement, my traditional prayers were directed to You as well as against You, Master of the Universe. What hurt me more: Your absence or Your silence?

In my testimony I have written harsh words, burning words about Your role in our tragedy. I would not repeat them today. But I felt them then. I felt them in every cell of my being. Why did You allow, if not enable, the killer day after day, night after night to torment, kill and annihilate tens of thousands of Jewish children? Why were they abandoned by Your Creation? These thoughts were in no way destined to diminish the guilt of the guilty. Their established culpability is irrelevant to my "problem" with You, Master of the Universe. In my childhood, I did not expect much from human beings. But I expected everything from You.

Where were You, God of kindness, in Auschwitz? What was going on in heaven, at the celestial tribunal, while Your children were marked for humiliation, isolation and death only because they were Jewish?

These questions have been haunting me for more than six decades. You have vocal defenders, You know. Many theological answers were given to me, such as: "God is God. He alone knows what He is doing. One has no right to question Him or His ways." Or: "Auschwitz was a punishment for European Jewry's sins of assimilation." And: "Isn't Israel the solution? Without Auschwitz, there would have been no Israel." I reject all these answers. Auschwitz must and will forever remain a question mark only: it can be conceived neither with God nor without God.

At one point, I began wondering whether I was not unfair with You. After all, Auschwitz was not something that came down ready-made from heaven. It was conceived by men, implemented by men, staffed by men. And their aim was to destroy not only us, but You as well. Ought we not to think of Your pain, too? Watching Your children suffer at the hands of Your other children, haven't You also suffered?

When we as Jews enter the High Holidays, preparing ourselves to pray for a year of peace and happiness for our people and all people, let us make up, Master of the Universe. In spite of everything that happened? Yes, in spite. Let us make up, for the child in me, it is unbearable to be divorced from You for so long.

Rabbi Joseph Dweck

Esther – A Study in Bravery

God is surprisingly not mentioned in the Book of Esther. Instead of imposing Himself through prophet or miracle in the story, He runs the world under cover, and guides it towards completion through natural events. This lack of overt intervention by God creates the space that allows human input to take centre stage. In the Book of Esther, God's interaction with the people reaches a state of maturity and is an example of how the relationship between God and Israel should be. Maimonides writes that there will come a day when all the books of the Bible will become obsolete, except for the Book of Esther, which will remain eternally relevant to the Jewish people.[1]

From our perspective, this mode of divine interaction can seem to run without rhyme or reason. The world looks as if it has no direction and meaning. Uncertainty develops, and it disturbs us. However, uncertainty also brings us precious gifts: freedom and opportunity for self-achievement come about when life lies before us, undetermined.

Thus, uncertainty and bravery are essential parts of God's world, and we read about both in the story. Lotteries, or *purim* in Hebrew, are prominent[2] in the book, along with other elements of doubt. For instance, when Esther is abducted and brought to the king's harem,[3] rather than beseech God and ask Him to intervene on Esther's behalf, we read instead that "Every day Mordechai would walk before the king's court to know about Esther's welfare and what might be done to her."[4] There are no assumptions that God will perform a miracle and save the day. There is, instead, firm

1. *Mishneh Torah, Hilchot Megillah* 2:18
2. Esther 3:7, 9:24, 26
3. *Ibid*, 2:8
4. *Ibid*, 2:11

recognition that this will need to be a joint endeavour with God, one in which they must respond to developments and make choices about which actions to take. The approach taken by Mordechai and Esther is an infrequent one in the Bible. They acknowledge the uncertainty of life and assert their free will in response to it. To act this way requires us to be vulnerable and take risks.

There are limits, though, to the liberties that freedom affords us. There are elements of reality that are "called out by God from the beginning"[5] and "will always stand,"[6] that are not susceptible to our choices. In understanding this, we come to terms with the fact that in our freedom we are not gods, but rather we are partners with God in Creation. God's determinations and our choices, run in tandem in a way that is showcased in the *megillah*. The story teaches us that while God is powering the world to have the result as He has planned, the particular course it takes and the people who will be involved with it, are entirely open.

The book presents this entire concept to us in one line. Mordechai tells Esther that no one can be certain as to why she might have become queen, but one thing is clear, "If you remain quiet at this time, salvation will come to the Jews from someplace else, and you and your father's house will be lost."[7] Mordechai insists that her actions will not affect the ultimate survival of the Jewish people. The only issue for her is whether she will take the opportunity to become the agent for that survival and, in doing so, bind herself and her line to the Jewish saga. The people would survive come what may, as God has planned from the outset. But would it be Esther's actions and Esther's story?

Her story and choice teach us that we are free beings who can bravely choose to live in an active relationship with God and become part of creation, or we can bow out of involvement and interaction. Either way, God powers the world and leads it to completion. The choice that is inviolably ours and that makes all the difference, is whether we will blend into the background and allow life to rush past us, or become partners with God as active agents in the grand tapestry of Creation.

5. Isaiah 41:4
6. *Ibid*, 14:24, Proverbs 19:21
7. Esther 4:14

Rabbi Mark Dratch

The Importance of Synagogue and Community in Contemporary Life

Facebook. Twitter. Instagram. Texting. Phone calls. Email. There are more ways today for people to connect with others than ever in history. And yet...researchers have suggested that, despite this increase in communication, the ease of travel, and the wealth of information that is now available at the push of a finger or the click of a mouse and despite the large number of "friends" we may have on Facebook, most people today are more lonely and more isolated than ever before.

We have a deficit of "social capital," a term used to refer to the resources – help, support, friendship, empathy, care, concern – that are available to us through our social connections. It is the opposite of isolation and loneliness. It is cohesion, friendship, and the support of an accepting community. And we need that friendship and support; the need is built into our very humanness. "It is not good for Man to be alone" (Genesis 2:18) is, as Rabbi Joseph Soloveitchik said in a different context, "a permanent ontological principle rooted in the very depth of the human personality."

Ecclesiastes (Chapter 4) put it best:

There was a man all alone; he had neither son nor brother.

There was no end to his toil, yet his eyes were not content with his wealth.

"For whom am I toiling," he asked, "and why am I depriving myself of enjoyment?"

This too is meaningless – a miserable business!

Two are better than one, because they have a good return for their labour:

If either of them falls down, one can help the other up.

But pity anyone who falls and has no one to help them up.

Also, if two lie down together, they will keep warm. But how can one keep warm alone?

Though one may be overpowered, two can defend themselves.

A cord of three strands is not quickly broken.

The need for community is utilitarian; we need others to help us meet the daily challenges of life. And the need for community is existential; we need others to help give meaning and purpose to our existence.

Our tradition prescribes many ways for people to relate. One is the area of *mitzvot bein adam la-chavero* (our social obligations) such as charity, visiting the sick, comforting mourners, refraining from *lashon ha-ra* (gossip and slander), and more. True service of God necessitates us to be of service to people, and loving our friends and neighbours as we love ourselves (Leviticus 19:18) expands our interests and concerns beyond our own physical and egotistical needs, and helps to connect us to others in significant and meaningful ways.

Our isolation is curtailed by being part of a community, where our joining together is not only a desirable outcome but a requirement in terms of prayer, to create the *minyan* required to respond "amen" to each other's blessings and *Kaddish*.

The Talmud (*Shabbat* 32a) castigates those who refer to the Torah ark as an "*arna*," a mere "closet," and those who refer to a *beit kenesset* (synagogue) as a *beit am* (a house of the people). The former is easily understood: the sanctity which surrounds the repository of our Torah scrolls can be diminished if pedestrian words are used to describe it. Similarly with a synagogue, some suggest it should not be called a *beit am* because it is the House of God, not the house of the people and suggesting otherwise is blasphemous.

Nevertheless, the synagogue *is* a place of gathering, it is the "People's House"! Our common term *beit kenesset* (house of gathering) implies that. There is, however, a fundamental difference between a *beit kenesset* and a *beit am*! A *beit kenesset* is a place not only where people are found, but a place where we connect.

A *beit kenesset* is not only a geographical place that exists at any particular moment in time, it is one in which we identify and bond with *Kenesset Yisrael*, the eternal Jewish people past, present and future. A *beit kenesset* is not merely a building which people pass through, but a home whose inspiring spirit passes through them. A *beit kenesset* is more than a place of entertainment and utilitarian functions; it is a locus of meaningful spiritual, religious, emotional, and interpersonal activities.

There is no better place – in fact, there is often no other place – in today's world where we can receive such great return on our investments. By investing our time, efforts, energies and talents in the Jewish community and in the *beit kenesset*, we can enjoy the returns on social *and* spiritual capital.

> *Dedicated by the author to his family who perished in the Holocaust and to the 80 escapees from the camp that did not make it.*

Jack Kagan

Surviving the Holocaust with the Jewish Partisans

I was born in 1929 in Novogrodek (Novardok) into a middle-class family. The town had a Jewish population of between 6,000 and 6,500, who made up half the town's inhabitants.

On 22nd June 1941, Germany attacked the Soviet Union. We knew that we would suffer under the Germans, but never imagined that they would try to liquidate us all. I remember the discussion between my father and my uncle. "There is no point in running. We are used to work. They won't kill us!" And so we stayed.

The Germans entered Novogrudok itself on 4th July 1941 and immediately started enforcing anti-Jewish laws. Yellow stars had to be worn on the front and back of our clothes and everyone from the age of 12 to 60 had to report for work.

On 5th December 1941, posters appeared ordering all Jews to assemble at the courthouse. It was a bitterly cold day, minus twenty degrees centigrade. 5,100 people were selected and we heard later that they had been taken to a forest and shot.

A further selection took place in August 1942, when a further 5000 Jews were murdered – mostly from the surrounding area – including many of my family. The remainder were then transferred from the ghetto into a work camp, enclosed by barbed wire and towers with searchlights and machine guns. But the young people began to escape. The four Bielski brothers had gone into hiding in the forest and were joined by other families. Once it became known in the ghetto that there was a place to run, people began to take the chance. I knew the youngest brother, Archik Bielski, very well, as we had been in the same class. Many of the escapees were helped by two Christians who were honoured as Righteous Gentiles after the war.

Getting out of the camp itself was still quite easy; the danger was that in winter you could freeze to death. Then there were the problems of food, and the fact that the outside world was unfriendly. People were ready to sell you to the Germans.

I became friendly with the Jewish warehouseman in charge of the store of boots. He had lost a son of my age and, therefore, wanted me to succeed in my escape. He risked his life and gave me a pair of beautiful hard felt boots. I told my parents that I planned to escape and they gave me their blessing.

On 22nd December, the gates were opened to allow lorries to unload raw material. I loosened my yellow star and number, and tore them off when I got nearer to the gates. There were no guards to be seen and I made my way to the small forest where a few people were already waiting. After dark, we started to skirt around the town to the rendezvous with the partisans. The going was very difficult, with waist-deep soft snow, and we had to cover approximately eight kilometres. We reached a little river and began to cross it. We felt the ice under the snow, but suddenly, it gave way and most of us fell in. I was the worst off; my felt boots immediately absorbed the water, and snow started sticking to them. Each step became more difficult and we reached the meeting place too late. But we knew the partisans were due to come back three nights later and had been advised to stay in the forest until then.

After a while though, I just wanted to sleep. I started to dream and realised that, if I fell asleep now, it would be forever. I made the decision that I must return to the camp and crawled to the road and was fortunate that a peasant passed by in his sleigh.

When we got near the camp, I jumped off and started walking towards the well, as I knew that in a few hours' time the first prisoners would come to fetch water. One of the water-carriers noticed me and alerted the rest of the group, who smuggled me back into the camp with them. When I entered the compound, my father tried to take off my boots but it was impossible – a sharp knife had to be used. My toes were black with frostbite but there was no doctor to help and no medicine; there was nothing we could do. After a few days the flesh started to rot, and my toes had to be amputated. Thus ended my first attempt at escape.

On the 7th May 1943, the Nazis selected another 250 Jews, mostly women and children, and showed them just outside the camp. Amongst them were my mother and sister.

That evening a resistance committee was formed and it was decided to dig a tunnel 100 metres (328 ft) long to the other side of the barbed wire, into a field of growing wheat. It would be a major engineering feat which would have to be carried out without discovery.

The work had to be stopped for a while because there was not enough oxygen for the lamps to burn inside the tunnel. Mr Ruk-ovski, one of the inmates, was an electrician. He found the camp's main power cable leading to the workshops, and made a hidden switchboard, so that the camp searchlights could be turned on and off, and the tunnel could be lit up.

The joiners among the prisoners prepared railway lines and a trolley, the tailors prepared bags and my father made the reins to pull the trolley. The loft was reinforced, and the dug-out earth hidden there and work went on secretly 24 hours a day, 7 days a week. The tunnel was 1.5 metres below ground, 60 centimetres wide and 75 centimetres high; just enough for a person to crawl through. However, in July, my father was sent to a labour camp near Baranovitz. He escaped from there in February 1944, but must have been killed en route to the partisans.

In August 1943, the tunnel was nearly ready when suddenly the Germans brought in a tractor and cut the corn. The fear was that the tunnel might collapse from the weight of the tractor, but it did not. However, if we had escaped then, probably none of us would have survived, as the German army had brought in 52,000 soldiers to launch a month-long raid on the Soviet partisans and the main German base was at Novogrudok. Once the cover of the corn field had been removed though, we were forced to extend the tunnel by another 150 metres.

The escape was set for the night of 26th September 1943. It was a dark, moonless, stormy night, as if made to order. At 9 PM, the line started moving forward. Fresh air was coming in from the tunnel as we broke through to the outside world. We made a big mistake, however, by leaving on the lights in the tunnel. Coming out into terrible darkness, some people became disorientated and ran towards the camp. The guards, not knowing what had happened, started shooting in all directions. But most of us ran towards the forest and freedom. Of those who escaped, about 170 made it to the partisans and about 80 were caught and killed.

The escape was three days before Rosh Hashanah and I subsequently found a German document which stated that the Novogrudok camp was to be liquidated after they dealt with the 2,000 Jews in Lida. Since the Lida Jews were killed on the 19th September, our execution date was probably set for Rosh Hashanah 1943.

In August 2012, a film producer organised a trip to Novogrudok for 50 people, to search for the tunnel. It included three escapees, my three children and ten grandchildren. We managed to locate the tunnel, which is 250 metres long, and has now been made into a museum.

Dr Naftali Loewenthal

Rabbi Israel Baal Shem Tov (1698–1760)

Rabbi Israel Baal Shem Tov, the founder of Chassidism, lived in Miedzyborz in the Ukraine in the 18th century. *Baal Shem* means "Master of the Name," referring to the Divine Name, since a Baal Shem would use kabbalistic amulets, which included names of the Divine, to heal the sick. But the Baal Shem Tov did much more than this. He changed the way people think about Judaism.

The Baal Shem Tov came from a poor family and was orphaned as a child. There are stories of him, as a young boy, going alone into the forest, meditating on the closeness of God. In his youth, he worked for a time as an assistant teacher, inspiring the children in his care, and his unique spiritual qualities were recognised by the learned scholar Rabbi Ephraim of Brody, who betrothed his daughter Chana to him. Her brother Rabbi Gershon of Kuty was a well-known kabbalist, who initially was disrespectful to Rabbi Israel, but later became his ardent follower.

When the Baal Shem Tov was still a young man, he led a circle of spiritual scholars in a study house in Miedzyborz. Unlike many great scholars of the time, he was determined to be accessible to ordinary people. He used his mystical knowledge to help the many people who would come to him for advice and blessing, both in material terms and spiritually. In addition, his help often had a practical basis: people would give him money when helped by him, which he used for the benefit of others, such as paying the ransom for Jews who had been imprisoned by the lawless Polish noblemen of the time.

In terms of his message, the Baal Shem Tov's main theme was *ahavat Yisrael* (love of one's fellow Jew). This crossed all borders:

young or old, learned or ignorant, rich or poor, pietist or sinner, and its basis was his spiritual perspective on life. His became known as the *Torah* of *Chassidut*. For example, we learn in the Torah that God created the universe by expressing a number of sayings, beginning with "Let there be light." The Baal Shem Tov taught that this was not a one-off event, but a continuous process; a flow of spiritual energy from God which continues to give existence to everything in the universe. If we look at the world from this perspective, we have a more "spiritual" view of reality because if God is constantly making everything exist, there is obviously an ongoing "Divine Supervision" of all that happens in the universe. Indeed, Nature itself is an expression of the Divine. Moreover, miracles are possible at any moment.

The Baal Shem Tov was aware of the darkness in life, of the concealment of the Divine, but he taught that the darkness itself is an aspect of God's presence during exile. Concealment, like revelation, is indissolubly part of God, even though at first we might find that difficult to understand.

Seeing things in this way can lead to a sense of closeness to God and even to a sense of joy, as a result of the appreciation of God's presence. This idea carries itself through into the practical realm of action. When people carry out *mitzvot* imbued with this spirit, they are filled with enthusiasm and equally are also careful to carry out the *mitzvah* meticulously, to ensure that the halachic teachings about the divine *mitzvah* are being fulfilled, since each commandment is an opportunity to enhance one's relationship with God.

Such enthusiasm and love are particularly expressed within prayer and Torah study. The Baal Shem Tov taught that in the Hebrew letters "there are spiritual worlds, and souls and Godliness." The individual letters join and become words, and the words, filled with spiritual radiance, rise and come closer to the Infinite.

Beyond the ideas that he taught, there were aspects of the Baal Shem Tov's experience which went far beyond ordinary consciousness, such as accounts of his trying to defend the Jewish people in spiritual realms. A unique letter from him describes an "ascent of the soul," which was a kind of spiritual journey into the higher worlds, including an encounter with the Messiah.

He asked the Messiah: "when will you come?" and the Messiah

answered: "When your wellsprings spread to the outside." The "wellsprings" mean the spiritual teachings of the Baal Shem Tov.

The rise of the chassidic movement was, in certain ways, a direct implementation of that message, with the idea that the sense of awareness of spiritual reality should not be reserved for only a small elite. It should be communicated to all. This was understood as something which would revive the Jewish people, bringing them closer to the spiritual essence of Judaism, and also hasten the coming of the Messiah.

In the following generation, the ideal of communicating spirituality, provoked strong opposition from those who believed that the message was easily misinterpreted, and feared that embracing kabbalistic spirituality would lead to abandoning the study of the classic areas of Torah and observance of *Halachah*. However, the subsequent history of Chassidism as a movement, showed that chassidic inspiration led to affirmation of Jewish law and custom rather than its abandonment.

According to one of the Baal Shem Tov's disciples, Rabbi Jacob Joseph of Polonoye (1710–1784), a key aspect of chassidic thought is the goal to unify the Jewish community. The scholars and the ordinary people form two distinct groups which should be drawn together. He believed the inspirational teachings of the Baal Shem Tov, and the new model of charismatic Jewish leadership which the Baal Shem Tov represented, were the means to achieve this.

The Baal Shem Tov's ideals of love of one's fellow, unity of the Jewish people, joy, study of the inner spiritual dimension of Torah and expressing love and awe of God in prayer, were also taught in the *Tanya*, a book written at the end of the 18th century by Rabbi Shneur Zalman of Liadi (1745–1812) who was a disciple of Rabbi Dov Ber of Mezeritch (d. 1772), the disciple and "successor" of the Baal Shem Tov. Rabbi Shneur Zalman, therefore, regarded himself as the spiritual grandchild of the Baal Shem Tov.

In our own time, we see that some of the values which the Baal Shem Tov taught have been affirmed by many diverse branches of Judaism, including some which could be considered at variance with his total message. To an extent, we could say that we are all influenced by his teachings and are all, somehow, his grandchildren.

Rabbi Dr Akiva Tatz

Free Will, Imagination, and Distortion

How does man's innate knowledge of what is right and good become distorted?

Rambam (*Moreh Nevuchim* 1:2) was questioned about a perplexing consequence of Adam's fall. Before the sin, he did not know good and evil, whereas after the sin, he gained that knowledge – the result of eating of "the tree of the knowledge of good and evil." Why did the sin lead to the acquisition of knowledge, a faculty previously denied him?

Rambam answered that there could not have been a greater fall. It was not the gaining of new knowledge; it was a loss of clarity. Prior to the sin, man did not know good and, evil; rather he knew only true and false. What we now call "good," he saw as true, as rock-solid reality. What we now see as "evil," he saw as essentially non-existent. To do evil then had as much appeal as the attempt to convince oneself that one plus one equals five. Man saw reality as it is, and his moral reality was as reliable and strong as logic itself.

After the sin, however, true and false were reduced to good and bad: good is not absolute; it may be right and obligatory, but it comes at a price and that price can be debated. Similarly, if bad is not absolute, while it may be immoral and prohibited, it certainly has benefits, potentially even worth the consequences. Man's sin did not lead to the acquisition of new knowledge; it led to the immense distortion of his clarity, a world where reality and illusion are both credible.

FIRST PERSON, SECOND PERSON

Furthermore, before the sin, man saw himself as primarily spirit.

His body was secondary, a vessel for expression of his spirit. When he thought of himself, his "I" was located in his spirit. The serpent – that represents bodily cravings and sensual distractions – addressed him as a separate being speaking from a distance, in the second person: "Would you like to taste sin?"

But after the sin, the body became primary in consciousness. When the body and its senses speak now, they speak from within, in the first person, and although it may be humiliating to acknowledge it, there is no denying that when a delicious opportunity tempts the senses, it always speaks in the first person: "I would like to taste that," and it is the conscience, when it speaks at all, that now speaks from a distance, in the second person: "You know you shouldn't do that."

The locus of man's awareness of self has moved down from mind to body. Awareness of the self began as Godly; the word *Ani* meaning "I" is one of God's Names. When man originally said "I," he conflated his identity with God in total sublimation. That was where man's consciousness resided. Now the "I" speaks from a lower place.

Indeed, the Talmud (*Succah* 52a) states that one of the names of the *yetzer* (lower self) is *tzefoni* (the hidden one), hidden deep in man's psyche; and very difficult to discover. What is meant here is that the dark side of man's nature has so thoroughly taken over that it is hidden: present in full view, masquerading as the one seeking him out.

With dark humour, one modern sage put it thus: "What is the right way to rob a bank? It isn't to enter with a mask and a weapon and use force. The correct method is to make an appointment with the manager, enter his office, gag and bind him, lock him in a closet, and then sit at his desk and run the bank."

That, in fact, is exactly what has been done to the higher self; it has been hijacked by the *yetzer*, who is now making the decisions in its name. What passes for the self is a motley assembly of vested interests and ulterior motives.

FALSE VISION AND THE WORLD OF APPEARANCES

"And the woman saw that the tree was good to eat." But surely one cannot see how a fruit tastes; what is meant here? Distortion of vision began the downward slide; a vision that saw clearly, became a vision that suggests. Fantasy replaced reality.

A clear vision would see God everywhere, but the eyes do not cooperate. When Hagar waited while her son was dying of thirst, a well miraculously appeared: "Then God opened her eyes and she saw a well of water." (Genesis 2:19). The verse does not say that God created the well; it says that He opened her eyes to see it. The problem is not the absence of a higher reality, it is the human inability to see it.

WEB OF FANTASY

Sin originally, therefore, had no intrinsic appeal. There can be no inner craving for a sensation that has never been experienced. Temptation begins as a flimsy illusion no more tangible than a spider's threads. Later, when the addictive pleasure is part of inner experience, it binds as firmly as the thickest rope. The process begins only as seeing and imagining. A young person's desire for his first cigarette is pure fantasy; there is no craving within him yet. When it is first tasted, it is not necessarily pleasant; it may leave him feeling thoroughly ill. But the fantasy is strong enough to overcome even that disappointment, and sooner or later what began as an experiment becomes a necessity.

God did not start the challenge with established addiction and then ask man to climb out of it; it was man's wide-eyed fantasy that built his own trap.

The imagination is free to wander endless paths; the constraints of truth do not apply to it. Whereas truth is always bound, falsehood has no limits (a mathematical problem has limited solutions, often only one; false solutions are endless).

TREE OF CONFUSION

In reality, therefore, the Tree of the Knowledge of Good and Evil that the woman saw was the tree where good and evil become intertwined, meshed ("knowledge" means intimate bond) for the one who tastes it. A proper name for it would be "the Tree of Doubt." Before man ate, he spoke to God face to face; after he ate, he found himself hiding among the trees from a God who surely sees through those trees – man became so confused that he believed he could hide from God. His clear vision had become hopelessly clouded.

Man created a world of illusion, and the illusion became as tangible as he imagined it to be – such that, when God appeared in the garden and found him hiding, He asked: "Where are you?" as if He did not see him. Man defines the terms of his relationship with God, and when he chooses to live in illusion, God steps behind the veil that man has created.

And even if a person experiences a flash of clarity today that shows the direction to be taken beyond all doubt; tomorrow he wakes up wondering how he could possibly have seen things that way yesterday. Almost as soon as perception clears, it changes until man can no longer trust his own vision and absolute truth is no longer visible. The result is that man is groping his way back to the garden, battling to separate good and evil, and our choices need to be viewed through a lens of absolute clarity, of truth, without which we are relegated to making choices in a world of confusion.

This is an extract taken from Rabbi Tatz's Book: *Will, Freedom, and Destiny* (Targum Press, 2014)

Dedicated to Rabbi Doron (Laurence) Perez in appreciation of his
magnificent contribution to South African Jewry and his commitment
to bringing about a revival of the World Mizrachi movement.

Rabbi Doron (Laurence) Perez

Identifying the Haggadah's
Wayward Son

The *seder* night is the quintessential Jewish educational experience
where grandparents, parents, and children sit together and retell
the story of our Exodus from Egypt and the birth of our people.

We are all familiar with the memorable description of the four
sons who find themselves at the Pesach *seder*. This famous paragraph appears at the beginning of the *Haggadah* narrative and in
many ways highlights its central educational message. I believe that
determining the identity of the enigmatic wayward son will offer
a fundamental insight into one of the major challenges facing the
Jewish people today. The *Haggadah* states as follows:

"The wayward son asks: "What is this service to you?" (Exodus
12:26) By saying "you," he excludes himself. And since he excludes
himself from the people of Israel, he has denied a fundamental
principle of our faith. You, in turn, should blunt his teeth (give a
sharp and blunt answer) and say to him – "because of what *Hashem*
did for me when I left Egypt, I do this" – implying for me but not
for him. If he (the wayward son) had been there (in Egypt), he
would not have been redeemed."

This paragraph from the *Haggadah* is most telling as to who
the wayward Jewish son is and, further, what our response to him
should be. The *Haggadah* describes the wayward son as the one
who sets himself apart from Jewish people and places himself
outside Jewish community life. His question, "What is this service
to *you*" implies that the service does not obligate *him* in any way.
Issues of Jewish identity – our collective fate, destiny and responsibilities – are seen as something which has no bearing on him. So
much so that the *Haggadah* uses the sharp terminology that, since

he has excluded himself from the Jewish people, he has denied a fundamental tenet of Jewish faith.

Remarkably, what emanates so succinctly from the *Haggadah* is the supreme importance of Jewish peoplehood. The community ethic is a core component of our identity and crucial to the meaning of Jewish life.

Pesach is the story of our people. It is where we explain to ourselves and our children what it means to be part of the collective Jewish experience. It is about the history of our people whose birth was forged in the houses of bondage and suffering in Egypt and continues with our freedom and redemption culminating in the ultimate messianic redemption. It is about our fate as a historic community. The crux of the Pesach story is sharing our common fate as a collective community and participating in the destiny of our people. Failure to embrace this reality excludes one from the Jewish community and, therefore, from being part of its destiny. One cannot claim to be either a religious Jew, or a universalist Jew, without being intrinsically connected to the particular fate and fortune of our people.

This is particularly relevant to one of the great contemporary challenges facing the Jewish people in general and the State of Israel specifically. Over the last 15 years, we have seen a dangerous and systematic delegitimisation campaign of the State of Israel, of her defenders and her supporters. This began with the horrific World Racism Conference in Durban in 2001, continued with the founding of the Palestinian BDS movement (boycott, divestment and sanctions) in 2005, and continued with the damaging Goldstone Report of 2009 and, most recently, during Operation Protective Edge in 2014. A global movement has been galvanised to single out Israel unfairly and unjustly and brand it as an "Apartheid State" with a clear aim of shaking and undermining the moral foundations of her right to exist.

What is most concerning is that some Jews are stridently siding with those who wish to uproot us. Some of these Jews such as Neturei Karta, claim to emanate from the extreme religious right, while other groups represent elements from the extreme secular left. These groupings form an unlikely and unholy alliance in which modern day Israel is the loser. Incredibly, these Jews claim to be proudly Jewish either through their religious or universalistic interpretation of their Jewish identity. Their tragic mistake though, is that they are excluding themselves from the fundamental tenet of the Jewish community and from our distinct and collective historic experience as a people. They are the wayward sons of our generation who want Judaism without Jewish peoplehood, faith without fate, universalism without bonds of unity with their people.

Having identified the wayward son, we now need to understand the bewildering reality of why it is that the wayward son who denies a sense of camaraderie with the Jewish community, is at the Pesach *seder* in the first place? After all, if he is so wayward, why does he want to be part of the Jewish experience? The answer is clear: he does want to have a connection to his Judaism, but without the commitment to a collective Jewish destiny. But the *Haggadah* teaches us that he cannot claim to be a good Jew, while at the same time separating himself from the pain and suffering of his own people. Of course, every good Jew must be sensitive to the suffering of all human beings. All are created in the image of God. This is without question a core Jewish value. But how can this possibly override the suffering of his own family, community and people? Kindness and charity must never end in the home, but they most certainly begin there.

The answer given to the wayward son in the *Haggadah* is most telling. We blunt his sharp criticism by highlighting the following important point: "Had you been in Egypt you would not have been redeemed." The wayward son needs to decide what side of Jewish history he is on. If his worldview does not contain this deep sense of Jewish peoplehood, then he has missed the point. Our Sages tell us that many Jews chose not to leave Egypt, but rather lost themselves during the plague of darkness. These individual Jews could not come to terms with the vision of redemption from Egyptian society: to journey to the homeland of their forefathers and to exercise their divine, religious, historical, and moral rights in their God-given land. Those who left Egypt committed to this narrative. Those who chose to stay behind rejected it.

We are encouraged by the fact that the wayward son is at the *seder* table and we, as his fellow Jews, bear a responsibility to both embrace and educate him as to the salient and eternal importance of the link between faith and fate – between Judaism and the Jewish people.

> *In memory of the Hundert and Kimel families, always remembered by those who survived them, and their descendants. Family Hunter.*

Rabbi Steven Weil

Confronting Providence in the Modern World

The Jewish people celebrate many holidays throughout the year. The objective of Pesach, Shavuot, Succot, Purim, and Chanukah is to inculcate in us an appreciation that the miraculous events that happened long ago to our People occurred because God is orchestrating our history hands-on. We recognise and celebrate numerous times a year the fact that God is a constant Presence in our lives and continuously engages His covenantal people. We do not merely conduct a Pesach *seder*, we relive the Exodus. We don't simply recall that God gave us a Torah, we re-enact the *Har Sinai* experience. By lighting the *menorah*, we recreate the experience of God's direct Providence in our national experiences. We do this to make sure we are aware that God's involvement in our lives is not consigned to history, but is continuous and happening in real time.

When we pray, we address God as both *Elokenu* and *Elokei avotenu*. *Elokei avotenu* means the God of our fathers who interceded on *their* behalf in the most obvious of ways. Our generation, however, addresses just as fervently *Elokenu* (our God) because we have borne witness to God in recent history. Our generation has two new holidays to celebrate, two recent occasions that have revealed once again the Hand of God in the experience of the Jewish people. *Yom HaAtzmaut* and *Yom Yerushalayim* – days that testify and celebrate that God is present and involved in the day-to-day journey of Jewish destiny.

In the spring of 1948, outnumbered and poorly equipped against five armies committed to Israel's destruction, the impossible occurred. After almost two millennia, the pitiful Israeli army, against all odds, won the war instigated by our neighbours and God allowed the Jewish people to return and re-establish our ancestral homeland. Despite the tremendous sacrifice of life, the Land of Israel became what God has always planned it would be, a place of refuge for Jews from the four corners of the earth and a light unto the nations on an ethical, philosophical and even technological level. To show our profound gratitude and appreciation for God's direct Providence in making this dream of a Homeland a reality, we celebrate *Yom HaAtzmaut.*

In June of 1967, just 22 years after the liberation of Auschwitz and Majdanek, we were facing a second Holocaust at the hands of our neighbours. Thirty thousand graves had already been dug in Tel Aviv alone, in preparation for the onslaught of the Arab armies. Just as the miracle of Purim occurred through the hidden Hand of God, stealthily guiding the politics and personalities, so too was the Six Day War won! Was it not the Hand of God that fateful Sunday morning, when the entire Egyptian air force was decimated by a limited number of planes with an even more limited amount of arsenal, all while the Egyptians went to eat their breakfast? Was God not whispering in the ear of Jordan's King Hussein when he chose to listen to Gamal Nasser's lies that Egypt was destroying Israel in the south so he should attack Israel's western front? Only because he ignored Prime Minister Levi Eshkol, who begged restraint, did we liberate the holy city of *Yerushalayim* along with the historical communities surrounding *Yerushalayim* on the west bank of the Jordan, when our soldiers – who fought with tremendous self-sacrifice – entered and captured these territories. To show our gratitude and appreciation for God's Providence in reinstating the capital for our Homeland, we celebrate *Yom Yerushalayim.*

Defeating armies ridiculously more powerful than ours is similar to defeating Pharaoh's Egyptian empire; having all of the minute details conspire in favour of our victory is no different than the victory over the Prime Minister of the Persian Empire; the miracle of *Har HaBayit* (The Temple Mount) is seen in the context of the miracle of the Maccabees defeating the Greeks who defiled the Temple. The miracles may be no different, but the people who witnessed the miracles are. On the fifth and the 28th of Iyar the witnesses were us and, therefore, our obligation and ability to praise, thank, and rejoice with our God whose nurturing and protection we personally experienced are so much more powerful. Just as Moses and Miriam led the Jewish people in a spontaneous outburst of song and praise after experiencing God's direct salvation at the *Yam Suf*, so too must we recognise and respond overwhelmingly and passionately to God's orchestration of our journey throughout history.

When the doors to our Homeland and our capital were flung wide open, we all marvelled at the miracle, but how many of us took the next step and entered? Many Jews from all parts of the world have made *aliyah* and settled in Israel, but certainly not all of us. Many of us celebrate *Yom HaAtzmaut* and *Yom Yerushalayim* in the Diaspora, but no matter where we are living, we can still reach out and hold God's Hand by partnering with Him to support our brothers and sisters who live in Israel and make the sacrifices for Jews everywhere. We can give money and time and expertise to help develop the land, assist its people and advocate for its security and protection. In this way, it is not only twice a year that we acknowledge God's direct involvement in restoring our Homeland and its capital, but every day we can seek out ways to tangibly recognise and appreciate the fundamental role Israel plays in our existence as a People.

We live in difficult times and the certainty of an independent Jewish State is not a given. We are attacked and threatened by annihilation, terrorism, bias, ignorance and baseless hatred. The only way to counter these frightening existential challenges is to keep the message of these holidays with us at all times – that God actively and constantly is involved with His people, He nurtures and protects, and He alone determines the destiny of all humanity.

Rabbi Dr Raphael Zarum

Isaiah – The Potency of Prophecy

The book of Isaiah is not a story; it is a polemic. Born at a time when Israel was divided into two, Isaiah son of Amotz watched the final destruction of the Northern Kingdom by the Assyrians as well as the beginning of the gradual demise of the Southern Kingdom, Judah. He outlived four kings of Judah and took them all to task.

Being a small kingdom in the midst of two superpowers, Egypt and Assyria, Judah's kings were convinced that the only way to survive was to play one off the other, switching allegiances as necessary. King Ahaz turned to Assyria for protection against the Northern Kingdom that had allied with Syria. Later, his son, Hezekiah, turned to Egypt for protection against Assyria which had become a threat. But Isaiah knew that human politicking ignored God's plan and implored the kings to listen:

> Turn away from man … for why is he worthy? … God is our Judge, the Lord is our Ruler, the Lord is our King, He will save us … Oh disloyal children! – declares God, making plans against My wishes, weaving schemes against My will, piling up sin after sin … (2:2, 33:22; 30:1–2).

If you were given a message that would outrage society, would you keep it to yourself or would you have the courage to speak? Isaiah spoke out for a full 66 chapters:

> Hear O heavens, and give ear, O earth, for God has spoken: I reared and raised children yet they have rebelled against Me. Even an ox knows its owner, an ass its master's crib; but Israel does not know, My people are thoughtless! (1:2–3).

Just as international politics must recognise God, so too must national aspirations be grounded in ethics. Thus Isaiah rails against insincere sacrifices and the injustice prevalent in Israel's society. His message is a deeply moral one:

> Wash yourselves clean, put away your wrongful ways... Cease to do evil, learn to do good. Devote yourselves to justice, relieve the oppressed, uphold the rights of the orphan and defend the cause of the widow (1:16–17).

He frames Israel's capital as the source of God's message on Earth, "For Torah will come out from Zion, and the word of the Lord from Jerusalem" (2:3). This message will have global influence, "Thus God will judge between the nations, and arbitrate for many peoples, and they shall beat their swords into ploughshares and their spears into pruning hooks" (2:4). The message will ultimately redeem all, "Nation shall not take up sword against nation, neither shall they learn war anymore" (*ibid*).

These words are carved onto a wall in the garden of the United Nations building in Manhattan. They are a 25 centuries-old testament to the values of real international cooperation. This utopian vision is meant to be transformative. It will unify adversaries, "The wolf shall dwell with the lamb" (11:6) and raise spiritual consciousness, "For the land will be filled with the knowledge of God, just as water covers the sea" (11:9).

But how do we get there? By remembering where we came from:

> Listen to Me, you who pursue justice, You who seek God: Look to the rock you were hewn from, to the quarry you were dug from. Look back to Abraham your father, and to Sarah who bore you" (51:1–2).

Our ancestors calibrate our moral compass and God will always be there to help:

> Listen to Me... you who I've carried since birth and supported since leaving the womb: Until you grow old, I will still be there; when you turn grey, I will still carry you. I made you and I will bear you (46:3–4).

Israel's role has a universal side too, for Isaiah challenges Israel to be, "a light unto the nations; to open the eyes that are blind, to bring out the prisoners from the dungeon" (42:6–7).

So rich is the Book of Isaiah that no fewer than 19 of the weekly *haftarah* readings come from its pages. Its popularity, however, has made it a target for revisionism. Chapter 53, concerning "God's suffering servant," is often misquoted as a reference to the Christian Messiah, "God has inflicted on him the sin of us all…he was cut from the land of the living for the sin of My people" (53:6, 8). In fact, a close reading of the whole book makes it clear that "*Israel* is My servant" (41:8) and the nation suffers as a whole when some have acted immorally.

Isaiah did not restrict his critique to Israel alone. In chapters 13 to 23, he surveys the neighbouring nations who have had dealings with Israel, and pronounces their fate. Babylon, Moab, Damascus, Egypt, Arabia, and Tyre are all included.

Isaiah's divine mission was his life's work. Even the names of his children attest to this. *She'ar Yashuv* (7:3) means "only a remnant will return"; and *Immanu-El* (7:14) means "God is with us."

According to Midrash (*Pesikta Rabbati* 4:3), Isaiah was put to death by King Manasseh for daring to criticise him. Unrepentant, he had been prophesying for some 40 years. But his beautiful and potent language lives on, every time we read and study his book.

The Book of Isaiah is not in chronological order and his first vision is, in fact, in Chapter Six. He saw winged angels, *seraphim*, attending God in the Temple. They were saying to each other: "*Kadosh, kadosh, kadosh* – Holy, holy, holy is the Lord of hosts, the whole earth is full of His glory" (6:3). This statement is at the heart of every *kedushah* prayer, the highpoint of the repetition of the *Amidah*.

However, like many of us when we pray, Isaiah did not feel worthy: "Poor me, I'm lost here, for I'm a person of unclean lips." (6:5) But when God asked, "Whom shall I make a messenger?" Isaiah immediately responded, "Here I am, send me!" (6:8). We too must answer the call that God gives us.

> *Dedicated to the memories of Charles Bloom and*
> *Nat Fox, the grandpas we hardly knew.*

Rabbi Yitzchak Schochet

The Definition of a *Mitzvah*

A *mitzvah* is the ultimate expression of how Judaism views religion. The word means either "commandment" from the root word *tzav*, or "connection" as derived from the word *tzavta*.[1] As with any relationship, forgoing one's own will for the sake of another is integral to establishing a bond. So too, it is through observing the divine commandments that one establishes a connection with God.

Moreover, the *mitzvot* govern every dimension of our lives, thus enabling us to bring God into every part of the human experience. From a kosher breakfast in the morning to a quick prayer before sleep, *mitzvot* provide the opportunity for maintaining an ongoing relationship with God beyond the confines of a synagogue and not limited to the awe-inspiring High Holy Days.

However, a *mitzvah* allows for more than simply a connection. The Midrash defines the purpose of this world's creation with the words, "God desired to have an abode in the lower worlds."[2] Thus, it is man's task to – in essence – establish an abode for Divinity in the terrestrial realm. How is this achieved? Man and the world are finite entities limited to the confines of time and space, whereas God is an all-transcendent Infinite Being. How can man expect to draw the Divine into the world?

The Midrash[3] states: "When God created the world, He decreed and said, "the heavens are heavens of the Lord, and the earth He gave to the offspring of man.'"[4] When He sought to give the Torah, He nullified the earlier decree and said, "The lower realms shall

1. See *Or HaChayim* on Numbers 27:23
2. *Tanchuma, Naso* 16
3. *Genesis Rabbah* 12:3
4. Psalms 115:16

rise to the higher realms and the higher realms shall descend to the lower realms, and I will be the Initiator.'"

Chassidism explains the midrash as follows: Before the giving of the Torah there was a great divide between heaven and earth such that the spiritual could not be manifest within the corporeal. After the giving of the Torah, God nullified the earlier decree enabling the lower realm to become united with the all-transcendent Divine.[5]

It is only through a *mitzvah* – a divine command to mortal man, that God endows man with the unique ability to draw divine energy into the physical and the mundane. Thus, we find that Abraham did not circumcise himself before receiving God's instruction, notwithstanding his foreknowledge of the *mitzvah*. For it is only through the precise commandment that he was able to establish a connection between the spiritual energy and his physical self.

Mitzvot are, therefore, the intermediary between man and the world and the Divine. They serve as the direct link between the upper and the lower, between God and man, in both directions; they make the channel through which the supernal effusions and emanations flow downward to sustain all beings, and they make the channel through which man attaches himself to the Divine.

This then, is the underlying significance of fulfilling *mitzvot*. Man's ultimate purpose is to manifest God's immanence in the physical world. The achievement of this manifestation establishes the ultimate unity of God, that is, that God is recognised to be the sole true reality. To that end, man was given *mitzvot* that instruct man precisely "the way in which he is to walk and the deed he is to do."[6]

Thus it is said, "God desired *le-zakot* the people of Israel and, therefore, He gave them Torah and *mitzvot* in abundance.[7] The term *le-zakot* means to refine and purify. The implication is that there is a refinement and purification of Israel's material reality so that it will be able to become attached and joined to holiness. This principle is alluded to in the saying, "A *mitzvah* brings about

5. *Likkutei Sichot*, vol. 15
6. See Exodus 18:20
7. *Makot* 23b

a *mitzvah*"[8]: Doing a *mitzvah* brings about, and leads to, *tzavta* (attachment and conjunction).

By means of *mitzvot*, therefore, man becomes like a channel or conduit for the supernal "spring" from which the beneficent abundance flows forth to that individual and to the whole world.

Any indwelling of the Divine requires a "receptacle," something to have a "hold" on these, something to which they become attached. For the holiness of a divine emanation is too intense to be absorbed as it is by man and the world. Thus, there is need for a medium through which it may vest itself below. This medium is the *mitzvot*.

Every *mitzvah* becomes, therefore, a deed of cosmic significance, serving as a bridge between Creator and creation. Thus, each deed is of infinite value unto itself. As Maimonides writes,[9] a single *mitzvah* performed by each individual could be the deed that tips the scales and brings redemption to the entire world and all of creation. Thus the value of a single *mitzvah* will not be diminished even if one is not committed to a fully observant life.

Aside from the intrinsic stand-alone value that each *mitzvah* has, *mitzvah* observance can also be contagious. This too is the meaning of "A *mitzvah* brings about a *mitzvah*." Agreeing to opt in, even just once, can have far-reaching effects. Countless Jews have made permanent changes in their lives for the better, on account of the fulfilment of a solitary *mitzvah*.

"Every individual is obligated to say, 'this world was created for me.'"[10] We are each charged with the individual task of bringing Divinity into our world. Through the fulfilment of each *mitzvah* we refine ourselves and the world around us and bring redemption one step closer. One *mitzvah* can, indeed, change the world.

---

8. *Avot* 4:2
9. Maimonides, *Laws of Repentance* 3:4
10. *Sanhedrin* 4:5

Rabbi Paysach Krohn

Deeds of Distinction

Republished with permission of Mesorah Publications from *In the
Footsteps of the Maggid*.

In 1940, Rabbi Binyamin Schachner was hauled from his home in
the small town of Susnofsza, Poland, to the first of seven concentration camps he was eventually to be in. Among the few possessions
that he managed to take along with him were his *tefillin*. Rabbi
Binyamin always kept a close watch on his *tefillin*, shielding and
safeguarding them as though they were his life's greatest treasure.
Every day, when he was sure that none of the Nazi guards were
looking, he would remove the *tefillin* from their hiding place, don
them on his hand and head and say the *Shema*.

Others in his barracks, inspired by his actions, would borrow
the *tefillin* and do the same.

Rabbi Binyamin was transferred from concentration camp to
concentration camp until he was eventually brought to a slave
labour camp in Markstadt. Aside from the toil demanded and
torture inflicted there daily, this place was an area of such filth
and of conditions so inhuman that survival was difficult. Food
was scarce and hard to come by and every day Jews perished from
disease and starvation.

When he first came to Markstadt, Rabbi Binyamin was con-
fronted by an SS guard who demanded to know whether he was
a carpenter. Instinctively he replied that he was, although actually
he had never built anything in his life except a family. Because he
knew that those deemed "useless" were put to death at once, Rabbi
Binyamin decided to claim that he was, indeed, handy. In order to
survive, he would try anything.

It was in the carpenters' woodshed, under a loose floor board, that Rabbi Binyamin hid his *tefillin* while he was in Markstadt. Throughout the weeks and months of his stay, every day without fail, he and others who dared, would disregard their privation and exhaustion and remove the *tefillin* from under the loose wooden plank. Each man would, in turn, wrap the *tefillin* around his hand and on his head and tearfully say the *Shema*, proclaiming, even in this most dire of situations, the uniqueness and Oneness of *Hashem* and *Kelal Yisrael*'s devoted loyalty to Him. Then the *tefillin* would be hidden away once again.

One day a particularly vicious SS guard walked into the woodshed unexpectedly and saw the *tefillin*. Realising that this must be a religious item of sorts, he began to scream in blood curdling tones, demanding to know what and whose they were. Frozen with terror, no one dared say a word.

The Nazi began to yell again, this time threatening to kill everyone in the room if he didn't get a reply.

Rabbi Binyamin's words somehow made it out of his throat. "This used to belong to a young boy who died recently," he said softly.

"But if he died, and you all kept these things here, then they belong to you now," the guard retorted in anger. And with that he ordered Rabbi Binyamin to come outside with him.

Rabbi Binyamin had no choice but to obey, for if he didn't comply he would be killed immediately. Outside, and within the hearing of those inside the shed, the guard began to beat Rabbi Binyamin mercilessly. His screams and cries pierced the hearts of everyone inside until they could stand it no longer. They ran to the barracks' *kapo* (Nazi-appointed leader – who in this case was a Jewish informer) and beseeched him to go out to the Nazi guard and beg for mercy. None of the regular inmates would dare ask the Nazi soldier for a favour; only someone who had the confidence of the oppressors could even make an attempt. Rabbi Binyamin's friends knew that only the *kapo* could intervene on his behalf.

The *kapo* pleaded with the Nazi guard, who finally agreed to stop beating Rabbi Binyamin. The Nazi then ordered Rabbi Binyamin to march back into the barracks. When he walked in, the others were shocked by his appearance. He was bleeding from multiple body wounds and was clutching his ear. (His hearing was impaired for the rest of his life from that beating.)

The guard ordered that the religious articles be burned at once and he announced that he would be coming back to see that it was in flames.

Rabbi Binyamin didn't say a word to anyone but went right over to the shelf where he had his tools and scraps of wood. He brought them to his workbench and, as fast as he could, he began to carve little square boxes to resemble *tefillin*. He glued the sides together as the others around him watched, astonished by his courage and ingenious idea.

A few men built a fire, and soon the boxes were tossed in. Two people removed their leather belts and threw them into the fire as well, to resemble the *retzuot* (straps) of the *tefillin* that had once again been hidden.

The guard came in, saw the fire, inspected it closely and walked out with a satisfied smile on his devious face. But the *tefillin*, now securely hidden, remained intact. Rabbi Binyamin and his friends cried as they thanked *Hashem* for this miracle amidst their agony.

Rabbi Binyamin guarded and protected his *tefillin* for the remaining time of his incarceration at Markstadt. When he was finally liberated, his treasured *tefillin* were still intact, and he was able to leave the camp clutching them tightly in his hands.

Now, decades later, the precious legacy of Rabbi Binyamin's adherence to the *mitzvah* of tefillin lives on. The *tefillin* were recently checked by a *sofer* (scribe) who verified that they are perfectly valid. However, he did advise against their being used on a regular basis. Today, every grandson of Rabbi Binyamin's is given the honour of putting on these extraordinary *tefillin* on the day of his bar mitzvah.

Tefillin have always symbolised the boy who becomes a man. *Tefillin* in this case symbolise how a man became a legend.

> *Dedicated in memory of my grandparents Chaim & Beila*
> *Hershkowitz who were murdered in the Holocaust – date unknown.*

Rabbi Aubrey Hersh

From East to West – The New Immigrants

The odds are that if you asked around for the most significant dates in the last 2,000 years of Jewish history, the list would include: 358, 638, 1096, 1492, 1516, 1939, and 1948. 1881 is an unlikely contender. Yet it was the year that not only radically changed the course of Jewish history in general, but the personal history of most of the readers of this article.

By 1795, two million Jews had been swallowed up into the Russian Empire, although the government was committed to keeping them away from society, to prevent 'holy Mother Russia' from becoming contaminated. Alexander I confined them therefore, to a large-scale ghetto – an area comprising less than five percent of the Empire – known as the Pale of Settlement. It was to remain in place for over 100 years.

Added to this political restriction, were severe economic regulations, which produced endemic and inescapable poverty. Even with everyone in the family working, often all they could manage was bread and potatoes, and it was not unusual for families to occasionally be without any food. Yet, as difficult as it was, things were destined to become far worse.

During the rule of Alexander III, antisemitism was transformed into a policy of violence. Starting on Easter Sunday in 1881, pogroms broke out all over south-western Russia. Over the next few weeks, mobs attacked the Jews in 150 cities and villages, looting, burning and killing, with the police passively looking on. Those that took part included workers, officials, peasants, women, and even children, and as the news reached communities further away, many of Russia's seven million Jews realised that no one was interested in defending them. The terror of these pogroms would recur almost annually, climaxing in 1903, in Kishniev, Odessa, and Kiev.

So the Jews left home due to poverty, political oppression, and religious discrimination.

> Imagine what it must have been like for a young father to make that decision. To quit the place he grew up in, to leave wife and children behind and strike out across the unknown countries of Europe, then to take steerage passage across the frightening Atlantic, and at the end of a harsh voyage, drop like some anonymous atom into the vast chaos of New York. Where would he sleep? What could he do to make a living? How would he make himself understood in a language he didn't know?[1]

One out of every three Jews in Eastern Europe emigrated, almost all under the age of 40, joining the 25 million Europeans who moved to the New World between 1880 and 1920. The 250,000 Jews of America, grew to four million by 1925. In the process, New York's Jewish community outnumbered Warsaw's – the world's second-largest – by five to one and Chicago and Philadelphia would become the third and fourth largest, outstripping Vienna, Budapest, and Kiev.

The immigrants arrived in America penniless, many ending up living in Manhattan's Lower East Side and working in the garment industries, especially the sweatshops.

Overcrowding was greater than that of the worst sections of Bombay, and since many small workshops were crammed into this area, the crowding by day was no less extreme than by night.

As a result of the mass immigration, unskilled wages had fallen sharply and even working a 14 hour six-day week would leave people with less than $10 for their efforts. For the vast majority however, there was no choice but to settle down to this hardship, with nostalgia as a constant companion.

Ironically, it was often Jews who were the harshest employers. In the 1880s, German Jews owned 225 of New York's 241 garment factories, and employed – and exploited – Jewish labour, in a

---

1. *Eastern Europe to America* p xii / p 277 – Milton Meltzer

country with few regulations. The industry turnover increased from \$60 million to \$850 million by 1920 and, unsurprisingly, Jewish immigrants often became the driving force in the early labour unions, ultimately affecting the entire labour movement.[2]

Accustomed to a harsh physical existence, they were unprepared for the spiritual difficulties that arose. America embodied a mix of the *Goldene Medina* (the Golden Land) and the *Treyfe Medina* (the non-Kosher Land) and whilst Jews had been granted equal rights and freedom of religion, that religion was not often practised. With a standard working week running from Monday to Saturday, people who wanted to remain Orthodox faced great difficulties, and many were forced to hunt down a new job every week or accept very low pay. Ephraim Lisitsky recalls: *I had only one friend in my loneliness, whom I met every day in the synagogue – the Talmud.*

The goal was to become American and a variety of publications were printed to achieve that, including a Yiddish version of the Declaration of Independence. But few of the Jewish immigrants escaped the clash of cultures. It was easy to Americanize your name and change your clothes, it was harder to actually contend with your past.

Some parents bitterly fought any change which might weaken the values they brought with them. Others, seeing it was a losing battle, resigned themselves to maintaining their culture for themselves and enduring their children's new behaviour. A third group, determined to keep close bonds with their children, gave up their own culture outright.

Not all elements of society, however, were entirely open to Jews. The universities resisted. Yale's shield is emblazoned with Hebrew, yet ironically, the Dean's instructions were: "Never admit more than five Jews and two Italian Catholics." However, by 1920, things were changing: 80% of applicants to NYC College, 29% in Hunter College, and 15% of Columbia University were Jews.

And then, almost as suddenly as it had started, the great immigrant wave came to an end. Principally, because of the abrupt changes to American immigration laws, post-WWI. Emma Lazarus' words: "Give me your tired, your poor..." may have still been

2. *The Immigrant Jews of New York*, p 82 – Irving Howe

inscribed on the Statue of Liberty, but from 1921 onwards, they became a notion rather than a practice.

Across the Atlantic, the UK's Jewish population more than tripled between 1880 and 1914. Jews arrived from both Galicia and Russia, often intending to continue onto – or sometimes assuming they were already in – America. They ended up in various towns across the UK although the vast majority settled in London's East End.

For most newcomers, it was a ghetto that they rarely left or wanted to leave, where their needs were provided for and where Yiddish predominated. However the influx of so many immigrants rubbed against the comfortable grain of the anglicised Jew, both religiously and politically. Even Chief Rabbi Adler spoke out against their arrival – somewhat out of consideration for the immigrants but equally to placate the wealthy and often assimilated indigenous Jews to whom he felt beholden:

> ...It is difficult for them to support themselves and at times they contravene the will of their Maker on account of poverty, and violate the Sabbath and Festivals. There are many who believe that all the cobblestones of London are precious stones, and that it is the place of gold. Alas, it is not so...I implore every rabbi of a community kindly to publicise the evil which is befalling our brethren who have come here, and to warn them not to come to the land of Britain, for such ascent is a descent.

Yet religious immigrants to England would be responsible for significant developments, especially in the area of *kashrut* – an area which would take much longer to rectify in the USA, where, even as late as 1925, New York State records acknowledged that over 40% of meat labelled and sold as kosher, was not. Kidney suet (which is biblically prohibited) was being sold in butcher shops which were licensed by the Chief Rabbi, and poultry had no markers to prove that they were kosher. Subsequent to a ten year dispute, matters were appropriately resolved.

In the USA and the UK, as well as South Africa and other pre-war immigrant destinations, the transition from peddler to retailer or banker and from sweatshop worker to garment manufacturer was not long in coming. And with the invention of motion pictures,

Jews were at first major consumers and then major producers and owners, of the new medium.

The new immigrant communities ended up dwarfing the existing ones and changing them forever, but arriving before the Holocaust, they planted the seeds that guaranteed survival into the 21st century. A cost was paid for acceptance in these new countries, in assimilation and intermarriage, but those who remained and identified within the fold established a strong identity and, subsequently, a network of philanthropic, religious and educational institutions greater than those that existed in pre-war Europe.

Rabbi Lord Jonathan Sacks

Religion and Science: The Great Partnership

If the new atheists are right, you would have to be sad, mad, or bad to believe in God and practise a religious faith. We know that isn't so. Religion has inspired individuals to moral greatness, consecrated their love, and helped them to build communities where individuals are cherished and great works of loving kindness are performed. The Bible first taught the sanctity of life, the dignity of the individual, the imperative of peace, and the moral limits of power.

To believe in God and faith and the importance of religious practice does not involve an abdication of the intellect, a silencing of critical faculties, or believing in six impossible things before breakfast. It does not involve reading Genesis 1 literally, as some Christian fundamentalists do. It does not involve rejecting the findings of science. Judaism is a faith in which we make a blessing over great scientists, regardless of their views on religion.

So what is going on?

Debates about religion and science have been happening periodically since the 17th century and they usually testify to some major crisis in society. In the 17th century, it was the wars of religion that devastated Europe. In the 19th century, it was the industrial revolution, urbanisation, and the impact of the new science, especially Darwin. In the 1960s, the "death of God" debate, it was the delayed impact of two World Wars and a move to the liberalisation of morals.

When we come to a major crossroads in history, it is only natural to ask who shall guide us as to which path to choose. Science speaks with aptitude about the future, religion with the authority of the past. Science invokes the power of reason, religion, the higher power of revelation. The debate is usually inconclusive and both sides live to fight another day.

The current debate, though, has been waged with more than usual anger and vituperation, and the terms of the conflict have changed. In the past the danger – and it was a real danger – was a godless society. That led to four terrifying experiments in history: the French Revolution, Nazi Germany, the Soviet Union, and Communist China. Today, the danger is of a radical religiosity combined with an apocalyptic political agenda, able, through terror and asymmetric warfare, to destabilise whole nations and regions. I fear that as much as I fear secular totalitarianisms. All religious moderates of all faiths would agree. This is one fight believers and non-believers should be fighting together.

Instead, the new atheism has launched an unusually aggressive assault on religion, which is not good for religion, for science, for intellectual integrity, or for the future of the West. When a society loses its religion, it tends not to last very long thereafter. It discovers that having severed the ropes that moor its morality to something transcendent, all it has left is relativism, and relativism is incapable of defending anything, including itself. When a society loses its soul, it is about to lose its future.

My argument is, therefore, that we need both religion and science – that they are compatible and, more than compatible, they are the two essential perspectives that allow us to see the universe in its three dimensional depth.

The human mind has an ability to do two quite different things. One is the ability to break things down into their constituent parts and see how they mesh and interact. The other is the ability to join things together so that they tell a story, and to join people together so that they form relationships. *Science takes things apart to see how they work. Religion puts things together to see what they mean.* Without going into neuro-scientific detail, the first is a predominantly left-brain activity (sorting and analysis), the second is associated with the right hemisphere (forming personal relationships).

One of the most difficult tasks of any civilisation – of any individual life for that matter – is to keep the two separate but integrated and in balance. That is harder than it sounds. There have been ages – the 16th and 17th centuries especially – when religion tried to dominate science. The trial of Galileo is the most famous instance, but there were others. And there have been ages when science tried to dominate religion, like now.

The new atheists are the most famous examples, but there are many others – people who think we can learn everything we need to know about meaning and relationships by brain-scans, biochemistry, neuroscience, and evolutionary psychology, because science is all we know or need to know. Both are wrong in equal measure. Things are things and people are people. Realising the difference is sometimes harder than we think.

Albert Einstein said it most famously: "Science without religion is lame; religion without science is blind."[1] It is my argument that religion and science are to human life what the right and left hemispheres are to the brain. They perform different functions, and if one is damaged, or if the connections between them are broken, the result is dysfunction. The brain is highly plastic and in some cases there can be almost miraculous recovery.[2] But no one would wish on anyone the need for such recovery.

Science is about explanation. Religion is about meaning. Science analyses, religion integrates. Science breaks things down to their component parts. Religion binds people together in relationships of trust. Science tells us what is. Religion tells us what ought to be. Science describes. Religion beckons, summons, calls. Science sees objects. Religion speaks to us as subjects. Science practises detachment. Religion is the art of attachment, self to self, soul to soul. Science is the conquest of ignorance. Religion is the redemption of solitude.

We need scientific explanation to understand nature. We need meaning to understand human behaviour and culture. Meaning is what humans seek because they are not simply part of nature. We are self-conscious. We have imaginations that allow us to envisage worlds that have never been, and to begin to create them. Like all

1. Albert Einstein, "Science, Philosophy and Religion" (1940), in Albert Einstein and Alice Calaprice, *The Quotable Einstein*. (Princeton, NJ, Princeton University Press), 1996.
2. See Jill Bolte Taylor, *My Stroke of Insight: A Brain Scientist's Personal Journey*. (New York: Viking), 2008.

else that lives, we have desires. Unlike anything else that lives, we can pass judgement on those desires and decide not to pursue them. We are free.

All of this, science finds hard to explain. It can track mental activity from the outside. It can tell us which bits of the brain are activated when we do this or that. What it can't do is track it on the inside. For that, we use empathy. Sometimes we use poetry and song, and rituals that bind us together, and stories that gather us into a set of shared meanings. All of this is part of religion, the space where self meets other and we relate as persons in a world of persons, free agents in a world of freedom. That is where we meet God, the Personhood of personhood, who stands to the natural universe as we, free agents, stand to our bodies. God is the soul of being in whose freedom we discover freedom, in whose love we discover love, and in whose forgiveness we learn to forgive.

Religion and science, the heritages respectively of Jerusalem and Athens, must now join together to protect the world that has been entrusted to our safekeeping, honouring our covenant with nature and nature's God – the God who is the music beneath the noise; the Being at the heart of being, whose still small voice we can still hear if we learn to create a silence in the soul; the God who, whether or not we have faith in Him, never loses faith in us.

Dedicated in memory of Daniel Rowe's grandparents:
Henry Pfeffer and Max and Hannah Rowe.

Rabbi Daniel Rowe

Is Judaism Still Relevant Today?

This question has been asked in almost every generation starting from the original exile from our land. In every generation since, Jews have been a small nation, more often than not with a weak voice and without a platform to promote their ideas further afield.

Yet, at the same time, their ideas have always been powerful, iconoclastic, and disproportionately influential, which caused many to write or agitate against them. And so they have been rejected, repeatedly, as belonging to some other era, with a presumption that the golden age of Jewish ideas lay in the past. The Roman historian Tacitus (*Histories* v (4–5)) objected to the Sabbath as promoting idleness and was reviled by the notion that Jews kept alive all children. Indeed, in most pre-monotheistic societies, children were killed if they were disabled, unwanted, or simply for population control. No less a thinker than Aristotle (*Politics*, Book 7) wrote: "There must be a law that no maimed or imperfect children be raised, and to prevent excess of population some children must be exposed."

History, however, has judged differently. These Jewish ideas seemed abhorrent at the time, precisely because they belonged to the future.

Like most social mammals, our genetics tend to lead us towards tribal groupings: small social groups who display strong links within the clan, but brutality to outsiders.

From at least the Neolithic revolution, humanity has been dominated by war, obsessed with power, and constructed hierarchical societies, entrenching the conquering class as the dominant caste with special laws. Babylonians divided society into three types of persons; the ancient Chinese had 20 classes. Even Athenian democracy permitted only a small class the right to vote. No ancient, medieval or early modern societies allowed for the spread of mass literacy, and so forth.

The Torah's monotheism radically transformed every society that it came into contact with. Genesis teaches of one God who created all mankind in His image, thus opposing infanticide, gladiatorial entertainment, and many other horrors of the pre-monotheistic world. Exodus teaches of God fighting for an enslaved people against the mightiest hierarchical empire on earth. In making God king, human power was to be limited, the citizens of Israel equal in the eyes of the law, and every child to be strongly educated.

The Torah's ideas spread to the world through other religions that incorporated many of its teachings, and through Western idealists that referred back to it as God's word. Though none of these were Jewish, and many were decidedly anti-Jewish, the messages carried forward have radically transformed humanity.

In the words of Paul Johnson: "To them we owe the idea of equality before the law, both Divine and human; of the sanctity of life and the dignity of the human person; of the individual conscience and so a personal redemption; of collective conscience and so of social responsibility; of peace as an abstract ideal and love as the foundation of justice, and many other items which constitute the basic moral furniture of the human mind. Without the Jews, it might have been a much emptier place."

The role of the Jew has always been to live up to Godly ideals in the deep belief that many of these would eventually become the norm. Torah is the constitution of humanity at the end of days. Judaism lives for the world as it is yet to be. In living the future today, we guarantee that Judaism will never quite be "with the times." It will attract the approbation of the best in humanity, and the venomous opprobrium of the worst.

But perhaps the most critical contribution is the vital belief that is carried in the Purim story. The deepest impact of belief in one God is belief that everything in this world is part of one plan. It is belief in history itself.

Purim tells of a story where God's acts are at no point directly revealed. There is no miracle, nor even mention of God's name. Yet the impossible comes to be. Through a series of apparent coincidences, the very source of would-be destruction of the Jews unwittingly conspires to destroy itself, save Israel and reveal God. Arch-antisemite Haman ends up dying because his own decree to kill all Jews turned out to be treason; the queen was Jewish. The former Queen Vashti was killed through the advice of a court adviser that tradition records as Haman himself. It was he who had inadvertently placed a Jewish queen there in the first place! It was even he who built the very gallows that he was to be hanged upon.

The power of the irony of evil ultimately destroying itself is only one part of the picture. For it could lead to complacency. Why need I intervene if, in the end, everything will work out? Purim teaches the very opposite.

In the critical moment, the Jewish leader begs Queen Esther to risk all to intercede on behalf of her people. In what appears to be the least persuasive line possible, Mordechai first declares, "If you stay silent now, salvation will come to the Jews from somewhere else!" before continuing, "yet you and your ancestral home may be obliterated; who knows if it was for precisely this moment that you became queen?" If the Jews will be saved anyway, then why ought she to intervene? And why would non-intervention lead to loss of her ancestry? Why should she feel the precious nature of "this moment"?

Yet that is precisely the point. The very fact that history must resolve itself means that there is a genuine "story" that history is telling. History is not a collection of unrelated acts, but a singular ultimate narrative within which each action plays an inextricable part in the plot, ultimately culminating in the fulfilment of creation itself. In such a scenario, to fail to take a stand is to walk away from history itself. It is to wipe out all that the past has bequeathed. That is what Mordechai tells Esther. When you stand before a moment, remember that history itself beckons; that we are part of a plot such that in the end things will work out. We cannot control the outcome of our choice, and what we hope for may not happen. But we know that no moment is ever lost. No person and no act is insignificant. And that is the greatest reason to step forward and play a role.

Looking back over history, it is staggering to consider the impact of one little nation; a revolution of human values that was wrought by no conqueror, but by the combined acts of many people just trying to live a Godly vision of human affairs.

Looking forward, we hear the call of Purim; that even when man struggles to believe in God, God continues to believe in man. That somehow every moment of creation can be transformed into a part of history. The call of Judaism is the call of the future. A worldview that is foreign to any moment in time, precisely because it belongs to all of time.

It is never relevant to anyone who lives for the here and now alone. But there could be nothing more relevant to one who lives with the consciousness of the past and the conscience of the future. It is to hear the call of eternity in each moment, and to recognise the power of each moment to shape eternity itself.

H.E. Ambassador Daniel Taub

Finding Our Jewish Voice in Our Own Land

Last year I accompanied a Holocaust trip to Poland. While I was there, I learned that in the rubble of the Warsaw Ghetto a blue and white box of the Jewish National Fund had been found.

I found this extraordinarily moving. The Jews of Warsaw, when they were herded into the Ghetto, were ordered to bring with them only their most essential belongings. For one of those Jews, this small collection box, with its dream of planting dreams and rebuilding a Jewish homeland in Israel, was an essential belonging.

Seven decades later, that dream is a reality. Indeed more than a reality. Even in the tumult and trauma of this past summer in Israel, we owe it to ourselves and to our forebears to remember the simple fact: there is not a day in Israel, no matter how challenging the security situation or how divisive the internal debates, that does not wildly exceed the greatest dreams of our ancestors.

But even as we celebrate this miraculous reality, we have to be aware that the history of our state, and in particular the Holocaust which preceded its re-establishment, places particular responsibilities on us, both as a people and as a country. I think there are three.

First, the survivors. Particularly at this time, we must not forget that living among us are those for whom the Holocaust is not history, but living memory. They are our human link to this darkest of periods, a truly remarkable generation and a treasure of the Jewish people. Incredibly, they not only survived the greatest of tragedies, but found the unfathomable resilience to renew and rebuild.

Here in the UK many of the most remarkable institutions of the Jewish community were established or revitalised by this special generation who found the will not only to raise their own families, but to create a vibrant and caring community for those who would come after them.

The resilience of this generation is nowhere more apparent than in the State of Israel, where just a few years after the horrors of the Holocaust, it was the survivors of that blackness who played the largest part in defending and building our own state. We do a disservice to that generation if we fail to recognise that the modern State of Israel was built in great degree by arms that had numbers tattooed on them.

We need to recognise honestly that we are in the twilight of this generation. By the time this project reaches its next decade, "80 for 80," it is likely that there will be few if any survivors among us. So the call to listen to them and to internalise their stories is more urgent than ever. As Elie Wiesel has written, "whoever listens to a witness becomes a witness."

Second is the need to learn to live together, to navigate our differing priorities and agendas as a united people. The dangers of the Holocaust, and the persecutions which preceded it, taught the Jewish people many lessons – but not all of these lessons live comfortably side by side. Every sector of our people has to learn to negotiate our different lessons to recreate a united peoplehood.

In Israel, this is both harder and more crucial than anywhere else in the Jewish world. During 2000 years of exile, many lessons were learned in order to survive. For some, the greatest threats were physical and the lesson learned was that only through becoming powerful, could Jacob out-Esau his opponents. For others, the gravest threats were spiritual, attacking not the Jewish body, but its identity. The lesson learned here was that ghetto walls needed to be higher in the hope that insulation would stave off assimilation. Each of these various strategies evolved in response to unique situations in a particular time and place, but today they find themselves competing for space in our sovereign state.

As we work to build a shared society, one of our greatest challenges is to navigate between the different historical imperatives we have been forced to learn over the centuries. In doing so, we must remember that the tragedy of the Holocaust, which made no distinction between Jew and Jew, has presented us with another, overarching historical imperative: to find that elusive path between the integrity we owe to the lessons that have shaped each of us and the sense of peoplehood that is critical to create room for a common society.

The third and final imperative is to regain our voice. The Holocaust was an attempt to silence the Jewish voice. Hitler felt that his goal was to "destroy the Ten Commandments," adding: "conscience is a Jewish invention; it is a blemish like circumcision."

Our response must be to find our voice once again, to give full expression to the uniquely Jewish contribution to humanity. The State of Israel provides an historic opportunity for us to do so.

The French philosopher Jean Jacques Rousseau once wrote: "I will never believe that I am hearing a serious argument by the Jews as long as they do not have a free country, and their own schools and universities where they can express themselves and argue without fear – only then can we know what they have to say." The State of Israel challenges us to give expression to this Jewish voice, in all fields of endeavour. To ask: what is an authentic Jewish social policy or Jewish foreign policy? What role should the Jewish spirit play in inspiring art, music, and film in a sovereign state? How do we build a society for all Israel's citizens, Jewish and non-Jewish, that is imbued with the most uplifting values of the Jewish State?

It is our shared history that gives us our greatest strength and inspiration. But it also presents us with these three great challenges: to learn from the voices of the past, to find harmony among our differing voices in the present, and to give voice to our own unique contribution to build a better future for the people of Israel and of the world.

Rabbanit Shani Taragin

Yirmiyahu: Man of Truth

Credited with authoring works of poetry and prose as he witnessed the tragic destruction of the *Beit HaMikdash* and deterioration of Judean monarchy 2,500 years ago, the prophet Yirmiyahu serves as a source of strength and bastion of truth for future generations.

He witnesses and mourns the vicissitudes of his generation: from a state of political autonomy to exile, from Temple worship to destruction, and from social order to chaos. Reminiscent of Moshe Rabbenu, Yirmiyahu reluctantly assumes the position of national prophet and accompanies the people for 40 years. But whereas Moshe led the People of Israel from Egypt to the Promised Land, Yirmiyahu sees them led from the Land into exile. Yirmiyahu shares his woes with the people and with God, even requesting respite from the burden of responsibility born of prophecy. Although threatened with death and attacked by his own brothers, he adamantly admonishes the people for their sins and explains the true reasons for the disasters they experience, with both integrity and perseverance.

Yirmiyahu assumes his role as prophet in the aftermath of King Yoshiyahu's initiation of widespread religious reforms, of the idolatrous practices of his father and grandfather. He is assigned by God to warn the nation of the impending disaster of destruction and exile, if the people do not adequately reverse the direction paved by the notorious King Menashe. Yirmiyahu was all but a *na'ar* (adolescent) when he was appointed by God, and responds to his mission with the reservation "לא ידעתי דבר" – I do not know how to speak, i.e., to interpret messages of prophecy (Jeremiah 1:6). God touches his mouth, instilling prophecy as an inextricable part of his being, and then demands of Yirmiyahu "מה אתה רואה" – "What do *you* – Yirmiyahu – see?" i.e., how do you interpret the current state of religious-political affairs of the people? Yirmiyahu is torn between the king's eschatological vision of redemption based on the repentance he initiated, and the simultaneous disillusionment with the insincerity with which many in Judea accepted those changes. For the last 18 years of King Yoshiyahu's reign, Yirmiyahu condemns the corrupt lifestyle of those living in Jerusalem and encourages them to reconnect to authentic worship of God.

Once Yoshiyahu falls in Megiddo, Egyptian control in the land begins, with his sons Achazyah and subsequently Yehoyakim as the puppet-leaders. An advocate of Egyptian prowess and culture, Yehoyakim encourages support for Egypt, leading the people to further corruption and a reversal of his father's reforms. Yirmiyahu responds with harsh rebuke and prophecies of impending tragedy. Yehoyakim attempts to quell the cries of Yirmiyahu by killing his peer Oriyah and threatens him not to appear publicly.

This is where the tenacity of Yirmiyahu shines through, as he risks his life to fulfil God's command to write and deliver his messages via Baruch his scribe, as a "last attempt" before the fall of Jerusalem.

As the Babylonian Empire becomes dominant in the Mesopotamian region and assumes control of Judea, Yirmiyahu calls for surrender to Nebuchadnezzar, King of Babylonia as he recognises that political independence cannot be restored through an Egyptian alliance. He urges Yehoyakim to subjugate himself to Babylonia in order to continue some semblance of religious autonomy. Yirmiyahu hopes the people will recognise their surrender as a punishment from God for their corruption and begin a process of religious reform, but Yehoyakim, indifferent to the reprimands of Yirmiyahu, continues to persecute him for undermining political stability.

Following the king's death, his son Yehoyachin is appointed, but surrenders shortly thereafter and is imprisoned and exiled. Nebuchadnezzar, understanding the pro-Egyptian sentiments amongst the leadership, then exiles the entire Judean aristocracy including senior military echelons, bourgeoisie, and many priests, and strips the Temple of its golden vessels. This marks the establishment of a Judean community on foreign soil, a devastating blow to the inhabitants of Jerusalem, but one that Yirmiyahu recognises as a necessary stage in the process of ultimate return to God and the Land of Israel.

Perhaps the most difficult times for Yirmiyahu are his final 11 years in the Land of Israel, when King Tzidkiyahu serves as the Judean vassal-king to the Babylonian Empire. The kingdom is split between the followers of Yirmiyahu, who begin to see the fulfilment of his prophecies of exile, and the pro-Egyptian nationalist faction, still determined to regain independence from Babylonia. The latter understand Yehoyachin's exile as a temporary political setback that will be overcome with Egyptian aid. For after all, how can Judean autonomy end after 850 years of settlement and divine promises? Again Yirmiyahu must answer these questions by relaying the truth of God's words – the nation merits autonomy when they are committed to God's edicts such as *Shabbat* observance, freeing of slaves and acts of justice and kindness.

Leadership is seized by power-seeking paupers, whilst Tzidkiyahu, who is young and weak both economically and politically, is caught between believing Yirmiyahu, and fearing for his life under the power-hungry officers who are confident in regaining autonomy. Isolated and oppressed, Yirmiyahu perseveres. He is told by God not to marry or bear children. He may not attend weddings or funerals, for they are all futile upon the eve of destruction. He walks around with a wooden yoke around his shoulders as one of the many symbolic acts he incorporates to corroborate his verbal prophecies of divine punishment. And who are his greatest enemies? Not the king, but the priests and false prophets. Yirmiyahu's most charismatic rival, Chananiyah the son of Azur, attempts to convince the masses of the imminent return of the exiles and restoration of glory. Yirmiyahu, unsure whether the people will believe Chananyiah, is sent by God once again to reveal the truth. The exiled will not return soon; they will remain in Babylonia for 70 years.

Yirmiyahu serves as a man of truth, articulating the messages of God while employing various literary and visual devices. His role as prophet is primarily to share the ominous possibility "to uproot and tear down, to obliterate and destroy." But he must also convince the people that they will subsequently return to "build and plant" (Jeremiah 1:10). As Jerusalem lay under siege, Yirmiyahu, imprisoned by the king in the court of the guard, is told by God that redemption will come soon after destruction and it is Yirmiyahu's responsibility to share the message of God's omniscience and involvement in historical and natural events – "Is there anything beyond Me?" (Jeremiah 32:27)

As he witnesses the destruction of Jerusalem's gardens, orchards, and palaces, I imagine Yirmiyahu wishing to be thrown in the flames with his beloved city. But nothing can compare to the pain he felt as he saw the Temple of God razed to the ground. *Chazal* teach us (*Bava Batra* 14b) that he authors four of the chapters of Lamentations over this event, not merely as a poetic expression of his own emotions, but as an attempt to elicit a response from the people.

Although he is treated royally by the emissaries of Nebuchadnezzar, he is seen as a staunch Babylonian ally and religious figurehead, and thus permitted to settle where he pleases. Yirmiyahu lives the truth he preaches: he remains a steadfast prophet – to God and to his nation. He encourages them to stay in the land and begin re-establishing a religious infrastructure, even after the destruction of the Temple and the subsequent assassination of Gedaliyah, the Jewish Babylonian-appointed governor. When the people resist his words again, he follows them down to Egypt as he delivers the prophecies of doom of the future that awaits them there.

All the elements of conflict in Yirmiyahu's *weltanschauung* (world view) and that of his generation can be found in today's political and religious debates. His personal destiny is forever intertwined with the national trajectory. We may not have the direct messages of God via the prophet's interpretation, but the words of truth of Yirmiyahu continue to resonate. The cries of our matriarch Rachel that he describes may be heard louder today than ever and the stones of his backyard in the city of Anatot still whisper longings of return. Yirmiyahu's assurance "Is anything too wondrous for God?" has materialised in the past 70 years, as we have witnessed destruction and redemption, uprooting and rebuilding. Yirmiyahu reminds us that the truth of God prevails even when we desist, and even when that truth is clouded by our own delusions. The cost of teaching and living with integrity is oftentimes heavy and arduous, and as we see from Yirmiyahu's life, at times even tragic; but it redeems us – in every sense of the word.

Chief Rabbi Pinchas Goldschmidt

The Future for Jews in Europe

Seventy years ago, our greatest tragedy, the Holocaust, came to an end, as the Allied armies freed Europe from Nazi rule. The war ended, the camps were liberated and some survivors decided that, perhaps, they should stay in Europe, that maybe there was still a future for Jews there.

Slowly but surely, they rebuilt their destroyed communities, their synagogues, and their families. They got married again, had children, and believed in the future. Indeed, for many decades, antisemitism in Western Europe was banned as politically incorrect, and if it ever surfaced, it did so in a camouflaged version, in guises such as anti-Zionism.

However, recent history has raised disturbing questions about long-term Jewish continuity and 2014 will go down as a year that Jews and Jewish targets were victimised across Western Europe – quite apart from the alarming gains made by many far right political parties at local and national elections.

In the space of just one week, eight synagogues in France were attacked. In Italy, the Jewish owners of dozens of shops in Rome arrived to find swastikas and anti-Jewish slogans daubed on shutters and windows. One slogan read: "Jews, your end is near." Windows were smashed at a synagogue in Belfast on consecutive nights, a rabbi was attacked in Gateshead, and the number of reported antisemitic incidents in the UK doubled. Four people were murdered at the Jewish Museum in Brussels in May and a Swedish Jewish woman was brutally beaten by ten Muslims, after she was spotted wearing a Star of David necklace. At the same time, hundreds of thousands turned out in the streets to protest against Israel and the Jews, even in defiance of government restraining orders.

"These are the worst times since the Nazi era," Dieter Graumann,

President of Germany's Central Council of Jews, told the British newspaper, *The Guardian*. "On the streets, you hear things like 'the Jews should be gassed' – we haven't had that in Germany for decades. Anyone saying those slogans isn't criticising Israeli politics; it's just pure hatred against Jews. Nothing else."

Beyond the immediate incidents, however, there is a more troubling development over the last few years, where we have witnessed a renewed attack on core Jewish rituals in Europe, most specifically *brit milah* and *shechitah*.

The origins of this assault appear, ironically, to lie partly with Europe's reaction to the large influx of Muslims into Europe. Over the last 40 years, as the European birth rate plummeted, immigration from Muslim countries reached unprecedented heights. Today, in France, there are now more Muslims going to mosques on Fridays than Christians going to church on Sundays. One-fourth of the children in the Dutch school system are Muslim and, as a result, many Europeans have taken a strong dislike to Islam. According to an *Ipsos/Le Monde* poll, 74% find Islam "intolerant," and 80% believe it is "forcing its ways on French society at large." A parallel poll conducted in Germany produced similar results, with 70% associating Islam with "fanaticism and radicalism," and 64% calling it "prone to violence."

What is equally important is that 53% of Germans foresee a battle between Islam and Christianity in Europe. This assessment is incorrect though, because the fight is not one between Islam and Christianity, but between Islam and an increasingly intolerant anti-religious Europe. And whilst Islam might be the current target of these prejudiced campaigns, European Jewry is the "collateral damage" in this offensive, in the words of Mati Wagner, Editor at *The Jerusalem Post*.

Shechitah and *brit milah* are under renewed attack in Germany, Poland, Norway, Denmark, and France (even in the UK, a recent survey found that one-third would favour a ban on circumcision, and 45% would outlaw *shechitah*), and the Conference of European Rabbis (CER), together with the local rabbinate, is working tirelessly at all levels to defend the religious freedom of the Jews of Europe. We need to be aware that Jewish ritual is being assailed across Europe, culminating recently with a recommendation by the Council of Europe's Parliamentary Assembly in October 2013, to ban male circumcision for minors.

And, although PACE only has advisory status, the Council is the continent's leading human rights organisation with a current total of 47 member states, and there is no question that this declaration is a direct attack against the Jewish faith and the Jewish people. The initiators of this resolution were fully aware (although other lawmakers may not have been as cognisant) that, were these recommendations to be turned into law, circumcision throughout Europe would be prohibited for any child under the age of 14.[1] Thus, the majority of the 1.7 million Jews living in Europe would be made to feel intensely unwelcome.

As the Chief Rabbi of Moscow, this resolution is reminiscent to me of the infamous Soviet law criminalising the teaching of religious texts to minors under the age of 16, as they were apparently too young to make that decision. And though history tends to repeat itself, I am seeing it happen in ways that we would have hoped would never occur during our lifetimes.

Circumcision remains as a defining factor for the majority of Jews, as the US State Department's special envoy on antisemitism stated in 2014: "Because circumcision is essentially universal among Jews, this [a ban] can shut down a community."

Professor Robert Wistrich adds that the latest attacks in Europe, which single out the ritual aspects of Judaism, are seen by the Jewish communities there as more dangerous to organised Jewish communal life than other forms of anti-Semitism, such as anti-Zionism. The new campaign against Jewish ritual in Europe is, in fact, often simply the new face of a politically correct antisemitism, as seen in remarks made by Bundestag Parliament member Marlene Rupprecht, when introducing this legislation in the European Council: "Circumcision is the "dark side" of the Jews' and Muslims' religion, traditions, and identity."

It is clear that a lot of work needs to go into explaining to the wider world the critical importance and significance of these practices for the Jewish people. Because, as Norway's Chief Rabbi

1. Muslims who circumcise at a later age – at the transition from childhood to adulthood – would actually find it easier to live with this law.

put it: "The vast majority of the population don't have a clue what ritual is. They see ritual in general as something which belongs to some dark evil – they have medieval conceptions [of rituals] which have nothing to do with modern society." But explanation alone will not staunch the tide, because there is a certain level of duplicity being used in the fight against Jewish ritual.

Admittedly, there are those who are – and those who claim to be – against circumcision because it is a medical procedure without apparent medical benefit. But firstly, this assumption is strongly contested by a broad part of the medical community. So that, whilst the debate concerning the medical efficacy continues, it is important to be aware that many within the global medical group do see strong prophylactic benefit in circumcision and not only as a safeguard against AIDS in Africa as, indeed, has been noted by the U.S. Center for Disease Control and Prevention.

Secondly, though, even assuming they make a good case for the lack of medical advantage, we must question their motives in singling out this particular medical procedure for scrutiny. Is it really the only procedure liberal secularists should care about? How about cosmetic surgery – given the dearth of positive medical outcome? Or is it simply because our Western culture has decided that a certain look is desirable that we can justify putting children under the knife?

Ronald Lauder, the President of the WJC, recently put out a salient question for consideration: "Can the Jewish renaissance in the heart of Europe continue if essential elements of Jewish life are declared illegal? Or will Europe's leaders stand up for the civil rights of their Jewish compatriots?"

Europe is not going to be saved by European countries and institutions adapting Middle Eastern practices of intolerance towards minorities. New Europe needs to send a message which defends the right of the individual to religious freedom, and which upholds the values of pluralism and mutual respect, in order to build a stable and broad-based future. The voice which calls the faithful in a mosque to bomb planes and the voice which calls an end to freedom of religion in Europe are equally dangerous to the future of Europe. We must remember, though, that we are dealing with a European-wide phenomenon and it is, therefore, imperative that local communities co-ordinate their responses with the European Jewish institutions.

As Europe redefines its society and its values 70 years after the end of World War II and the Holocaust, we hope that there will always be a place for us here, and that democracy and freedom will be upheld. It is somewhat sobering to realise that this hope requires more goodwill than is currently being manifest.

This essay has been sponsored by Joy and Stanley
Cohen OBE together with all their family.

Sir Nicholas Winton

Rescue

In 1939, a British stockbroker called Nicholas Winton undertook the unthinkable, and rescued 669 Czech children from their fate under the Nazis, but, incredibly, his achievement went unrecognised for more than half a century: for 50 years, most of the children did not even know to whom they owed their lives. His story only emerged when his wife pieced together all the files that were in their attic, containing lists of the children and letters from their parents.

Winton was a 29-year-old clerk in 1938, working at the Stock Exchange, who visited Prague at the invitation of a friend at the British Embassy. He had been alarmed by reports of the violence against the Jewish community in Germany and Austria during *Kristallnacht* in November of that year, and when he arrived in Czechoslovakia, the British team asked him to help. He was subsequently introduced to Doreen Wariner, who arranged for him to visit refugee camps filled to capacity with Jews and political opponents. He saw first-hand the conditions they were living under, in the depths of a freezing winter.

He was also informed of the efforts of Jewish agencies in Britain to rescue German and Austrian Jewish children through the *Kindertransport* (through which 10,000 unaccompanied children were brought to safety in Great Britain). Winton then summoned a small group of people to organise a similar rescue operation in Czechoslovakia, and courageously decided to make every effort to get the children outside the reach of Nazi power.

"The commission was dealing with the elderly and vulnerable, and people in the camps kept telling me that nobody was doing anything for the children," Nicholas Winton later recalled.

Using the name of the British Committee for Refugees from

Czechoslovakia, and initially without any official authorisation, he set up office at a dining room table in his hotel in Wenceslas Square in Prague and began taking applications from parents. Word got out about the "Englishman of Wenceslas Square," and parents flocked to the hotel to try to persuade him to put their young children on the list, desperate to get them out before the Nazis invaded. "It seemed hopeless," he said years later. As his operation expanded, he opened an office. Soon, thousands of parents lined up outside on the street seeking a safe haven for their children.

Winton then returned to London to organise the rescue operation at that end. Working round the clock, he persuaded the Home Office to let the children in. However, even when they agreed to accept a child, they were often slow about processing the paperwork, and with the situation in Czechoslovakia deteriorating, on occasion, Winton resorted to forging the necessary documents. For each child, he also had to find a £50 guarantee (in those days a small fortune), as well as raise money to help pay for the transports, when contributions by the children's parents couldn't cover the costs. As importantly, he had to find British families willing to care for the refugee children.

He approached the Americans as well – even writing to Roosevelt for help – but they responded that they were unable to offer him any help.

In nine months of campaigning as the war crept closer, Nicholas Winton managed to arrange for 669 children to leave Prague safely for London. His first transport left by plane for London on 14th March 1939, the day before the Germans occupied the rest of the Czech lands. Winton managed to organise a further seven transports out of Prague, even after the Germans established a Protectorate in Bohemia and Moravia, sending the children across Germany to the coast and then by ship across the English Channel to Britain. At the train station in London, British foster parents waited to collect the children.

The last trainload of children left Prague on 2nd August 1939 and all rescue activities ceased when Germany invaded Poland, and Britain declared war on Germany in early September 1939.

Nicholas Winton never forgot the sight of the exhausted children from Czechoslovakia piling out of the trains at London's

Liverpool Street station. All wore name tags around their necks, and one by one, English foster parents collected the refugee children and took them home, keeping them safe from the war and the genocide that was about to consume their families back home. Winton, who gave these children the gift of life, watched from a distance.

Tragically, the ninth and biggest transport was due to leave Prague on 3rd September, but the train never left the station. "Within hours of the announcement, the train disappeared," Winton later recalled. "None of the 250 children on board were seen again. We had 250 families waiting at Liverpool Street that day in vain. If the train had been a day earlier, it would have come through. Not a single one of those children was heard of again, which is an awful feeling." During the war, more than 15,000 Czech children were killed.

Nicholas Winton, one of the unsung heroes of World War II, known as the Schindler of Britain, is revered as the father who saved scores of "his children" from the Nazis. But it wasn't until 1988 that Winton had his first encounter with some of those whom he had saved. The setting was a British television programme called *That's Life*. The host displayed a scrapbook that listed the names of the rescued children, and she pointed to the woman seated beside Winton. "Vera Gissing is here with us tonight and I should tell you that you are actually sitting next to Nicholas Winton," she said. The woman beside Winton embraced him; he wiped away a tear. The host asked, "Is there anyone in our audience tonight who owes their life to Nicholas Winton? If so, could you stand up, please?" The entire audience rose. He got up and he looked around absolutely amazed, seeing the effects of his rescue efforts 50 years on. It is reckoned that today, there are over 10,000 descendants of those 669 children.

Gissing, who has written a biography of Nicholas Winton, says: "Very few of us met our parents again; they perished in concentration camps. Had we not been spirited away, we would have been murdered alongside them. I owe him my life and those of my children and grandchildren. And having the chance to thank Nicky was the most precious moment in my life."

But Winton insists he wasn't anything special, adding, "I just saw what was going on and did what I could to help."

The survivors, many of whom are now grandparents, still call themselves "Winton's children." This includes film director Karel Reisz, who met Winton 45 years after his rescue. "I had never heard of him. I thought the Red Cross had organised it," he said. "I took my children and grandchildren – I think it brought it alive to them to learn where their grandfather came from. It was very emotional."

Nicholas Winton was awarded the Order of Marsaryk by President Vaclav Havel, for outstanding contributions to the development of democracy, humanity, and human rights. In 2002, he received a knighthood in Britain, and in 2007, he was awarded the Czech Republic's highest military decoration.

Incredibly, Winton had no experience in this field, but he saw something that needed to be done and did it. When asked what gave him the ability, he replied: "I work on the motto that if something is not impossible, there must be a way of doing it." Perhaps even more incredible is the simplicity he exhibited. Having achieved all he did, he simply went back to living his daily life. A lesson for all of us to live by.

Dedicated and with thanks, to those whose devotion
and sacrifice has given the Jewish people their homeland.
Gaby and Howard, Lucy and Joshua Morris.

Sir Martin Gilbert

The Beginnings of Zionism

Based on extracts from *Israel: A History*

Ideology, politics, diplomacy, and war each have their place in this narrative, as do the stories of many individuals – some famous, others not – who contributed to the building of the State. The original pioneers came mostly from the Russian Empire, but they were supported by Jews from across the Jewish world.

Since the destruction of the Second Temple by the Romans in 70 CE, the dispersed Jews prayed for a return to Zion. "Next year in Jerusalem" was the hope expressed at the end of every Passover meal. However, for two millennia that dream seemed a fantasy, and Zion, which had been under almost continuous Muslim rule since the seventh century, and under Ottoman rule since 1516, was possible only for a few.

In addition, the perils of the journey could be severe. Of 1,500 Jews who travelled from Eastern Europe to Palestine in 1700, as many as 500 died on the way. Nevertheless, the imperative to return never died. In 1777, more than 300 chassidic Jewish families made the journey from Poland and in 1812, some 400 followers of the Vilna Gaon journeyed from Lithuania. Such that by the middle of the 19th century, about 10,000 Jews lived in Palestine, mostly in Jerusalem with a few hundred in Jaffa, Safed, and Tiberias. There was also a small community in the town of Peki'in which had a tradition of continuous Jewish settlement since Roman times.

But in the second half of the 18th century, things changed dramatically. In 1862, a German Jew, Moses Hess, proclaimed in his book, *Rome and Jerusalem*, that Jewish "nationality" was connected "inseparably" with the Holy Land and the Eternal city and advocated their return. And in 1876, the British Christian writer George Eliot stated in her novel *Daniel Deronda*: "Revive the organic centre; let the unity of Israel ... be an outward reality." It was to make its impact on many Jews, among them Eliezer Ben-Yehudah and I L Peretz.

At the same time, in Russia, following an upsurge of violent attacks against the Jews, two movements were founded, urging the emigration of Jews to Palestine. One was known as Bilu, from the Hebrew initials in the biblical phrase *Beit Ya'akov Lechu Ve-nelcha* (House of Jacob, come and let us go!). The young men and women of Bilu, being secular and socialist in outlook, omitted the concluding words of the phrase: "in the light of the Lord." The second Russian-born movement was *Chovevei Tziyon* (Lovers of Zion).

As a result, over 25,000 Jews reached Palestine between 1882 and 1903, in what became known as the First Aliyah. The Jewish population of Jerusalem tripled, having already been a majority there since the 1850s, whereas others lived by tilling the soil and by recourse to the financial support of the Rothschild family. Jewish migration saw the steady settlement of small groups of pioneers on the land. These *moshavim* – often named for Zionist or biblical leaders and places – gradually transformed the landscape. Philanthropy also played a very strong part in the building up of the Jewish community. The Bezalel art school was funded by a German philanthropist, and an American Jew, Nathan Straus, provided the funds to set up a Jewish hospital in Jerusalem.

Yet among the sophisticated and assimilated Jews in Western Europe, there was little interest in Zionism. Palestinian Jewry was seen as an exclusively religious community, although the trial of Alfred Dreyfus would change that, especially for one man: Theodore Herzl. An assimilated Jew, who had not circumcised his own son, he was shocked by the harsh antisemitic tones of the criticism of Dreyfus.

The trial was actually a watershed for many Jews generally. They asked themselves what had gone wrong; what caused this antisemitism? Three ways out seemed to present themselves: to assimilate into the nation with whom one was living, to fight for a revolutionary socialism that would cure all the evils of the world including antisemitism, or to seek a "normal" Jewish life in a Jewish land with a Jewish government. Herzl was drawn to the last option, especially when Vienna, where Herzl lived, elected Karl Leuger – who headed an antisemitic political party and openly denounced the Jews – as mayor in 1893.

Some of those to whom Herzl expounded his ideas considered him insane. The first Rothschild whom he approached ignored his letter. But he found an ally in the physician and philosopher, Max Nordau, who told him, "If you are insane, we are insane together!" Herzl's *Judenstadt* was a major influence in the emergence of political Zionism. He pointed to the part played by antisemitism in bringing the Jews to their existing situation. "We have honestly endeavoured to merge ourselves in the social life of surrounding communities and to preserve only the faith of our fathers. We are not permitted to do so. In vain we are loyal patriots."

He formed a congress in Basel in 1897, and on 3rd September wrote in his diary, "Were I to sum up the Basel Congress in a word, it would be this: at Basel, I founded the Jewish State. If I said this out loud today, I would be answered by universal laughter. Perhaps in five years, and certainly in 50, everyone will know it."

One of the attendees at the second congress was a 23-year-old bio-chemist from Ukraine. His name was Chaim Weizmann, and in time he became President of the World Zionist Organisation and eventually of Israel itself. Concerning the Jews, he said: "We have, throughout our history, not disappeared among the nations with whom we have lived. We have remained different: different in religion, different in outlook… The moral effect of this situation, combined with an age-long tradition of attachment to Palestine, has made us what we are."

In the ten years following Herzl's death (1904), the Turkish government was unwilling to grant the Jews any autonomous region in Palestine, but Jewish settlement – especially from Russia and Romania, where there was unabated persecution – continued to grow. In 1906, David Gruen emigrated to Palestine, having been twice arrested during the Russian uprising in 1905. On arrival, he took on the Hebrew surname Ben-Gurion.

In 1909, a town was established on the sand dunes just north of Jaffa. It was called Tel Aviv, and became known as "the first all-Jewish city." In the north, a Romanian-Jewish poet, Naphtali Herz Imber, wrote a poem, *Hatikvah* (The Hope), which was to become the Zionist hymn. Imber read the poem to the farmers of Rishon le-Zion, one of whom, Samuel Cohen, set it to music.

The religious aspect of Zionism was actively personified by Rabbi Abraham Isaac Kook (1865–1935), who became the first Chief Rabbi of Palestine in 1921. He was a noted Jewish thinker and scholar, who tried to build channels of communication and political alliances between the various Jewish factions. As a result, in 1913, he led a group of the most distinguished rabbis of the Old Yishuv – representing the full gamut of Orthodoxy – to tour the new *moshavim* in the Galilee and Samaria. Over the course of one month they visited over 20 settlements, to inspire the pioneers to the importance and eternity of Judaism and Torah, whilst simultaneously demonstrating to the accompanying rabbis, the idealism of these young secular Zionists.

World War I eventually brought with it the Balfour Declaration, but did not address the issues of Arab nationalism. When the militantly radical Haj Amin el-Husseini became the leader of the Palestinian Arabs in 1921, any possibility of dialogue between the Arabs and Jews in Palestine was lost and it led to the Arab riots of 1921, 1926, 1929, 1933, 1935, and 1936.

Eventually, in 1936, the Peel Commission raised the idea of partition, a plan that was accepted by the Jews and rejected unilaterally by all Arab parties (as was the case with the UN vote for partition in 1947) and the years that followed brought about an increasingly hard-line attitude from the Arabs to Jewish immigration, even as Hitler's plans were coming to fruition. In 1945, with a new Labour government in Britain, Zionist aspirations to independence suffered a setback, which would bring about a bitter fight in Palestine for two years, and would not be adequately addressed until the UN vote in November 1947.

From ISRAEL: A HISTORY by Martin Gilbert
Published by Doubleday
Reprinted by permission of The Random House Group Ltd

Rabbi Dr Harvey Belovski

All You Need Is Love: Does It Matter What Jews Believe or Just What They Do?

One responsibility in my first rabbinic position was to administer a bar/bat mitzvah test. It encouraged young adults to cover a syllabus of basic Jewish knowledge prior to their "big day." I wrote the test myself and after some predictable questions such as "when is Pesach?" and "who was married to Abraham?" I posed one that was met with surprise by every examinee: "does Judaism have beliefs and not just rules?"

With hindsight, it was a poor question, but it was intended to challenge adolescents to start thinking about belief and action in their lives. It is well known that Judaism includes both a detailed code of practice and a sophisticated belief system, although the relationship between them is often little understood.

For many modern, thinking Jews, successfully navigating the tensions between belief and action will determine our commitment to Torah observance and pursuit of Jewish aspirations for ourselves and our families. How important is it to believe in core principles (e.g., existence of God, historical truth of the Sinaitic revelation), or is it only observance that counts? Put succinctly, does it matter what Jews believe or just what they do?

Where better to begin our investigation than the Talmud? Rabbi Tarfon and the elders were reclining in the attic of Nitzah's home in Lod, when the following question was posed to them: "is study or action greater?" Rabbi Tarfon spoke up and said, "action is greater." Rabbi Akiva spoke up and said, "study is greater." They all spoke up and said, "study is greater, as study leads to action."[1]

1. *Kiddushin* 40b.

"Study" here cannot refer to learning those laws that govern behaviour (since without knowledge, one would simply have no idea what to do), but rather to the beliefs that inform these laws, as well as the concepts that underpin the entire halachic system.

Rashi explains that only Rabbi Akiva's position allows one to have both study and action "in hand,"[2] and Rambam adds that "while study leads to action, action does not lead to study,"[3] asserting a unidirectional relationship between the two. Apparently, belief is indispensable to determining what we do, but action will not lead us to appropriate beliefs.

What is certain is that belief is never enough on its own. We live in a material world which God wishes us to advance and improve by implementing the Torah's master plan in practice, not just in theory. Unlike Immanuel Kant, who presumes that "it is not with the actions which we see that we are concerned, but with those inward principles of them which we do not see"[4] – our performance as Jews is measured by the extent to which we "resolutely pursue justice"[5] in our interactions with others and "walk modestly"[6] with God.

Returning to belief and action, the assertion that belief leads to righteous behaviour is common. According to Plato in his *Meno* dialogue, Socrates insisted that if one knows what is right, then one will naturally behave in a virtuous way.[7] And in his famous essay *The Ethics of Belief*, William Clifford refers to belief as "that sacred faculty which prompts the decisions of our will."[8] In fact, so convinced is Clifford of the inevitable influence of belief on action that he rejects as a legitimate belief anything "which has not some influence upon the actions of him who holds it."[9]

---

2. Rashi's commentary *ad loc, s.v.* "she-ha-talmud."

3. Rambam, *Mishneh Torah, Hilchot Talmud Torah* 1:3.

4. Immanuel Kant, *Fundamental Principles of the Metaphysic of Morals*, trans. by Thomas K Abbott (Merchant Books, 2009), p 29.

5. Deuteronomy 15:20.

6. Micah 6:8.

7. Plato, *Five Dialogues: Euthyphro, Apology, Crito, Meno, Phaedo*, trans. by G M A Grube (Indianapolis, IN: Hackett Publishing Co Inc, 2002) p 92.

8. William K Clifford, 'The Ethics of Belief,' in *Ten Essential Texts in the Philosophy of Religion: Classics and Contemporary Issues*, ed. by Steven M Cahn (Oxford: Oxford University Press, 2005), pp 367–72 (p 370).

9. Clifford, p 369.

Yet despite the views of these great thinkers, experience suggests that it is rather complex to manage the interaction between the two polarities of belief and practice to ensure the best possible result. The desirable outcome is a Jewish lifestyle which maximises the benefits of both belief and practice while minimising their downsides.[10]

Let us briefly investigate those benefits and downsides. Some prefer to concentrate on practice because they find core beliefs of Judaism hard to accept. But the inadequacy of Judaism without an underlying belief system is self-evident. Rules and rituals quickly become devoid of meaning and spirituality, something denounced by Isaiah: "with their mouth and lips they honour Me, but they have distanced their heart far from Me; their fear of Me is a commandment of men learned by rote."[11] Yet, at the same time, focusing exclusively on beliefs denudes Judaism of its unique commitment to programmatically changing self and society and restricts it to the realm of thought and mood, ignoring the need to tame and elevate very real human passions. Neither a Judaism of garbled prayers and empty ritual, nor one purely of ideas and ideals is meaningful, nor can it be sustained or communicated. Since neither one will naturally lead to the other, how is it possible to create a harmonious balance between the two polarities?

It is fascinating to note that the great 20th century Jewish philosopher and talmudist, Rabbi J B Soloveitchik, never notices "any sort of tension...between...the ideals of cognition and action."[12] This is because in reality, this equation of knowledge, will, and action with one another is one of the principles of *imitatio Dei* (emulating the Divine). By imitating this marvellous identity, man becomes like Him and also cleaves to Him.[13]

Imitating God is the clue to the puzzle. God, by definition, is a unity, exhibiting no division between knowledge and action;

10. Harry Johnson, *Polarity Management: Identifying and Managing Unsolvable Problems* (Amherst, Mass: HRD Press Inc, US, 1996), pp 65, 82.
11. Isaiah 29:13.
12. Alex Sztuden, 'Behaviorism and the Unity of Knowledge, Love and Action in Halakhic Man,' *The Torah u-Madda Journal*, 16 (2012), p 98.
13. Joseph B Soloveitchik, *And from There You Shall Seek*, trans. by Naomi Goldblum (Jersey City, NJ: KTAV Publishing House, 2009), p 73.

we as human beings must emulate Him and overcome the gulf we perceive between belief and thought. But how is this to be done? Quite simply, through love – we must love ourselves, love others, love the world, love Judaism, and love God. When we love unconditionally, we shatter the barrier between belief and action, because "love … is irreducibly and conceptually tied to actions…"[14] and as such, "cognition and action are conceptually unified through love."[15]

This is a fascinating outcome: more than any other emotion or belief, love cannot be confined to the realm of theory – it only exists when it is demonstrated in practice, something that anyone who has experienced true love will do automatically.

For Rabbi Soloveitchik, love performs the impossible, creating a mystical union between our polarities of belief and practice, allowing us to embrace the two simultaneously. This, in turn, lays the ground for developing healthy and harmonious relationships between our thoughts and behaviour in other areas.

So what we believe matters as much what we do. Acknowledging the complex relationship between belief and behaviour and then focusing on loving thoughts and actions, allows us to grow as human beings without sacrificing one for the other.

Finally, Mahatma Ghandi's adaptation of a poem by the Chinese philosopher Lao-tzu, explores the relationship between belief and action:

> Your beliefs become your thoughts,
> Your thoughts become your words,
> Your words become your actions,
> Your actions become your habits,
> Your habits become your values,
> Your values become your destiny.

I conclude by adding a Jewish spin to this Hindu-Taoist concoction, completing the circle:

> Your destiny becomes your beliefs.
> To square this circle, all you need is love.

14. Sztuden, p 92.
15. Sztuden, p 97.

Rebbetzin Lori Palatnick

Bringing Israel to Every Home

I have a Jewish neighbour that I know not to wish a "*Chag Sameach*" on *Yom HaAtzmaut*. It's not that they are anti-Zionist or anti-religious, they are just your average Jew, not negative or apathetic, just disconnected. They are the children of the rapidly disappearing "Jewish middle class."

My siblings and I were the same. Our parents were that middle class – grew up as first generation Jewish Canadians, told to marry Jews, eat bagels, and make bar mitzvahs. And they did. And they assumed their kids would do the same. But they and their peers were shocked to see their children view their bar and bat mitzvahs as their graduations out of Judaism (instead of in). When told to marry Jews, they asked "why?" and received uninspiring answers that involved Bubby rolling over in her grave.

According to the recent Pew study, 90% of American Jewish adults are not Orthodox, and their intermarriage rate is 74%. In the same study, over half of secular Jews say that they have little or no emotional attachment to Israel.

When I quote these stats to Israelis, they are shocked and dumbfounded. And then I tell them that my mother-in-law says that she and her peers do not struggle over whether or not to go to the intermarriage of their children. Now they struggle over whether to attend the christening of their grandchildren.

Welcome to the "new normal."

So how did three out of four of the kids in my family beat the odds? We not only married Jews, we became committed Jews. My brother and his family made *aliyah*. So did our daughter. Our son served as a soldier in the IDF.

The answer: *Eretz Yisrael*. Israel. The eternal home of the Jewish people.

Israel is awesome, but the real challenge is for Diaspora Jews to see Israel for what it really is, how it occupies centre stage in the life of every Jew, how the connection is at one and the same time eternal and vital, yet readily achievable. Just coming to Israel is not enough though, because the experience can be "touristic" or life-changing.

My sister came to Israel first, many years ago, to learn about her Judaism. When I was 23 and backpacking through Europe, I ended up in Israel and didn't initially understand why I wanted to stay and live there forever. So I left. But one year later I returned and not only toured, but studied my heritage. Now I stayed and knew why. I continued to study, and eventually met my husband. Our journey as a family eventually brought us to the US.

In the past five years, I have led thousands of women there. More than half have never been to Israel, and of the other half, their primary memory of visiting in their youth is "the soldiers were so cute." But now they are grown up mothers, responsible for raising the next generation of the Jewish people. And they have no tools.

From the moment they get off the planes, they can feel connection – to the land, to their Judaism and to each other. Nira is a perfect example, "It's amazing how one 'little' trip became the impetus to huge changes in our lives!" She was born in Israel, but left when she was five and now lives in Maryland. While on a trip, she realised what her family was missing. She called up her son and told him to get on a plane. Soon Brandon, then 21, was studying Judaism in Jerusalem. Then he joined the IDF, and is now at the IDC School in Herzliya.

Back in Maryland, Nira brought Israel, spirituality, and Judaism into her home and to her community. *Shabbat* became central and meaningful and, with Brandon in the IDF, the whole family got involved with the local Friends of the IDF (FIDF).

Sheryl's initial trip served as an inspiration to her entire family and when she came back a second time, she brought her sister Suzy who is blind. Suzy's husband said his wife has now been to Israel twice – once before she became blind, and once after. As he put it: "She saw more of Israel the second time than the first."

Israel's Ministry of Diaspora Affairs is now also involved in partnering these connections between Diaspora Jews and Israel

PHILOSOPHY AND CHAGIM

through trips – partnering organisations who create meaningful bridges. Families disenfranchised from Jewish communities are not only back "in," but have become active and inspired members.

Recently, a potential financial supporter went to the Ministry, to hear about this project. She was intrigued but asked the Ministry, "I don't understand. Are you doing this in order to get these families to make *aliyah*?"

"No," they said. "We do not expect them to move here. We are doing it because we are a family and a people." Those profound words hung in the air.

And my neighbour? This year I think I will wish her a "*Chag Sameach*," along with an explanation, and an invitation to join us "This Year in Jerusalem."

> *Dedicated to my parents, Eli and Chava Fachler on the occasion of their 70th wedding anniversary. They escaped Germany just in time to build a dynasty of their own.*

Rabbi Dr Jacob J Schacter

Holocaust Memory and Holocaust Commemoration

The 70th anniversary of the liberation of Auschwitz provides us with a most important opportunity to explore the issue of Holocaust memory and Holocaust commemoration. As time passes, and as the survivors pass on to their eternal reward, this matter becomes more crucial and urgent for our community.

Towards the end of November 1942, word reached the *Yishuv* in Israel for the first time about the full magnitude of the destruction of European Jewry that was, by then, well under way. In response to this terrible news, Rabbi Yitzhak HaLevi Herzog, Ashkenazic Chief Rabbi of Israel since 1937, announced that 2nd December 1942/23 Kislev 5703 would be a day of fasting and prayer. On that day, a massive crowd of thousands, including several hundred rabbis led by the revered Rebbe of Gur, gathered first in the Hurvah Synagogue in Jerusalem's Old City and then at the *Kotel*. They heard sounds of the *shofar* and recited prayers including verses from the Book of Lamentations and selections from the *kinot* (elegies) recited on the Ninth of Av.

It was around this time that Rabbi Herzog paid a visit to Rabbi Yitzhak Ze'ev HaLevi Soloveitchik (known as "the Brisker Rav"), who had recently escaped from Europe and settled in Jerusalem. Rabbi Herzog inquired whether Rabbi Soloveitchik would support the establishment of such a "day of mourning" (*yom evel*) for the tragedy and destruction that was underway in Europe. Rabbi Soloveitchik disagreed with Rabbi Herzog's initiative, based on a passage in one of the *kinot* recited on the Ninth of Av dealing with the destruction wrought by the Crusades at the end of the 11th century. The *kinah* describes the devastation of the German communities of Speyer, Worms and Mainz and, although explicitly noting that they were destroyed during the months of Iyar and Sivan, goes on to state that the appropriate time to commemorate these tragic events is on the Ninth of Av. "Since one may not add a time [to commemorate] destruction and conflagration...therefore, today [i.e., the Ninth of Av] I will raise my cries of woe." One does not institute new days of commemoration for tragedies that followed the destruction of the Temples as they are already commemorated on one day in the Jewish calendar and that day is the Ninth of Av.

Rabbi Soloveitchik applied the principle delineated here in the context of the Crusades, to the situation he was facing in 1942. On the basis of this statement, he concluded that establishing a special – even temporary – day of mourning for the Jews being exterminated in Europe would be contrary to Jewish tradition.

Indeed, this principle expressed by the Brisker Rav, proved to be a very influential one in later generations, particularly in the context of Holocaust commemoration. After the war, the question moved to establishing a new ritually mandated fast day – or even just a day of commemoration – as a way of permanently remembering the unprecedented tragedy that had taken place. In opposing this practice, many halachic authorities such as Rabbi Joseph B Soloveitchik, Rabbi Moses Feinstein, and Rabbi Menaham M Kasher, cited the above *kinah* written in the 12th century.

But there is an alternative model, one that also brings us back to the 12th century. In the early spring of 1171, a Christian in the French town of Blois, reported that he had just seen a Jew disposing of the corpse of a Christian child. The charge was taken seriously and, less than three months later, on the 20th of the month of Sivan 1171, some 31 or 33 Jews were burned there as a punishment for this allegedly grievous act.

In the aftermath of the catastrophe, Rabbi Ephraim of Bonn noted that a fast on that day was mandated by none other than the great 12th century Tosafist and communal leader, Rabbenu Tam. It has been subsequently argued, and mostly accepted by scholars, that Rabbi Ephraim of Bonn was mistaken; that, in fact, Rabbenu Tam never did establish a new fast day on this date, but, nevertheless, it was assumed that a date had been set aside as a separate commemoration for the event, and that it was not subsumed under that of the Temple's destruction.

Almost 500 years later, starting in 1648, Bogdan Chmielnicki and his followers attacked dozens of Jewish communities in Eastern Europe and killed thousands of Jews. In 1650, the *Va'ad Arba Aratzot*, the organisation in charge of governing the Eastern European Jewish communities at the time, wanted to commemorate the catastrophe. Rabbi Nathan Nata Hannover wrote in *Yeven Mezulah* that a decision was made the date on which the massacres began in the city of Niemiròw as a fast day, the 20th of Sivan, the same date that had earlier been associated with the martyrs of Blois in 1171.

A new day of fasting was thus established in Ashkenazic Europe as a result of this calamity, separate from the Fast of the Ninth of Av.

This Fast of the 20th of Sivan played a central role in support of the arguments made by those in favour of the establishment of a special date for commemoration of the Holocaust. In a responsum written a few months before the end of the war, Rabbi Herzog cited the existence of this fast as a precedent in support of establishing a separate fast day to commemorate the Holocaust. It was also cited as the only historical precedent for the establishment of a national *Yom HaShoah* commemoration in Israel, in the first speech delivered on this topic in the Knesset in 1951, and various dates were suggested for this purpose. The Chief Rabbinate of Israel designated the fast day of the tenth of Tevet as *Yom ha-Kaddish ha-Kelali*, the day to be set aside annually for the recital of *kaddish* by all those who did not know the date of the murder of their loved ones, and the 27th of Nisan was designated by the Knesset as *Yom ha-Shoah ve-ha-Gevurah*.

The debate as to whether or not Holocaust commemoration should be subsumed under the Ninth of Av or should merit its own independent day continues into the 21st century. Regardless, we need to commit ourselves to remember the Holocaust, especially as the survivors – first-hand witnesses – are becoming fewer in number. We need to remember those who were killed and we need to implore the Holy One, Blessed Be He, to remember both the individuals and the holy communities who were murdered and destroyed in the conflagration that consumed six million of our people. *Hashem yikom damam.*

Rebbetzin Tziporah Heller

Daniel in the Lion's Den – A Modern Day Hero

As a nation, we have been hated, and we have learned to live with it. The roots of the hatred that we still face are diverse. The responsibility of being chosen and the resentment that the role has created is as ancient as we are, yet as contemporary as the UN's double standards when Israel is in the picture. The miracle of our survival is then a continuing drama.

The first rule of survival – both physical and spiritual – is to recognise that there are enemies out there. No one likes defending their right to exist and we yearn for the acceptance and validation that other nations enjoy, but which, in the history of our 2,000-year-old exile, we have found to be elusive. We fear being perceived as paranoid and as xenophobic. However, this fear is often our Achilles heel, the inability to stand our ground unapologetically. To determine our fate, we need to look for heroes and role models from the past.

One of the real heroes of our continued struggle for survival is Daniel (of lion's den fame). He faced both of the kinds of enemies we have faced: those who want us to disappear, and are willing to sacrifice every bit of their own humanity to make it happen, and those who want us to survive by becoming mirror images of them. They are willing to let us be, as long as we don't really exist. Daniel survived without committing the cardinal sin of the persecuted: becoming what we hate.

He was separated from his family at the beginning of the Babylonian exile. With the fall of the monarchy and the destruction of Jerusalem, the Davidic royal family was expelled to Babylon, where Daniel was chosen to be one of the "privileged" children who would live in King Nebuchadnezzar's palace. Nebuchadnezzar's goal was to redefine the best and brightest of the Jewish children so that their energy, drive and brilliance would become part of the Babylonian regime. Their Judaism would be forgotten, and they would adopt new identity willingly. Daniel's name was changed to Belteshazzar.

The question was though, whether he would make the decision to remain Daniel or whether he would become Belteshazzar.

His first move was to refuse to eat the food that came out of the royal kitchen. This would not be an easy choice even for an adult. It would be almost impossible for most children, but Daniel understood that Judaism has to do with real world choices that affect your life. The servant in charge of the children's maintenance was appalled. He would be held accountable for what he saw as an almost suicidal choice. Daniel refused to compromise. He survived on fruits and nuts and seeds.

His next move was to face up to Nebuchadnezzar, who knew about his stubborn determination to remain Daniel. The Midrash tells us (*Bereishit Rabbah* 88:13) that Nebuchadnezzar had an unusual pet. He kept a snake which would consume anything that came too close. Daniel asked permission to approach and took out a bag of straw mixed with nails. The snake consumed the offering and died at Daniel's feet.

Daniel was responding to Nebuchadnezzar's symbolic message. Nebuchadnezzar was declaring that his civilisation could swallow up any rival culture. He had conquered the entire known world, and the very idea of resistance was foreign. Daniel "answered" by showing him that when the snake consumes nails, it would fail. The core personality of the Jews as a whole is as strong as steel, and survives those who endeavour to devour it whole.

In the course of time, Daniel's intellectual brilliance took him to the highest levels of governance. Belteshazzar was a name that everyone knew. Daniel was still the core identity of Babylon's rising star. Nebuchadnezzar's ministers instituted the concept of a national religion. Their intent wasn't religious by its nature; it was political. Religion was to become a means of taking the disparate members of Babylon's polyglot population and homogenising them. Daniel made a point of praying at the window of his residence facing Jerusalem. He could have chosen the path of least resistance and prayed in a room where his rebellion against the latest decree would remain his own business. Instead, he decided to make a statement of principle.

If your grandparents had a charity box where their coins went to rebuilding Israel, at a time when Israel was a concept rather than a reality, then they too had a bit of Daniel within them. His resistance led to the famous "lion's den" story. Daniel was sentenced to death, but his fate was in the hands of God, not the hands of humans. His survival was a miracle but, to tell you the truth, your survival as a Jew is not less of a miracle.

The issue that faces you isn't physical survival. The vast majority of people who read this article are not in imminent danger of being killed. You are endangered by the difficulty of living in a tolerant society and still choosing to be Daniel rather than Belteshazzar. The only way to make the choice more authentic is to learn more about what the Daniel within you represents. You have been exposed to Belteshazzar for as long as you remember. But to make a truly educated choice, you owe it to yourself and to the generations past, to choose to be educated!

> *In loving memory of Minky Rochel bas Boruch Zvi Ha Levi.*

Rebbetzin Rivkah Slonim

Niddah and Jewish Sexual Ethics

Most people have heard the popular claim that men think about sex every seven seconds (around 8,000 times a day!). But there is no scientific research to back that assertion. The recently released and only definitive study to date (Ohio State University) found the median number of sexually related thoughts per day for men to be about 19, and half of that for women. The study subjects were told to also chart the number of times they thought about food and sleep and, surprisingly, the numbers did not vary greatly from thoughts about sex.

So why does sex take up so much mind and heart space? Why does it saturate popular culture and media? Why does it pervade advertising? Why have otherwise sane individuals sabotaged very successful career paths and family units because they were blinded by carnal desire?

We seem to be built this way. The first description of man in the Bible is sexual: "Male and female He created them." On the scale of human urges, sexuality is second, trumped only by the will to survive.

The mystics understood this to be a reflection of the most important mission man has in life, and the deepest desire of the soul. Far from being one of many lifestyle choices, marriage and child-bearing are a holy obligation for the Jew. It is the way in which one half soul is joined with its other half and thus – in tandem – given the ability to make a distinct contribution in the unfurling of God's universe and design. This is the soul's most important mandate.

The soul's most urgent desire – even as it is in the physical world – is to taste *Olam HaBa* (the World-to-Come). And this drives man's utter infatuation with intimacy, for the closest we get to "tasting" *Olam Haba* in this world is through our human coupling – *done right*.

How so?

Our tradition teaches that happiness is born of the feeling that one is on "the right path." More than anything else, man craves knowledge of a point of departure, a point of return and a plan for getting there. If joy is being on the right road, then arrival is the ecstasy for which we hunger.

Human intimacy done right gives us that feeling; with this person, joined as one – in soul, spirit, mind and body – there is no tension, no fissure, no dissonance. In this union, there is just the perfect endpoint; I am home. And that is what the soul feels in *Olam HaBa*.

How do we do intimacy right? This is an important question. It is all too easy to conflate sex, lust, hormonal overdrive, and oxytocin flooding the blood stream with the intimacy we are hardwired to desire. Indeed, a cursory look at society shows how widespread this confusion is and the havoc and heartbreak it can wreak. The mystics teach that that which is sourced in the highest realm can fall lowest. Sex is the quintessential double edged sword: it can be a fountain of great joy and ultimate contentment, and can, God forbid, bring the worst type of pain and trauma. It is the atomic energy of our lives.

From the perspective of Jewish theology, sexual intimacy is a unique language shared by two people partnered in a holy union called marriage. Undoubtedly, people can and do have sex outside of that framework, but the Torah teaches that, unlike animals, we are capable of so much more. With discipline and restraint, we can taste heaven on earth. To do so, we must be careful not to separate physical intimacy from its celestial framework – from consecration, commitment, and the true love that flows from it.

Even within marriage, sexuality must be modulated to be an enduringly nourishing factor. The laws of *Niddah* outlined in the Torah help calibrate true intimacy with the innate sexual desire. Biblical law prohibits wife and husband from engaging in sexual intercourse during the time of her menses and until after her immersion in a *mikveh* (ritual pool), which takes place seven days after her menses have ceased.

Spontaneity is alleged to be crucial to sexuality and can sometimes make for an especially enjoyable interlude, but statistics show that married couples have sex more frequently than unmarrieds and that setting aside special time actually makes sex happen. This is especially true within the *mikveh* dynamic, when there is a limited amount of time each month during which husband and wife can be intimate. The time is precious, and charged with sexual energy. It coincides with the time of the cycle during which a woman is most primed physiologically, as well as emotionally, to enjoy sex. During the other half of the cycle they are acutely aware that they cannot have each other. For that time, they each become the "forbidden woman" or "forbidden man" to the other, injecting a powerfully romantic element into their married lives and never letting it get dull.

No matter how many years they have been married, this routine leaves husband and wife pining for reunion. The off time gives them the opportunity to deepen their communication skills and strengthen their friendship. After immersion in the *mikveh*, the pent up passion fuels their physical intimacy so that each month there is a deepening, a slightly higher level of fusion. The most common and insidious threat to healthy human sexuality is a meaningless context; marriage provides the context. The most common and insidious threat to marriage – sexual boredom – is all but obviated by the biblical rhythm of *mikveh*.

But there is even more.

Jewish ethics teaches that the spectacular, God-given gift called "human sexuality" is more than just one of the most powerful forces of nature; it is a sacred partnership with God. It is the Holy of Holies.

When sex is centrifugal, when it is tethered to the Divine – when we move beyond operating solely on the level of our own desires and agenda – this powerful animalistic urge turns into an unstoppable energy, an agent for all that is good and healthy and healing. A strong family unit is a source of light, warmth, and joy to all who behold it. It nurtures a sense of security and, at the same time, of deep wonder. It causes the onlooker to ask: what lurks above all this we call life? Who created this miracle called love and devotion?

In a very real sense, our private lovemaking has profound, cosmic repercussions. Now that's something worth thinking about multiple times a day!

Chief Rabbi Yisrael Meir Lau

Out of the Depths

I was officially registered as a "Polish child" in the Buchenwald Concentration Camp rather than a Jew, and owed my life to the saving power of the letter P, but daily life was still difficult. Yet within the darkness, there were several points of light. One image that is constantly in my memory is that of my older brother, Naphtali, repeatedly coming to the barbed-wire fence that surrounded my block. Each time he looked worse than he did in the previous visit, more gaunt, more emaciated. I, Lulek, his eight-year-old younger brother, would give him a slice of bread spread with margarine, which I guarded vigilantly for him. I recall watching with great satisfaction as he ate the thin slice, proud of my success – I had obtained a slice of bread for my saviour, I was permitting him to eat, and, perhaps due to me, he lost a little less weight.

Naphtali's continual updates kept me informed of what was happening among the Jews in the camp. Since I was very young, and never had the opportunity to learn about Judaism during the war, my knowledge of these customs and holidays was very limited. As Passover approached, Naphtali and his friends were determined to do anything to avoid eating leavened foods during the holiday. Although the only food available to them was the daily ration of three and a half ounces of bread, they were determined to observe the laws of Passover at all costs. Months in advance, at the beginning of January, they began to prepare by collecting potatoes. They told me about their arrangements and tried to explain their significance. Some of the prisoners had organised a trade in potatoes: three potatoes were worth the daily bread ration.

One day, a feeble Naphtali dragged his feet toward Block 8 and stood next to the barbed wire fence. He pulled a few potatoes from his pockets, and explained that he could not carry them because they hindered him while working with the bodies in the crematorium, so he was bringing them to me to guard carefully, because they had been set aside for Passover. Then he explained to me, for the first time, why they were so important to him in this concentration camp, adding a few words about the prohibition against eating *chametz* on Passover. I guarded those potatoes with my life.

Meanwhile, Purim arrived and the Jews in Buchenwald decided to commemorate Purim as best they could. They had no food to fulfil the *mitzvot* of sending gifts to friends or to the poor, or to eat a festive meal with, but they could attempt to read the *megillah* (Scroll of Esther). Obviously no one in Buchenwald possessed an actual scroll, yet they did not give up. Several days before Purim, some of the older Jews in the camp held a meeting in secret. They resolved to shake off their despair and try to reconstruct the *megillah* from memory. Each man would write whatever verses they remembered by heart, and a group of the elders from the block would try to reconstruct the proper order of the text. Everyone remembered the most important verses, such as "In the days of Ahasuerus"; "For the Jews there was light and happiness, joy and glory"; and "Mordechai would not kneel or bow." They wrote out the verses with charcoal on yellow paper torn from discarded sacks of millet and, on Purim Eve, the Jews of Buchenwald read the improvised scroll which they had dredged up from memory.

At the end of the evening, they sung the traditional Purim song of *Shoshanat Yaakov* (the Rose of Jacob) whose symbolic lines were charged with meaning: "You have always been their salvation, their hope in every generation." When they sang: "Cursed is Haman who sought to destroy me," no one had any doubt to whom the verse referred, and the phrase "Blessed is Mordechai the Jew" inspired everyone with great hope.

The next morning, the Jews were marched out at dawn to forced labour. Many had trouble walking and those who stumbled were buried in the snow, or else the Ukrainian guards beat them with the butts of their rifles so that they would never get up again.

But the same Jews who told me about the Purim celebrations, also spoke of a religious chassid of Gur named Avraham Eliyahu. He was a tall man with broad shoulders, powerful and with an unusual personality to boot. Unlike most of the Jews, he had little problem walking to his work, upright and with confidence. But instead of leading the line from the barracks, he insisted on bringing up the rear, and the whole way, he would support the backs of those who had trouble walking. *Avrum deh shtipper* (Avrum the pusher), they used to call him in Yiddish. He picked up the weak, straightened the bent, and pushed them forward. If he saw one of his fellow Jews sway and fall, he would grab him quickly and give him a push so that the man could continue walking on his own. Everyone thought of him as a remarkable figure, even the Ukrainian guards.

The day after Purim Eve, after the reading of the improvised scroll, one Ukrainian guard, who had great respect for the tough Jew, could not restrain himself, and whispered two words in Avrum's ear: "Hitler *kaput*" (Hitler is done for). Within a minute, the announcement spread like wildfire from Avraham Eliyahu, at the end of the line, all the way up to the front. At once, even the weakest *Muselmanner* straightened their backs and began to walk unassisted. Someone in the middle of the procession began to mumble and the others joined in: "The Rose of Jacob rejoiced and exulted... Cursed is Haman who sought to destroy me." The song of the previous night returned the next morning – a month before our liberation. This was the only time the Jews sang on their way to forced labour in Buchenwald.

The Jews also celebrated a Passover *seder* in Buchenwald that year. Over and over, they sang the holiday song *Karev Yom* from memory: "The day is approaching that will be neither day nor night and the darkness of the night will be lit like the light of day." They had no *Haggadah*, no wine, and no *matzah*. Still there was no leavened food to be seen among them – only potatoes. In the impossible conditions of the camp, these Jews tried as best as they could to preserve their Judaism – truly heroic people.

Dedicated to Teresa & Josef Szyjowicz. Wonderful people and like so many Holocaust survivors had a special strength and humanity that is rarely found today. We love them forever. Rita Tucker and Sigi Szyjowicz.

Chief Rabbi Michael Schudrich

An American in Poland

When I came to Poland for the first time in an official capacity in 1991, the question was, "Why are you going there? There are no Jews." Now people ask, "Is the community viable?" This reflects positive developments in Poland, but my answer is, "Who knows?" There is nothing logical about how Jewish communities function and survive.

As long as there is a community, I, as a rabbi, feel an obligation to be there, and currently the community is growing. Moreover, the average age of the Warsaw *kehillah* has recently fallen from 65 to 45 and there are thousands of stories of men and women of all ages and backgrounds who are only now returning to Judaism. This year more than 100 people sought me out to discuss their Jewish roots, while many others went to other rabbis.

For decades it was often not a good idea – or even a safe one – to admit to being Jewish. Poland has known democracy only since 1989 and fear dissipates slowly. A few months ago, a man of about 60 approached me and said that his Jewish mother had died. They had buried her next to his non-Jewish father in a non-sectarian cemetery. He told me that he had never done anything Jewish, but now felt the need to say *Kaddish*. So, on a Friday morning, I taught him this prayer for the dead, then said, "*Shabbat* begins this evening. Why don't you come to the synagogue?" He mentioned that his wife was also Jewish, and, therefore, also their 21-year-old daughter. I invited all three of them. They came and were moved.

Another story: a young woman, in her early 20s, discovered that her mother's mother was Jewish. She became observant, met a young Jewish man from the United States, and they fell in love. Her mother wants the wedding to be in New York so that the neighbours won't see that they are having a Jewish wedding. This does not so much concern current antisemitism, but mainly what might happen again, and is based on what people have experienced during most of their life.

But just how did an American rabbi from New York's Upper West Side become the Chief Rabbi of Poland? I made my first trip there in 1973, and was told that there were only a few thousand old Jews left, which didn't make sense. If 10% of three and a half million Polish Jews survived the war and 90% of the survivors emigrated, that would still leave about 30,000 Jews in Poland. Where were they?

In 1976, I returned to Poland, and in 1979, after three years in rabbinical school in Israel, I decided to study Polish at the Jagiellonian University for the summer (I nicknamed it an *ulpanski*). That summer, I met several young Jewish dissidents, such as Staszek and Monika Krajewski and Kostek Gebert, and realised that there were, indeed, some young Jews left, and they were asking for my help to gain Jewish knowledge. Yes, this is ironic, because before World War II, American rabbis would come to Warsaw to study Torah with the greatest talmudic scholars of their time. This city was the heart of Jewish tradition. Now an American rabbi has to come here to help the Polish Jews.

But another sign of the Jewish community's development is the recent increase of rabbis living in Poland. There are now 13, of which seven are traditional, three are Reform, and three are Chabad emissaries. One of the traditional rabbis is Polish-born Rabbi Mati Pawlak, who discovered that he was Jewish at the age of 16. In such a small community, we make great efforts to avoid division. On Israel's *Yom HaZikaron* (Memorial Day), I invited both the rabbi of Beit Warszawa and the local Chabad rabbi to participate in the ceremony, because part of what keeps the Jews in Poland united is that we don't want Hitler to have won the war. And perhaps one day, Poland's Chief Rabbi will be Polish, although it doesn't seem likely to happen in the immediate future.

My main obligation obviously, is toward the living Jewish community. The economic and social status of the Jews is such that there are no philanthropic Polish Jewish billionaires, such as the Jewish oligarchs in Russia or Ukraine, and at present, we remain significantly dependent on Jewish foreign aid.

Obviously, there is also a profound Jewish past in Poland,

whose memory must be preserved and material sites protected, although this heritage raises many complex issues. For example, how many synagogues can we possibly afford to restore? What should the community's attitude be toward the 1,300 unattended Jewish cemeteries? We cannot save all of them because we cannot raise such massive funding. But if no one has paid attention to a Jewish cemetery for 50 years, there is an inclination to build over it. So my first priority is to prevent further desecration.

It is unacceptable, for example, for somebody to build a road over a Jewish cemetery. In Ostrów Mazowiecki, one-third of the Monday flea market is located on the old Jewish cemetery. Yet the mayor told me that if I said this was wrong according to Jewish law, he would move the market. Indeed, over the last ten years, I have found increased sensitivity to our tradition among the authorities. I only encountered one substantial exception, in Leżańsk, where the great chassidic master, Rabbi Elimelech is buried. Thousands of chassidim and other Jews visit Leżańsk every year but, despite that or perhaps because of it, the town has too often been insensitive to Jewish needs.

In recent years, we have learned that there are hundreds of unmarked Jewish mass graves all over Poland. There is a Baptist fellow, a very unusual denomination in Poland, who now travels by bicycle through villages in eastern Poland, asking old people if they know where Jews are buried. Since he is a Pole, elderly witnesses speak to him more easily and often are relieved to talk.

A very different issue is that of assisting Righteous Gentiles. We cannot do enough to help these precious people. There is a Jewish Foundation for the Righteous that assists some of them, and there are also some other organisations. The last few hundred remaining in Poland should be enabled to live out the rest of their lives in dignity and some comfort. And there are small groups of non-Jews who want to "do something Jewish": save a synagogue, celebrate a Jewish festival, teach about Jewish history, etc. Adept at identifying and fighting antisemitism, we are far weaker at identifying potential allies and friends.

As far as Jews are concerned, I have always believed that our work in Poland is to revive the Jewish identity of individuals. I want to give people the chance to decide to be Jewish.

Until a few years ago, the problems in Poland were predominantly post-Holocaust, post-Communist matters. As far as we can look ahead, the Jewish community will continue to live in the shadow of the Holocaust. Yet most problems are becoming more "normal" and familiar. A young woman says to me, "Rabbi, I am 23 years-old. I know all the boys in the community and don't like any of them. How am I going to get married?" Or parents will say, "Our son is 15. He has decided to become Orthodox, but he has no Orthodox friends. What is he supposed to do?" These are the typical problems of a normal small community.

In memory of Naftali and Jutta Felber,
Jasha and Dora Lepski, and Alan Morgan.

Rabbi Steven Burg

Uniting Jews in Our Time

It is no secret that in our generation, there is a perception of a divide between Jews who observe the precepts and commandments of the Torah and Jews who, while they may not implement the laws of Judaism in their daily routine, feel culturally Jewish. Each side is guilty of finger pointing in the direction of the other. Both feel that the other side wrongly sits in judgment of them.

One of the most common phrases mentioned by survivors of the Holocaust is that "Hitler didn't discriminate." If you were a Jew, that was enough reason to be targeted and killed. No one checked your level of religiosity or commitment and even Jews who had converted to Christianity were targeted by the Nazis. Secular and religious Jews were placed side by side in concentration camp barracks. Why is it, though, that Jewish unity is so often predicated on having a common enemy? The Bible is replete with stories of Jews coming together for the express purpose of fighting evil. Even today in the modern State of Israel, we are quick to form united coalition governments in the time of war. We are also just as quick to dissolve them at the close. Why can't the Jewish nation come together as easily in times of peace?

Whilst I cannot answer for the past, I would suggest that the following story offers a formula for uniting Jews around the world in the future, irrespective of their level of commitment. During the Mandate, when the British ruled over Israel, there was a very special prison chaplain named Rabbi Aryeh Levine. Rabbi Aryeh Levine was what would be described today as an ultra-Orthodox Jew. He wore a long black coat, had a flowing white beard and the chassidic hat called a *shtreimel* on top of his head. Rain or shine, Rabbi Levine would show up at the prison every *Shabbat* to lead

221

the services, visit the inmates and bring messages to and from the families of the Jewish prisoners.

Out of respect for the rabbi, the prisoners would not desecrate *Shabbat* in front of him. One fellow, who was a dedicated communist, got very upset at his fellow inmates. He told them they were all hypocrites because they pretended to be observant in front of Rabbi Levine, even though they would smoke cigarettes and desecrate *Shabbat* immediately following his departure. Finally, this young man could not take it anymore. The next Saturday morning, he stood at the front gate and shouted at Rabbi Levine, "Don't you know that these men are all liars. They only put their *kippot* on their heads when they see you coming?"

Rabbi Levine answered immediately, "My son, I never look at their heads to see if they are wearing *kippot*. I only look to see what is in their hearts. The young man was very taken aback by Rabbi Levine's answer. From then on, every *Shabbat* morning, this ardent communist would sit in the front row of the prison synagogue, listening to every word Rabbi Levine had to say.

I believe that this philosophy of Rabbi Aryeh Levine should be widely adapted. As Jews, when we connect with each other, we should strive to see what lies in someone's heart. Too often we focus on the outer dimensions and don't take the time to see what lies beneath the surface. We need to see the person not the veneer.

There is a movement in Orthodox circles called "outreach" which exists to show non-observant Jews the depth and beauty of religious Judaism. But, I believe that, as a community, the word outreach, since it connotes a scenario where we are on two different playing fields, should no longer be used.

I recently attended the most spectacular retreat for the staff of Tribe, the youth movement of the United Synagogue in the United Kingdom. I believe that they understood this issue better than anyone I have ever encountered. They had large signs made up that said in big letters the word "engage." The word "engage" means that we are meeting each other with no preconceptions. The word "engage" means that while I have something to teach you, I believe I can learn from you as well. The word "engage" means the coming together and building of a real relationship.

I sincerely believe, that for the Jewish people to be unified, we must engage with each other regardless of religious level. As part of the process of engagement, we must be able to see past the exterior and look into each other's hearts, just as Rabbi Aryeh Levine did for the Jewish men at the prison, without compromising who he was. I believe that, in our long history, Jews have demonstrated that they have deep and loving hearts. We are always amongst the first to contribute philanthropically. You can find Jews helping humanitarian causes around the world; the State of Israel quickly dispatches medical teams to help after natural disasters in all corners of the globe.

Our challenge must be to engage each other with a loving heart and a powerful embrace. We must create unity built on the appreciation that we have for each other. If we are successful in Jewish engagement, then Jewish unity will quickly follow.

Rabbi Dr Michael Harris

What Does Judaism Say about Theodicy?

The term "theodicy" comes from the Greek words for "God" and "justice" and literally means "justifying God." In contemporary philosophy and theology, the term "theodicy" is used to describe attempts to "justify" God, as it were, in the face of the existence of evil and suffering in the world. This conundrum, usually referred to as "the problem of evil," commonly takes the following form in the Western philosophical tradition: how can evil exist if God is omnipotent, omniscient, and perfectly good?

The distinguished contemporary philosopher Eleonore Stump, has persuasively argued that it is preferable to refer to the problem of *suffering* rather than the problem of evil; after all, if bad things happened in the world, but people did not suffer as a result, it would bother us much less.

Tisha Be-Av, as the prophet Zechariah assures us, will one day be transformed from the darkest moment in the Jewish calendar to a time of joy. In the meantime, we recall on Tisha Be-Av the destruction of the two Temples and other great tragedies in our history which have brought great suffering in their wake. How does our tradition understand suffering and reconcile its undoubted existence, pervasiveness, and (something that particularly bothered *Chazal*) its apparently unjust distribution (*tzadik ve-ra lo, rasha ve-tov lo* – the righteous suffer and the wicked prosper) with our belief in a wholly good, all-powerful, and all-knowing God?

There are several kinds of approach to suffering in Jewish tradition. Suffering is too deep and complex a phenomenon, and Judaism too rich and insightful a faith, for any single or simple prescription to be whole.

Sefer Iyov, the Book of Job, is the book of *Tanach* which is most directly relevant to the theme of suffering. Job's friends adopt a theodicy in response to his suffering that has strong intuitive religious appeal and which apparently provides a clear answer to the question of why suffering occurs. They argue that suffering is always divine punishment for sin. This is what contemporary philosophical discussion calls a "punishment theodicy." Yet as many have noted, the biblical text makes clear that God prefers the questions of Job to the answers of his friends. At the end of the book (42:7), God tells Job's friends that they "did not speak to me correctly as did my servant Job." As Professor David Shatz puts it: "[T]he book of Job is cogently read as a *protest* against the view that suffering implies sin." Sin can lead to suffering, but the presence of suffering does not necessarily entail that there has been sin.

While there are sources that advocate a punishment theodicy by linking all suffering to sin, other teachings of *Chazal* reject this idea (see, for example, *Shabbat* 55a–b). Moreover, particularly in the Babylonian Talmud, *Chazal* offer other possible explanations for suffering that resist such linkage. Perhaps the most intriguing of these is the concept of *yisurin shel ahavah* (sufferings of love), which are visited on righteous people in order to allow them greater reward in the World-to-Come. But the discussion of *yisurin shel ahavah* in the Babylonian Talmud (*Berachot* 5a–b), perhaps suggests that often the absence of suffering is better. In one of several similar and beautiful episodes recounted there, Rabbi Yochanan goes to visit the sick Rabbi Chiya bar Abba. Rabbi Yochanan asks: "Are your sufferings precious to you?" Rabbi Chiya replies: *lo hen ve-lo secharan* (neither they nor their reward). Rabbi Yochanan asks Rabbi Chiya to give him his hand, whereupon "he took his hand and healed him."

Importantly, as early as the Mishnah itself, *Chazal* suggest that, in fact, no satisfactory intellectual resolution of the problem of suffering, no compelling theodicy, is available to us: "Rabbi Yanai said: "We are unable to explain either the tranquillity of the wicked or the suffering of the righteous" (*Avot* 4:15). Rabbi Yanai's statement anticipates an influential position in contemporary philosophy of religion known as "sceptical theism."

Philosophers often distinguish between two kinds of suffering in their discussions of theodicy. One kind is suffering caused as a result of events in the natural world such as earthquakes and hurricanes. The other type is suffering caused as a result of evil perpetrated by other human beings. The Holocaust comes immediately to mind here, and recent Jewish thinkers have grappled extensively with the issue of theodicy in this context. Eliezer Berkovits, for example, draws on the Torah's concept of *hester panim*, (God's 'hiding of His face') to argue for what philosophers call a free will theodicy: God allows human beings freedom to choose how to act, and people sometimes choose radical evil.

Thus far, the question on which we have focused is: "Why does suffering occur?" The position of one of the 20th century's greatest Jewish thinkers, Rabbi Joseph B Soloveitchik, is that this is the wrong question. The most appropriate religious question about suffering is not *why* it occurs, not the search for the most satisfactory theodicy, but rather *how* to respond to suffering.

In his essay *A Halachic Approach to Suffering*, Rabbi Soloveitchik makes three basic claims. First, suffering and evil are real, and they are bad. Judaism does not pretend otherwise. Secondly, we must never make peace with evil and suffering, but rather defy and oppose them with all the power at our disposal. That is why Jewish tradition is so enthusiastic about medicine, with its power to cure and to diminish suffering, and about scientific advances which enable us to control our environment. The third claim is the traditional Jewish insistence that ultimately evil and suffering will be defeated. We may lose battles, but we will win the war. "He will swallow up death for ever, and the Lord God will wipe away the tears from every face" (Isaiah 25:8).

In memory of Susi and Freddie Bradfield,
Sarah Gittel bat Mordechai Menachem and Yaakov ben Zvi.

Professor Deborah Lipstadt

Valley of the Shadow of Darkness

I do not pray consistently, though there have been occasions when prayer has been for me a source of strength and comfort. As the adage goes: there are few atheists in fox holes. So it has been with me. On occasion, I have stood outside an intensive care unit while a loved one was hovering between life and death. Then prayer came easily to my lips. I vowed that when this situation passed, I would pray not just *for* something but also in expressions of thanksgiving. Of course, that rarely happened.

But my prayers have not *only* emanated from places of pain and desperation. Sometimes, I allow myself to be transported to a spiritual place, a place that I am always surprised I can access. Rarely, however, has prayer spontaneously enveloped me without my actively deciding *to* pray.

On the morning my trial was to begin,[1] my legal team – barristers, solicitors, paralegals, experts, and researchers – gathered in my barrister's chambers. After five years of preparation, there was a heightened degree of anticipation in the room. The lawyers reviewed last minute details. The clerks checked to make sure that the correct documents were at hand. Mobile phones rang incessantly. The copier was humming. The adrenalin in the room was stupefying. Everyone was moving at full speed. Everyone, except,

---

1. In 1996, David Irving sued Lipstadt and her publisher, Penguin Books, for libel in an English court, after she characterised writings and public statements of his as Holocaust denial in her book *Denying the Holocaust*. Although English libel law puts the burden of proof on the defendant (rather than the plaintiff), Lipstadt and Penguin won the case and demonstrated in court that Lipstadt's accusations against Irving were substantially true and therefore not libellous. *The Times* (14th April 2000, p 23) said of Lipstadt's victory, "History has had its day in court and scored a crushing victory."

that is, for me. I had nothing to do. Even though I was at the eye of the storm, I had no "real" job.

At first I was glad for this respite. After the many years of intense preparation, I appreciated this chance for a brief reverie. But I found it hard to relax. I was beset by thoughts of the people – from historians to leaders of the Jewish community – who had urged me not to fight this battle. The academics had sloughed off David Irving's claims as akin to the "rantings of a flat earth theorist." Why, they wondered, would I waste my time on this? The communal leaders feared Irving would garner so much media attention that, irrespective of the outcome, he would emerge the real winner. What if they were proven right? Sitting there, I realised that if we won, lots of people, including those in the room, would deserve the credit. But if we did not win, the loss would be mine.

Then I thought of the survivors and their emotional investment in this battle. In the preceding months they had reached out to me almost in desperation. They feared that they and, more importantly, their relatives who had been killed, would be subjected to a "double dying," one at the hands of the Nazis and another at the hands of the deniers. I tried to tell them that, irrespective of the legal outcome, their history was secure. These experiences could not be diminished by a decision rendered by a British court. That, however, did not assuage them. "No," they had replied, "you *must* win."

Beset by these fears, I felt as if I was about to freefall into an emotional abyss. Then as abruptly as this descent had come upon me, the words of the 23rd psalm began rumbling through my head. I had not sought them out. They simply were there. This, I thought, must be what my theologian friends call spontaneous prayer.

In Jewish tradition, this psalm serves to offer comfort at frightening and melancholy moments. I was surprised to find it roaming around in my head. Psalms do not spring easily to my lips. My mother, on the other hand, had kept a copy of the Psalms next to her bed. She had relied on them when my father suffered through a long illness and during her own difficulties. I had always been in awe of her ability to find comfort in them. I, in contrast, found little comfort in these words. I could not relate to the shepherd, who despite feeling exposed and vulnerable as he camps alone in the Valley of the Shadow of Darkness, proclaims: *lo ira ra* (I will fear no evil). How, I wondered, could he be so unafraid? Was he so certain that he was such a worthy person that God would intervene on his behalf? I felt no such certainty. Unlike the shepherd, my fears felt palpable. I was sure everyone in the room could see them.

I struggled to find comfort in the shepherd's words. Maybe what he was saying was: "I have very good reason to be afraid – and so do you. If this trial does not end up as you hope it will, many people will be upset, particularly those who already suffered so much. But take courage from the fact that you are doing the right thing. And therefore, *lo ira ra.*"

And then the rest of the psalm seemed to fall into place, as if it had been written for just this moment. *Shivtecha u-mishantecha hemah yenachamuni* (your staff and your shield comfort me). All around were people who brought me comfort. Some – such as the legal team surrounding me – by their professionalism and utter competence; some by stepping forward to give to my defence fund. Others had reassured me, "Though your name is on the court documents, *our* history is on the line. We are with you in this battle." Emory University, a place with Methodist roots, had not only given me a paid leave and funds to cover my travels, but had ensured that courses on the Holocaust would be taught while I was gone, so a Holocaust denier would not cause students to be deprived of learning about this event. As we worked our way through the crowds of people gathered outside the courtroom, many of them reached out to wish me luck. *Hemah yenachamuni* (I was comforted).

As we entered the courtroom, the lawyers indicated that I was to sit at a large table right in front of the judge. My opponent was similarly situated on the other side of the room. *Ta'aroch lefanai shulchan, neged tzorerai* (You have prepared for me a table against my enemies.) By now, a psalm which had first seemed to mock my fears seemed to have been written for me. Then I reached the final lines. *Dishanta ba-shemen roshi* (You have anointed my head with oil). I tripped over that for a moment. Then I realised there was something affirming about this struggle. I had been given the chance to stand up to someone whose antisemitism was undeniable, who was at the heart of the denial movement, and who caused those who had already suffered terribly even more pain. I had been given the chance to return the figurative blows inflicted on the Jewish people measure for measure.

While I could rejoice in the opportunity to fight, it seemed a bit premature to declare *Kosi revayah* (my cup runneth over). Not quite yet. Though I did not know it then, in time that too would arrive.

Rabbi Michael Laitner

How a Conversation Changed the World

Could one ancient conversation begin to change history and continue to affect us today? The biblical book of Ezra[1] records such a conversation in Babylonia (modern day Iraq), which occurred around 2,500 years ago and put in place a sequence of events which would ultimately lead to the contemporary society that we recognise today.

THE HISTORICAL BACKGROUND AND CHARACTERS

The participants were Artaxerxes, King of Persia, and Ezra, a courtier and outstanding young Jewish scholar of the vibrant Babylonian Jewish community, which had developed after the destruction of the First Temple. The king instructed Ezra to travel to Jerusalem, with a royal decree authorising him to revitalise the Jewish community and fledgling Second Temple there. Nehemiah, another great leader, later worked together with Ezra; their respective biblical books sit side-by-side.

Whilst the king may have had his own political considerations in dispatching Ezra, perhaps to keep the western peninsula of his kingdom loyal in the face of growing Greek power across the Mediterranean, Ezra's stay in Jerusalem provided him with the opportunity to establish a flourishing Jewish life through enactments which remain vital to Judaism until this day. We shall focus on just one of these, *Keriyat ha-Torah*, the public reading of the Torah.

To understand the impact of *Keriyat ha-Torah* and the broader

1. Chapter 7.

picture of how it was to affect history, I will present the teachings of the great British Jewish scholar, Rabbi Dr Irving Jacobs.[2]

EZRA'S ACCOMPLISHMENTS

One of Ezra's most influential accomplishments is described in the Book of Nehemiah,[3] and occurred on Rosh Hashanah. The city walls had been rebuilt but the Temple was still not fully functioning. To mark the festival, Jerusalemites gathered near the water gate of the city, close to the southern side of today's Old City walls.

Ezra's efforts to inspire the people religiously had started to make an impact. On that holy day, the people yearned to know more and asked Ezra to read the Torah to them. Although the *Kohen Gadol* read aloud sections of the Torah every year on Yom Kippur, and the king was commanded to read the book of Deuteronomy in the Temple once every seven years, this innovation of Ezra created a weekly reading of the Torah in the context of a prayer service for all communities and an ongoing connection to the five books of Moses. It was the precursor to *Keriyat ha-Torah* taking place in synagogue services.

For us, this is not unusual. Yet for those Jews, many of whom were assimilated and mostly unaware of their heritage, the Torah was a book for scholars, not the regular Jew. The verses describe how Ezra read and also explained the Torah to all those present. It was, perhaps, the first community adult outreach education programme in history, to put it in our terms. It was staggeringly successful.

Ezra, Nehemiah and the *kohanim* continued to teach the people in the same way the next day when they returned.

EZRA'S IMPACT, THEN AND NOW

How, though, did this change history? In a world with few books (scrolls in those times), much Torah study was done through listening. With *Keriyat ha-Torah* as part of the service, any Jew who was able to, could listen to the Written Law just by coming to synagogue. The effect was astonishing. By the time the Second

2. A former principal of Jews College in London and the current rabbi of the Neve Shalom David Ishag Synagogue in Wembley, Greater London.
3. Chapter 8.

Temple was destroyed in 70 CE, the Torah had become a text that was very familiar to Jews across Israel and the Diaspora.

Ezra's actions directly impact on us too, due to the placement of *Keriyat ha-Torah* in services, especially on *Shabbat* and *yom tov*, where a larger attendance is likely. Without this, we might only rarely see a *Sefer Torah* or encounter its words.

As we noted, Ezra did not just read the Torah. He also explained and taught it. This set the scene for what we know as the rabbinic sermon and explanations in synagogue services, and the many commentaries such as Rashi, for example. This great change went beyond the Jewish community, though, because the initial concept that sprang from Ezra's work was that of *Targum*, (translation of the Torah as it was read, rather than broader explanation).

Targum, however, allowed not just Jews to understand, but also anybody else who was interested in the Torah and came to synagogue. It might surprise us to learn that there were a significant number of such non-Jews. Many non-Jews (although pagans) were fascinated by Judaism, because it was a structured religion in contrast to most pagan practices. They were also amazed by the tenacity of Jewish practice: how the Jews had not only survived the destruction of the First Temple, but were even flourishing again both in the Land of Israel (with a rebuilt Temple) and in Babylonia and elsewhere.

These non-Jews were attracted to elements of Jewish practice and some began to adopt such practices. Rather than just hearing about pagan cults, such as the one that worshipped Osiris in Egypt (which, curiously enough, taught of a young god who died and was resurrected), those pagans were also hearing the Torah and its messages. This can begin to explain why those pagans who became the early Christians saw themselves as "new Jews" and saw the biblical texts, rather than pagan myths such as Osiris, as their primary religious inspiration. It also explains why they confined their teachings to the *Tanach* (Written Law) as opposed to the Oral Law, since the Oral Law was not read out in public, but rather studied in the academies of learning. This served to preserve the authentic interpretation of Torah to those who had studied all elements, whilst still allowing outsiders to be introduced to the concept of monotheism. As Christianity spread through the

Roman Empire, Europe, and beyond, the same thing happened in those lands.

The catalyst for all of this was Ezra. Without his journey to Jerusalem, the Jewish community in Israel may well have withered, and it is likely that many Jews may not have become familiar with the Torah, and the religions of the non-Jewish world, which we are most familiar with, might have existed in a very different format. It is a fascinating thought.

So, next time you hear the Torah being read, think of Ezra and his achievements. Think of how we, his descendants, can also positively change the world by listening to and applying the words of the Torah as understood by thousands of years of Jewish teachings. By doing so, we too might learn how to make our own contribution to the ongoing adventure of the Jewish people.

In memory of the lost generations of The Holocaust. In honour of the generations today. In celebration of the generations to come.

Chief Rabbi Ephraim Mirvis

The Path to a Jewish Life

"*Shimon HaTzadik* (Simon the Just) used to say: the world stands on three things, on Torah, on *avodah* and on *gemilut chasadim*" (Ethics of the Fathers 1:2).

Torah is the source of our laws and traditions. *Avodah* is service of the Almighty through prayer. *Gemilut chasadim* is achieved through acts of charity and loving-kindness.

Shimon HaTzadik's teaching defines how we should think, speak, and practise Judaism. These three principles constitute the tripod supporting all human existence. If any one of these key supports is removed, the very structure of life will collapse. As Jews, we have a unique responsibility: through studying Torah, we stimulate the growth of our intellects and we learn Jewish values. Through *avodah*, we articulate our closeness to our Creator. Through *gemilut chasadim*, we emulate God's ways, inspiring us to better our communities, society, and the world through all that we do.

Our Patriarchs were the original and outstanding exponents of these three key features of Judaism. Each one, through his unique character, highlighted the essence of one of these three principles.

Abraham excelled in *gemilut chasadim*. He dispensed kindness and hospitality, fed the hungry, defended the vulnerable, and prayed for strangers, even the unworthy. Isaac prayed and meditated in the fields. His life was a continuous act of devotion to God; he was even willing to be offered upon an altar. Jacob, the "dweller of tents," was the consummate Torah scholar, whose knowledge and learning inspired him to spiritual greatness.

Echoes of this teaching can be found in Rabbi Abraham ibn Ezra's fascinating introduction to the Ten Commandments. Ibn Ezra (1089–1164) divides all the commandments of the Torah into three categories:

235

MITZVOT HA-LEV – commandments concerning thought and feeling, such as loving God, cleaving to God, loving our neighbours as ourselves, not hating others in our hearts, and not bearing a grudge.

MITZVOT HA-LASHON – commandments concerning speech, such as prayer, the prohibition of slander, the priestly blessing, reciting the *Shema,* and Grace after Meals.

MITZVOT ASEH – commandments involving action, such as giving charity, wearing *tzitzit* and *tefillin,* lighting *Shabbat* candles, and going on pilgrimage to Jerusalem.

The Decalogue was given on two tablets. The precepts which relate to our relationship with God are on the right hand side, while commandments relating to our responsibility to our fellows, appear on the left. If we look attentively, we see that the Ten Commandments are structured in a remarkable chiastic order (i.e., ABC CBA):

COMMANDMENTS ON THE RIGHT HAND-SIDE:

Believe in God (*thought*)
Don't believe in idols (*thought*)
Don't take God's name in vain (*speech*)
Keep *Shabbat* (*action*)
Honour parents (*action*)

COMMANDMENTS ON THE LEFT HAND SIDE:

Don't murder (*action*)
Don't commit adultery (*action*)
Don't steal (*action*)
Don't bear false witness (*speech*)
Don't covet (*thought*)

Nechama Leibowitz explains the rationale behind this intriguing pattern. The Torah begins with the obvious and proceeds to the less obvious. With regard to God, it is well known that we should believe in the Almighty and not pay homage to any other purported power. It is less obvious, however, that our belief in God should be reflected in the way we speak. Our choice of words and our manner of speech are integral to the sacred life we lead. Least obvious, is the recognition that our belief in God must be translated into meaningful and responsible action. Ultimately, a good person is not one who thinks correctly or who merely talks about doing the right thing, but rather one who acts correctly in his or her daily life. Sound beliefs and appropriate expressions necessarily precede good conduct.

When it comes to our dealings with our fellows, the opposite order applies. It is well known that we are required to behave appropriately. We must not murder, commit adultery, or steal. It is not obvious to everyone, however, that our words form an important part of our responsibility to others. Slander can destroy reputations. Relationships can fail through insensitive communication or can be strengthened through kindness, consideration and appreciation. Least obvious of all is the importance we ascribe to our motivations in our relationships with others. There is only a small step from inappropriate thoughts to their actualisation.

The cultivation of positive habits of the mind, accompanied by a kind-hearted and genial disposition towards others, are essential elements of a healthy, meaningful and socially responsible life.

What we think, what we say and what we do are, therefore, equally important components of a Jewish life, as represented by Torah, *avodah,* and *gemilut chasadim.*

JEWISH THOUGHT requires us to identify with just causes and to empathise with the needy and downtrodden, in tune with the spiritual aspirations and the prophetic challenges of our tradition. Jewish pride, including pride in the State of Israel and genuine causeless love for others, are ennobling components of responsible Jewish thought.

JEWISH SPEECH includes prayer and blessings, but it is also practised in constructive sentiments, in making others laugh, in brightening their lives, and realising happiness, which is one of God's greatest gifts to humankind. Saying the right thing at the right time and curbing insensitive and harmful remarks, are all part of appropriate Jewish speech.

JEWISH BEHAVIOUR is the ultimate hallmark of a Jewish life, as embodied in our tradition. Contrary to popular belief, Jewish law does not forbid kneeling. Indeed, we kneel and prostrate ourselves before God on the High Holy Days. However, our tradition regards kneeling as a passive form of worship, paying homage to the Creator while doing nothing. Similarly, Jewish ethics demands that we stand up and be counted, that we are tireless and passionate in our pursuit of what is right.

These principles help orientate us and should form the basis of a Jewish Life. *Shimon HaTzadik* taught that the survival of the world itself, depends on these three principles. His example, and the noblest achievements of subsequent generations, teach us that our lives should revolve around these three vital ingredients: Torah, *avodah,* and *gemilut chasadim.*

Professor Yaffa Eliach

A Girl Called Estherke

It was the new month of Sivan, 5704, Spring 1944. Ida, her father, mother, brothers, and sisters were ordered to the train station with the rest of the Jewish community of their Czechoslovakian town. Jews had lived there for generations, but their history was all coming to an abrupt end with a single train ride to Auschwitz. The cattle cars were sealed. More than 80 people were squeezed into a single wagon. Ida and her family managed to stay together, and they comforted each other amidst the choking heat, filth, and fear of the unknown. "Papa, where are they taking us?" Ida asked. "My children, once there was an altar on Mount Moriah in the holy city of Jerusalem. God commanded a father to take his only, beloved son and sacrifice him upon that altar, in order to test his faith in God. As the father was about to fulfil God's command and lifted the knife, the Lord God spoke to Abraham and said, 'Lay not thy hand upon the lad.'"

"Today, my children, there is another huge altar, not on a sacred mountain but in a profane valley of death. There, man is testing his own inhumanity toward his fellow man. The children of Abraham are again a burnt offering, this time by the command of men. But man, unlike God, will not stop the knife. On the contrary, he will sharpen it and fan the altar flames so that they may totally consume their sacrifice. A man-made fire, a knife held by man, must be stopped by man, by a human voice, a human hand. My children, be human in this inhuman valley of death. May the merit of our father Abraham protect you, for whoever saves one Jewish soul, it is as if he saves an entire universe."

On the eve of the holiday of Shavuot, Ida and her family arrived in Auschwitz. The skies above Auschwitz were red. Ida's father

239

spoke as if to himself: "On this day, millenniums ago, God came down to man in fire and smoke and gave his commandments. Today, man is commanding in fire and smoke, 'Thou shalt kill!'"

The Auschwitz platform separated Ida forever from her father, mother, young sisters, and brothers. Ida and her older married sister passed the selection and were put to work for the German civilian population and the Reich's war machine. Ida sorted the clothes of the gassed, folded them neatly, and placed them in symmetrical piles according to size and quality, ready for shipment to Germany to be used by the German people.

One day, as Ida was sorting the clothes, an SS officer walked over to her and said: "Why do you smile, Jewish pig?" Before Ida had a chance to respond, she saw a black boot flying into her face, felt a piercing pain and the gush of blood, and looked down to behold her front teeth on the floor in a puddle of blood. "Pretty white teeth look better on the floor than in a filthy Jewish mouth," said the SS officer. He commanded Ida to wipe the blood off the boot that knocked out her teeth and cheerfully walked away, humming a tune.

Ida quickly assessed her condition. She realised that a gaping hole in her mouth was a sight that an SS officer at a selection would not cherish. She walked over to the pile where thousands of dental bridges were thrown and hastily selected one. She placed it in her swollen mouth and returned to her assigned spot.

That night in the barracks it was especially difficult to fall asleep. Heartbreaking screams were piercing the night, mingled with the wailing of children and mothers as they were torn away from each other. Slowly, the screams subsided and gave way to the usual deadly sounds of the Auschwitz night. Most of the girls in Ida's barracks fell asleep.

Then there was a noise under Ida's three-tiered bunk bed where 36 girls slept, 12 per bed, packed together like sardines. "All we need are rats, just to give them another reason to shoot us," someone said. "Shut up, I am tired," another voice complained. The noise persisted. "Ida, you are the brave one, go down and see what it is." All the other 11 girls had to turn so that Ida could move from the spot where she had wedged herself in.

Under the bed, in a corner, curled up like a frightened porcupine, was a little girl. She told them that when the children's *Aktion* began, she managed to run away and hide in the latrine among the piles of chlorine cans. When it became dark, she ran into the barracks and hid under the bed.

The girl's name was Estherke. She had big, blue, frightened eyes, beautiful blonde curls, and two deep dimples. Ida became instantly attached to the child and kept showing her off to all the others girls, exclaiming: "Doesn't she look like a little actress?" The *blockova* told Ida that she must give up the child, otherwise she, her sister, and maybe all the girls in the barracks, would pay with their lives for harbouring a little criminal. Ida stood there clutching the child. "I will never give her up," she said with determination. She walked over to the *blockova* and asked to speak to her privately. "I know that your boyfriend is Jewish and assumed a false Aryan identity. Killing me, my sister and others will not help. Other girls, and even men outside of this barracks, know it too. We will all keep quiet if you will help to save Estherke. During the day when we are at work, you must keep Estherke in your private room." The *blockova* agreed. Ida had won her first battle for Estherke's life.

Ida loved the child. All her thoughts focused on Estherke. To save that child became her obsession and purpose for living. Rumours began to circulate that *Lager* (camp) C, in BII, Ida's camp, would be evacuated. Ida became frantic. She knew that Estherke would not pass the selection for transfer from one *Lager* to another. With the help of her older sister, whom Estherke called Grandma, and men from the nearby *Lager*, Ida worked out a plan.

When the evacuation materialised, Ida wrapped Estherke in a blanket and threw her over the electrified fence into the waiting arms of a male inmate in the adjacent men's camp, BIId. Later that afternoon, a package flew once more over the fence into Ida's waiting arms. She got back her Estherke. Ida was now in *Zigeunerlager* (gypsy camp).

During that selection, however, Ida was separated from her sister, who, with a group of other girls, was taken away to an unknown destination. Again rumours spread in the camp that the eastern front was nearing and the entire camp was going to be evacuated. Ida began to plan once more how to save her little Estherke. On 18th January 1945, the camp was evacuated. Ida put

Estherke into a knapsack that she had "organised" for this purpose. With Estherke on her back, she set out with the others on the dreadful death march.

The winds blew, the frost bit, the snow fell, and her stomach growled from hunger, but Ida marched on. At night, she shared with Estherke whatever stale bread she had managed to conceal. She comforted the little girl, warmed her tiny frozen hands, and promised her that one day they would be free. After many days of marching and travelling in open cattle cars, a few of the original group that began the death march on 18th January 1945, reached Bergen-Belsen. Ida and her beloved Estherke were among them.

In Bergen-Belsen, Ida found conditions even more difficult than in Auschwitz. With the evacuation of camps in the east, thousands of evacuated inmates were driven into Bergen-Belsen. Absorbing all the evacuees was far beyond the camp's capacity. Water was scarce; a few crumbs of stale bread and inadequate toilet facilities made life almost impossible. Filth, lice, starvation, and epidemics took over. Ida managed to find a job, for which she was given a piece of bread and a warm drink that they insisted on calling coffee. One day, as Ida was cleaning the latrines, she heard a familiar voice calling her name. She looked around, but saw no one she knew. A face covered with blotches and lice, a body covered with rags, was coming closer to her while calling her name. Ida stepped backward. "Ida, don't you recognise your own sister?"

Estherke was overjoyed. "Grandma" was back, the three of them were once more together, just like in Auschwitz. While Ida was out searching for food, Estherke and "Grandma" stayed together. But their happiness did not last long. "Grandma" succumbed to typhus.

Estherke did not leave her side and tried to ease her suffering. One day, while Ida was trying to get some coffee for her dying sister, the squad that came daily to collect the dead took the sister away with the other corpses. Estherke protested, insisting that her "grandma" was still alive. She pleaded, but to no avail. Estherke followed the squad, and when "Grandma" was dumped on the big pile of corpses, Estherke managed to pull her out from under the corpses and did what she could to warm her body with her own.

When Ida returned with the coffee and discovered that Estherke and her sister had been taken away with the dead, she felt her knees giving way as if she would collapse, but her weakness did not last long. Ida was not one to give in to despair. She took the coffee and began to search for Estherke and her sister, and there, near a pile of corpses, she found them. Ida wasted no time. She gave the coffee to Estherke to guard. After mouth-to-mouth resuscitation, massage, and a few drops of coffee on her sister's parched lips, Ida revived her. Thousands were dying, but with Ida's and Estherke's love, "Grandma" recovered. Their joy knew no limit.

On 15th April 1945, Bergen-Belsen was liberated by the British Army. The two sisters and Estherke made their way back home to Czechoslovakia, together with throngs of other refugees. They were all trying to go home, all hoping that perhaps other relatives had also survived and families could be reunited. After finding a temporary shelter in Prague, the three set out in different directions to search for other surviving members of their families. Estherke travelled to Bratislava, hoping that her father, mother, or some of her eight brothers and sisters had survived. Ida and her sister left with similar hopes for their family. The parting was painful for Ida. She and Estherke had not been separated since that fateful night in Auschwitz. The three agreed upon a time and place to meet no matter what the outcome of their search might be.

The two agreed-upon weeks passed. Ida and her sister returned to Prague as planned. But Estherke failed to return. They waited a few more days, but still there was no trace of her. Then Ida launched an intensive search. She travelled to Bratislava, but no one recalled seeing a child who matched Estherke's description. Ida then contacted all children's homes and refugee centres, but to no avail. Estherke had vanished without leaving behind a single trace or clue. After months of searching, Ida gave up. She met and married a young man, a survivor like herself. Her sister was fortunate too, for her husband had managed to survive the camps and one day they ran into each other on a street in Prague.

The sisters parted once more. Ida and her husband went to America. Her sister, her husband, and their newly born baby, became part of the illegal immigration to Israel. They out-manoeuvred the British blockade and finally reached the shores of Palestine.

In the early 1950s, Ida travelled to the young State of Israel to ity and the Judean hills, Ida stepped forward and led her beloved Estherke to the bridal canopy.

There was a strange presence in the air. Ida was sure that her father was present at this very holy moment in Jerusalem. She could even see the smile on his face and hear his gentle voice: "Whoever saves a single soul, it is as if he saves an entire universe."

Based on interview by Marcy Miller with Mrs Ida Hoenig, 16th April 1976.

BUILD THE FUTURE

Build the Future

Rabbi Andrew Shaw

Seventy days ago, you embarked on a period of commemoration, building a personal memorial day by day, and learning in memory of those who perished in the Holocaust. Seventy days later, we hope that you have developed a greater understanding of your Judaism and the active role in it which only you can fulfil.

Just over 70 years ago, who would have believed there could be any positive future for the Jewish people? Entire communities wiped out, historic synagogues destroyed, hundreds of years of Jewish life eradicated as if they had never existed, and more than six million of our people lost.

However, just as we did after previous tragedies such as the destruction of the temples in Jerusalem with enormous loss of life, we rebuilt. After the ashes of the Holocaust, the State of Israel was formed, communities were recreated and the vibrancy that had been part of our history began to flourish. Now we can marvel and thank God for how far we have come in such a short time.

It is true that antisemitism has not disappeared and its global rise is very worrying. However, over the last 70 days, all across the world, we have dedicated ourselves not just to remembering what antisemitism can lead to if unchallenged, but we have engaged in strengthening that which the antisemite wishes to crush – our Jewish identity.

There are many days of celebration in the Jewish calendar. For example, Chanukah celebrates the Jews' victory over the mighty Greek empire, while Purim celebrates the day we remember our victory against Haman, despite the odds. Both times, it seemed that the Jews or Judaism were destined for destruction. Miraculously, we survived and the Jewish nation triumphed.

Today is the first day of Pesach – when the Jewish people were liberated from Egypt to begin the journey to the Promised Land. Seventy years ago the Jews of Europe were liberated too, and began their journey forward. Some – like Estherke (see Essay 70) – made it to the Promised Land.

So today, on Pesach, the festival of our freedom, you have even more to celebrate – simultaneously remembering our past and celebrating both the completion of this book and the start of further exploration into the fascinating world of Judaism. The remarkable festival of Pesach is a perfect time for this with its evocative rituals and literature which teach its messages.

Last night was *Seder* night. You sat around your table and heard the four questions that we have been asking for millennia. As Jews, we have always asked questions. Some have been mundane, others central to our existence and survival. Today, ask yourself two more: First, what have I achieved from this project? This answer is self-evident: you have completed the sacred task of learning in memory of another Jew, reclaiming a "number," and replacing it with a name. Second, what's next? This is the challenge that faces us all.

There is a custom in Judaism to make a *siyum*, a celebratory meal, upon the completion of a segment of Jewish learning. Most commonly a *siyum* is made upon finishing a tractate of Talmud. We recite two Aramaic words after completing the tractate, "*Hadran alach*," meaning "we shall return to you." There is a powerful message here: at soon as Jews finish a segment of learning they commit to return to their learning, to continue the journey, to capitalise on the momentum already achieved.

Seventy days ago, we began this project together. We have studied and remembered together. Now, as we end the book and the project, we should collectively assert, *Hadran alach* – we shall return to you. We have only provided a taste of each topic. We cannot distil all the wisdom of Judaism into 70 topics; it is for all of us to take the studying further. That, I believe, is our challenge.

With that in mind, I want to turn your attention to "Day 71 – Building the Future." After *Yom Tov*, the 70 Days website will be transformed. By logging into the website, you will be able to continue your own learning, wherever you are in the world, via numerous resources. If you have not done so already, please sign up to the Build the Future campaign by visiting www.70for70.com from *Chol HaMoed*, Pesach 5775, and make sure that your 70 days of learning are a springboard to further engagement with our remarkable heritage.

And finally, thank you for taking part in a project which I hope has been a fitting commemoration to the victims of the Shoah, 70 years ago. To emphasise the importance of further engagement, I will conclude with the words of Rabbi Lord Jonathan Sacks which opened this book: 'If each of us in the coming year makes a significant personal gesture to show that Judaism is alive and being lived, there can be no more momentous signal to humanity that evil does not have the final victory, because *Am Yisrael Chai* – the Jewish people lives.'

Build the Future Photos

With thanks to: Ganzach Kiddush Hashem, Yad Vashem & USHMM for permission to print these photos.

Poland – 1945. *Desecrated Torah scrolls, lying in the street after liberation.*

Feldafing – 1946. *Demonstrations in support of immigration to Eretz Israel in a DP (Displaced Person's) camp in Germany. The British refused to increase entry quotas for Jews to Palestine after WWII and 100,000s of Jews languished in camps all over Germany and Austria.*

Poland – 1946. *These children were retrieved from Polish non-Jews and from monasteries and convents by Leib Zamoscz (pictured).*

Prague – August 1946. *Chief Rabbi Herzog is met by child survivors under the care of the* Vaad Hatzalah, *who are making* aliyah.

Athens 1946. *10 married couples just before their aliyah*

Teenage survivors of the holocaust at prayer, soon after their arrival in Israel

Biographies

Rabbi David Aaron is Rosh Yeshiva of Yeshivat Orayta and founder and Dean of Isralight, an organization that strives to inspire Jewish living through Education and Leadership Training. He has taught thousands of students and reached hundreds of thousands through appearances on TV. www.rabbidavidaaron.com

Dayan Yonason Abraham was born in London before moving to Australia in 1985 to join the Lakewood Kollel Beis Hatalmud in Melbourne. In 1995, he became Rabbi of the Caulfield Hebrew Congregation in Melbourne and in 1997 became a member of the Melbourne Beth Din. Dayan Abraham was invited to join the London Beth Din in 2001.

Rabbi Hershel Becker, Rabbi of Young Israel of Kendall, Miami, was born to Holocaust survivors who maintained a deep love of Torah and Judaism. He is the author of *Love Peace: Blueprints for Lasting Relationships*, which provides the tools for establishing harmonious homes, organizations, and communities.

Rabbi Dr Harvey Belovski is the Rabbi of Golders Green Synagogue, London and principal of Rimon Jewish Primary School. He teaches at LSJS in London, is the rabbinic consultant to University Jewish Chaplaincy and is a guest lecturer at King's College, London. He is an author and a regular broadcaster on BBC Radio 2.

Dayan Ivan Binstock is Rabbi of St John's Wood Synagogue, having served a number of London communities since 1972. He joined the London Beth Din in 1989 and is Principal of the North West London Jewish Day School.

Rabbi Davey Blackman and his wife Deborah helped to found the Jewish Learning Centre (JLC) in Sydney, Australia. They have served as the senior Rabbi and Rebbetzin team of the JLC since its inception 18 years ago.

Dr Erica Brown is an educator and author who consults for the Jewish Agency and The Jewish Federation of Greater Washington and is a faculty member of the Wexner Foundation. She is the author of eight books, including *Leadership in the Wilderness*.

Rabbi Steven Burg is the Eastern Director of the Simon Wiesenthal Center & Museum of Tolerance. He worked for NCSY for 22 years, starting out as Programme Coordinator for the Central East Region of NCSY and then serving as International Director.

Cantor Albert Chait is currently the Senior Minister at United Hebrew Congregation in Leeds. He is also the Jewish Chaplain to the Leeds Hospitals NHS Trust and a well-respected and highly sought after international cantor.

Elana Chesler teaches regularly on behalf of United Synagogue Living and Learning and holds an MA and BEd in Jewish Studies. Elana is currently employed by Capita PLC.

Father Patrick Desbois is a Roman Catholic priest, Head of the Commission for Relations with Judaism of the French Bishops' Conference, and Consultant to the Vatican. He is the co-founder and President of Yahad-In Unum, an organization founded 15 years ago, to locate the sites of unknown and unmarked Holocaust mass graves across Europe.

Rabbi Mark Dratch is the Executive Vice President of the Rabbinical Council of America. After serving as a pulpit rabbi for 22 years, he founded JSafe: The Jewish Institute Supporting an Abuse Free Environment. He served as Instructor of Jewish Studies and Philosophy at Yeshiva University.

Avraham Duvdevani is the Chair of the World Zionist Organization. He previously served as the Co-Chair of JNF and worked for the World Zionist Organization. He is a member of the Jewish Agency Executive and chairs the Holocaust Restitution Committee.

Rabbi Joseph Dweck is Senior Rabbi to the Spanish and Portuguese Jews' Congregation of London, England.

Professor Yaffa Eliach is a historian and author, and is probably best known for creating the "Tower of Life," made up by 1,500 photographs for permanent display at the US Holocaust Museum in Washington, DC. She is the author *of Hasidic Tales of the Holocaust.*

Sir Martin Gilbert is Winston Churchill's official biographer, and a leading historian of the Holocaust and of Israel. He is the author of 88 books. He is an Honorary Fellow of Merton College, Oxford.

Rabbi Mordechai Ginsbury is Rabbi of Hendon United Synagogue, Principal of Hasmonean Primary School, and Director of P'eir, the United Synagogue's training facility for US Rabbis and Rebbetzins.

Chief Rabbi Pinchas Goldschmidt is the Chief Rabbi of Moscow, Russia since 1993, head of the rabbinical court of the Commonwealth of Independent States (CIS), president of the Conference of European Rabbis, and an officer of the Russian Jewish Congress (RJC).

Chief Rabbi Dr Warren Goldstein is Chief Rabbi of South Africa and a *dayan*. He has created various educational and humanitarian initiatives across the country and published numerous books on government, morality, and society. He has a PhD in human rights and constitutional law.

Rabbi Micah Greenland is the International Director of NCSY, the youth movement of the Orthodox Union, and is a sought-after speaker on a variety of Jewish topics.

Ruth Ellen Gruber is an American author and journalist who has chronicled Jewish developments in Europe for more than 25 years. She is the recipient of a Guggenheim Fellowship, Poland's Knight's Cross of the Order of Merit, and other awards. She coordinates the web site www.jewish-heritage-europe.eu.

Rabbi Dr Michael Harris is Rabbi of The Hampstead Synagogue, London. He is a Research Fellow at The London School of Jewish Studies and an Affiliated Lecturer in the Faculty of Divinity, University of Cambridge.

Rebbetzin Tzipporah Heller is a faculty member of Neve Yerushalayim College in Jerusalem. Her areas of expertise include textual analysis of biblical literature and Jewish philosophy with an emphasis on the teachings of Maimonides and Maharal. She is the author of a number of books and writes a weekly column.

Rabbi Malcolm Herman is the Associate National Director of seed UK. Rabbi Herman developed seed's pioneering network of educational programs for parents in Jewish schools across the UK. He is a sought after speaker across the UK and beyond, known for inspiring audiences with both humour and wisdom. www.seed.uk.net

Rabbi Aubrey Hersh is an editor of the *70 Days for 70 years* book and an international lecturer, based at the JLE in London, where he has taught since 1996. He also runs educational and history tours to most European cities. www.aubreyhersh.com

Anthony Julius is a British lawyer and academic, known for his actions on behalf of Diana, Princess of Wales, Deborah Lipstadt, and Heather Mills. He is Deputy Chairman of the London law firm Mischon de Reya.

Jack Kagan grew up in Novogrodek, in modern day Belarus. He escaped a death camp and joined the famous band of Jewish resistance fighters headed by the Bielski brothers.

Rabbi Ari Kahn is Director of Foreign Student Programs at Bar Ilan University and a senior lecturer in Jewish Studies. He is also a senior lecturer at MaTaN, Jerusalem. Rabbi Kahn is a renowned speaker worldwide, authors a weekly analysis of the weekly Torah reading, *Explorations,* and has a readership of thousands.

Rabbi Shaya Karlinsky is the Dean of Darche Noam Institutions, Yeshivat Darche Noam/Shapell's and Midreshet Rachel for Women in Jerusalem.

Rabbi Paysach Krohn is a *mohel,* author and international lecturer on topics related to ethics and spiritual growth. He has written the *"Maggid"* series of books inspired by the stories of Rabbi Sholom Schwadron, who was known as the "Maggid of Jerusalem".

Rabbi Michael Laitner is the Director of Education for United Synagogue Living and Learning and an assistant rabbi at Finchley Synagogue, London. He is a qualified solicitor.

Rabbi Dr Norman Lamm, former Chancellor and President of Yeshiva University and *Rosh HaYeshiva* of Rabbi Isaac Elchanan

Theological Seminary, is one of the most gifted and profound Jewish thinkers of our time. He is a prolific author in the field of Jewish philosophy and law and a distinguished academician.

Chief Rabbi Yisrael Meir Lau is the Chief Rabbi of Tel Aviv, Israel, and Chairman of Yad Vashem. He previously served as the Ashkenazi Chief Rabbi of Israel from 1993 to 2003. Lau was rescued from the Buchenwald concentration camp and immigrated to Mandate Palestine with his brother Naphtali in July 1945.

Rabbi Eli & Rebbetzin Lauren Levin are associate Rabbi & Rebbetzin at the popular South Hampstead Synagogue in London, UK. Lauren is also the Dean of the Judi Back Women's Institute for Torah Studies and serves as Community Educator and *Yoetzet Halachah* at Finchley Synagogue, London, where she advises women on issues of women's health and halachah.

Rabbi Dov Lipman was elected to the 19th Knesset as a member of the Yesh Atid party. He holds rabbinic ordination from Ner Israel Rabbinical College in Baltimore, Maryland and a masters in Education from Johns Hopkins University. He has published four books about Judaism.

Professor Deborah Lipstadt is Dorot Professor of Modern Jewish and Holocaust Studies at Emory University, Atlanta. She has been appointed by both Presidents Clinton and Obama to the United States Holocaust Memorial Council and she chairs the Holocaust Council's Committee on Holocaust Denial and Antisemitism.

Dr Naftali Loewenthal lectures in Jewish Spirituality at University College London (UCL). He authored *Communicating the Infinite: the Emergence of the Habad School* and directs the Chabad Research Unit.

Chief Rabbi Ephraim Mirvis is the 11th Chief Rabbi of the United Hebrew Congregations of the Commonwealth. He has previously served as Chief Rabbi of Ireland and as Rabbi of Finchley Synagogue, London. He is the founding rabbi of Sacks Morasha Jewish Primary School as well as of the Kinloss Learning Centre. He is also President of LSJS and a frequent contributor to the media.

Rebbetzin Lori Palatnick is an international speaker, author, and media personality. She is the Founding Director of The Jewish Women's Renaissance Project (JWRP), an initiative that has annually brought thousands of women on subsidised programmes to Israel, from a total of 18 countries, to inspire them with the beauty and wisdom of their heritage.

Rebbetzin Holly Pavlov is the founder and director of She'arim College of Jewish Studies for Women in Jerusalem. Rebbetzin Pavlov is an author and international lecturer and is recognised as one of the foremost educators in the world of adult education today.

Rabbi Doron (Laurence) Perez is the Head of the World Mizrachi Movement based in Jerusalem. He was formally head of the Mizrachi Movement of South Africa, the Senior Rabbi of the Mizrachi Shul and Head of Yeshiva College School.

Professor Laurence Rees is a former Head of BBC TV History Programmes and Creative Director of BBC TV History. He has written seven history books on the Second World War. His career as a writer and filmmaker, specialising in the Nazis and WWII, stretches back nearly 20 years and has won him several awards. www.laurencerees.com

Sara Yoheved Rigler is the author of three best-sellers and is a popular international lecturer on Jewish spirituality. She is one of the most popular authors on Aish.com.www.sararigler.com

Rabbi Dr Shlomo Riskin is the founding Rabbi of Lincoln Square Synagogue, New York, which he led for 12 years; founding Rabbi of the Israeli town of Efrat. He is also the founder and Chancellor of the Ohr Torah Stone Institutions, a network of high schools, colleges, and graduate programmes in the United States and Israel.

Rabbi Shaul Robinson has been the Senior Rabbi at Lincoln Square Synagogue, New York since 2005. Rabbi Robinson was formerly the Rabbi of Barnet Synagogue, London. rabbi@lss.org

Rabbi Dr Jonathan Rosenblatt has been the Senior Rabbi of the Riverdale Jewish Center for almost 30 years. He holds degrees in Comparative Literature and Modern British Literature.

Rabbi Daniel Rowe is Education Director at Aish UK. He holds a BA in philosophy from University College London (UCL). Rabbi Rowe is considered one of the most dynamic Jewish speakers in the UK, teaching in campuses, communities, and schools across the country.

Dr Robert Rozett has been Director of the Yad Vashem Libraries since 1993 and has worked at Yad Vashem in various capacities since 1981. He has been researching, writing about, lecturing, and teaching about the Holocaust for more than 30 years.

Rabbi YY Rubinstein. In 2000, *The Independent* newspaper cited him as being amongst five people in Britain to turn to for advice. He is the author of eight books and teaches at Yeshivat Sh'or Yoshuv in New York. In addition, he writes a regular column for *Mishpacha* magazine.

Rabbi Lord Jonathan Sacks is a global religious leader, philosopher, and the author of more than 25 books. For 22 years, until September 2013, he served as Chief Rabbi of the United Hebrew Congregations of the Commonwealth. Currently a professor at Yeshiva University, New York University, and King's College London, Rabbi Sacks is a frequent contributor to national and international media. www.rabbisacks.org

Rabbi Dr Jacob J Schacter is University Professor of Jewish History and Jewish Thought and Senior Scholar at the Center for the Jewish Future, Yeshiva University.

Chief Rabbi Michael Schudrich is currently Chief Rabbi of Poland, having previously served as Rabbi of Warsaw and Lodz. Born in the USA, he also served as Rabbi of the Jewish Community of Japan.

Rabbi Yitzchak Schochet is Rabbi of Mill Hill Synagogue, London. He served on the previous Chief Rabbi's Cabinet and as Chairman of the Rabbinical Council of the United Synagogue. He has a popular weekly column in the *Jewish News* and can often be seen on television, including the BBC as a panellist for The Big Questions as well as on CNN.

Rabbi Andrew Shaw is the Director of Living and Learning at the United Synagogue. He is also the Director of US Futures and the Community Development Rabbi of Stanmore Synagogue, London. He is the co-founder of Tribe and was the general editor of the *60 Days for 60 Years* series.

Rabbi Yaakov Asher Sinclair is a lecturer in talmudic logic and philosophy at Ohr Somayach/Tanenbaum College in Jerusalem, and is a senior staff writer of the Torah internet publications *Ohrnet* and *Torah Weekly*, as well as *Seasons of the Moon*.

Rebbetzin Rivkah Slonim is the Education Director at the Rohr Chabad Center for Jewish Student Life and an instructor of Jewish Bio-Medical Ethics at Binghamton University. She is an internationally known and much sought after teacher, lecturer, author, and activist.

Rabbi Gil Student is a Torah pioneer on the Internet; his award-winning Hirhurim blog has transformed into the popular Torah Musings website. He worked as Managing Editor of OU Press and has published widely on the interface between Torah and contemporary issues in newspapers, magazines, and journals.

Rabbi Gideon Sylvester is the United Synagogue's Rabbi in Israel. Prior to making *aliyah*, he served as Rabbi of Radlett United Synagogue. Rabbi Gideon has also worked as an adviser at the Office of the Prime Minister of Israel and teaches Torah and Human Rights in Jerusalem. He tweets @GideonDSylveste

Rabbanit Shani Taragin is currently pursuing her PhD in Tanach while teaching Tanach in Midreshet Lindenbaum and at MaTaN, Migdal Oz, Sha'alvim for Women, Lander's College, and the Women's Beit Midrash in Efrat. She is a graduate of Nishmat's Keren Ariel Program as a halachic advisor in issues of family purity law.

Rabbi Dr Akiva Tatz is a physician, author, and lecturer and has written a number of books on the subject of Jewish thought and philosophy which have been translated into various languages. He teaches at the Jewish Learning Exchange (JLE) in London and internationally, and recordings of his lectures are widely distributed.

H.E. Ambassador Daniel Taub is a British-born Israeli diplomat, lawyer, and writer who currently serves as Israel's Ambassador to the United Kingdom. He is an expert in international law, with specialisations in counter-terrorism and the laws of war.

Rabbi Hanoch Teller is a modern-day *maggid* (storyteller of yore). He has written 28 books and is a senior docent at the Yad Vashem Holocaust Museum in Jerusalem. He has also produced a number of DVDs on Jewish history and Jewish life.

Rabbi Dr Abraham Twerski is descended from distinguished rabbinic ancestry. He is a resident psychiatrist and an Associate Professor of Psychiatry. A prolific author, he has written more than 50 books on topics such as stress, self esteem, spirituality, drug and alchohol dependency. He appears regularly as a radio and television guest.

Rabbi Steven Weil is Executive Vice President of the Orthodox Union. Rabbi Weil began his career teaching, and then moved to pulpit work. Rabbi Weil is a popular teacher and lecturer, having delivered invocations for former President Bush and Governor Schwarzenegger, amongst others.

Rabbi Berel Wein is the founder and director of the Destiny Foundation, and has popularized Jewish History via his 15 books, documentary films, lectures, history courses and educational tours.

Elie Wiesel is a Romanian-born professor and political activist. He is the author of 57 books, including *Night*, a work based on his experiences during the Holocaust in the Auschwitz, Buna, and Buchenwald concentration camps. He was awarded the Nobel Peace Prize in 1986.

Sir Nicholas Winton MBE, is a British humanitarian who organised the rescue of 669 children from Nazi-occupied Czechoslovakia on the eve of the Second World War. The British press has dubbed him the "British Schindler."

Rabbi Dr Raphael Zarum is Dean of the London School of Jewish Studies (LSJS). He has an MA in Adult Education from the Institute of Education in London and a PhD in theoretical physics in 1999. He is the creator of the *Torah L'Am* crash course.

Rabbi Shraga Feivel Zimmerman is the spiritual head of the Gateshead Jewish community. He lived previously in New York where he was a Dayan in Washington Heights and a community rabbi and teacher in Monsey. He is recognised as an authority in *Halachah* and is a much sought-after speaker in the UK and abroad.

Glossary

A"h (Alav – Male, Aleha – Female Hashalom)   Shortened way to write "Peace Be Upon Him/Her". Written after the name of a deceased Jew.

Ahavat Yisrael   Love of one's fellow Jew.

Aliyah   Emigrating to Israel.

Amidah   The central, quiet prayer in Judaism. It is recited three time a day. Also known as the "*Shemonah Esreh*".

Aron Kodesh   Holy Ark. The Ark is the holiest place in the Synagogue. In most synagogues the *Aron Kodesh* is on the Eastern wall, so that when we face the ark, we are facing the holy city of Jerusalem, where the Holy Temples once stood.

Ashkenaz/Ashkenazic   Referring to practices of Jewish communities which developed in Germany and Eastern Europe.

Avodah   Service. Often refers to Prayer.

Baal Shem Tov   Rabbi Yisrael ben Eliezer (1760 CE), often called Baal Shem Tov or Besht, was a Jewish mystical rabbi. He is considered to be the founder of Chassidism.

Bar Kochba   Simon bar Kochba (died 135 CE) was the Jewish leader of what is known as the Bar Kochba revolt against the Roman Empire in 132 CE, establishing an independent Jewish state which he ruled for three years as Nasi ("Prince"). His state was conquered by the Romans in 135 CE following a two and half-year war.

Bar Mitzvah   A boy who has reached the age of 13 and is consequently obligated to observe the commandments; also a ceremony marking the fact that a boy has reached this age.

Bat Mitzvah   A girl who has reached the age of 12 and is consequently obligated to observe the commandments; also a ceremony marking the fact that a girl has reached this age.

Beit HaMikdash   Holy Temple (twice destroyed) in Jerusalem.

Birkat Kohanim   The priestly blessing, also recited in some prayers and given as a general blessing at significant times.

Brit Milah The ritual circumcision of a male Jewish child on or after the 8th day of his life, or of a male convert to Judaism.

Chag (pl. Chagim) Festival/s.

Chanukah An eight-day festival celebrating the miracles and re-dedication of the Second Temple in Jerusalem after it was defiled by the Greeks.

Chassidut/Chassidism (adj. Chassidic) Pious ones. Usually used in reference to a particular segment of Orthodoxy founded by the Baal Shem Tov in Poland in the mid–18th century. There are various groups, each of which follows their own *rebbe* as their leader.

Chesed An act of kindness.

Chumash A Torah in printed book form, as opposed to the Torah scroll. The word comes from the Hebrew word for five – *chamesh*. A more formal term is *Chamishah Chumshei Torah*, "five fifths of Torah".

Chuppah/To perform a Chuppah The wedding canopy or wedding ceremony.

Daven (pl. Davening) To pray.

Elul The 6th month in the Jewish calendar. It precedes Rosh Hashanah and is a particular time for self introspection and preparation for the *Yamim Noraim* (High Holy Days).

Eretz Yisrael The land of Israel.

Esau The elder son of Isaac.

Eshet Chayil Woman of Valour. Also the name of a song found at the end of the biblical Book of Proverbs. It is widely sung on Friday night before the Sabbath meal and details the attributes of a virtuous wife or ideal woman.

First Temple The First Temple, was the Holy Temple (*Beit Ha-Mikdash*) in ancient Jerusalem, on the Temple Mount (also known as Mount Zion), before its destruction by Nebuchadnezzar.

Gemara Commentary on the Mishnah. The Mishnah and Gemara together form the Talmud.

Geshmak Yiddish word for 'delicious'.

Haggadah A Jewish text that sets the order of the Passover Seder. Reading the *Haggadah* at the Seder table is a fulfillment of the

Scriptural commandment to each Jew to "tell your child" of the Jewish liberation from slavery in Egypt.

Halachah (**adj.** *Halachic*) The complete body of rules and practises that Jews are bound to follow, including biblical commandments, commandments issued by the Rabbis and binding customs.

Hallel A collection of psalms said on joyous days in the Jewish Calendar, such as *Yom Tov* and *Rosh Chodesh*.

Har Sinai Mount Sinai. The mountain at which the Jewish people received the Torah.

Hashem The Name – a common way to refer to God outside of prayer.

High Priest See *Kohen Gadol*.

Holy of Holies The inner sanctuary of the Temple, in which the Ark of the Covenant was kept.

Ishmael Abraham's first son, born of Abraham's marriage to Sarah's handmaiden Hagar.

Jacob The third of the the Jewish Patriarchs. The son of Isaac and Rebeccah, and the younger twin brother of Esau.

Kabbalah/Kabbalistic/ Kabbalist Jewish mystical tradition.

Kaddish A prayer sanctifying God's name, often associated with mourners.

Kadosh Holy.

Kedoshim Holy people/martyrs.

Kedushah The central part of the repetition of the *Amidah*.

Kehillah A community which provides Jewish facilities for its members from cradle to grave.

Kelal Yisrael 'The Whole of Israel'. A Hebrew expression used to define the Jewish Nation.

Kenesset Yisrael The concept of the Jewish people being defined as one community.

Kiddush The prayer that is recited at the beginning of a festive meal on *Shabbat* and festivals, over a cup of wine.

Kiddush Hashem   Sanctifying God's name. Often related to the concept of giving up one's life for God.

***Kippot* (sing. *Kippah*)**   Head covering worn by Jewish men.

***Kohen* (pl. *Kohanim*)**   Jewish priest/s.

Keriyat Ha-Torah   Public reading of the Torah from a *Sefer Torah* during services.

Kugel   A savoury dish of potatoes or other vegetables often eaten on *Shabbat* or Festivals.

Lashon ha-ra   The halachic term for derogatory speech about another person. *Lashon ha-ra* forbids the use even of statements which are true but negative.

Levi/Levite   A member of the Hebrew tribe of Levi, whose original function was to provided assistance to the priests in the Holy Temple.

Maimonides   See Rambam.

Ma'ariv   The evening service.

Maharal   Acronym for Rabbi Judah Loew ben Bezalel, (c. 1520–1609), widely known as the Maharal of Prague, the Hebrew acronym of "*Morenu ha-Rav Loew*," ("Our Teacher, Rabbi Loew"). An important talmudic scholar, Jewish mystic, and philosopher in Bohemia.

Mazel   Luck.

Megillah   Scroll. There are five *megillot* (pl.) including Esther which is read on Purim and Ruth which is read on Shavuot.

Megillat Ruth   The Scroll of the Story of Ruth.

Melachah   The 39 categories of defined creative activity that are forbidden on *Shabbat*.

Menorah   A sacred candelabrum with seven branches used in the ancient temple in Jerusalem. Nowadays often used in connection to Chanukah.

Messiah   The messiah (king) will bring all Jews back to Judaism and the Land of Israel. His eventual redeeming of the Jewish people serves as one of the 13 attributes of faith.

Midrash   Stories or short teachings elaborating on incidents in the Bible to derive a principle of Jewish Law or provide a moral lesson.

Mikveh   A special pool of water, used for the purpose of attaining ritual purity.

Minchah   The afternoon service.

Minyan   The quorum necessary to recite certain prayers, consisting of 10 adult Jewish men.

Miriam   Sister of Moses and Aaron, and the daughter of Amram and Yocheved. She appears first in the Book of Exodus in the Tanach.

Mishnah   A foundation Jewish legal text of the Oral Law. The structure of the Mishnah was compiled by Rabbi Yehudah Ha-Nasi in approximately 180 BCE.

Mitzvah (**pl.** *mitzvot*)   Any of the 613 commandments that Jews are obligated to observe; it can also refer to any Jewish religious obligation, or more generally to any good deed.

Mohel   A Jew who performs the rite of circumcision.

Moses/Moshe   The person who led the Jewish people out of exile in Egypt, through the desert to Mount Sinai where they received the Torah. The greatest of all Jewish prophets.

Muchni   A mechanism designed to lower the laver into contact with the water table. A term used to describe an in-depth educational talk.

Musar   A thousand-year-old Jewish system for personal growth, specifically in the realm of character improvement. *Musar* provides a distinctively Jewish answer to the sorts of questions thinking people are likely to ask about life.

Ne'ilah   The closing service of Yom Kippur.

Nun   14th Letter of the hebrew alphabet.

Oral Law   Jewish teachings explaining and elaborating on the Written Torah, handed down orally until the 2nd century CE, when they began to be written down in what became the Talmud.

Orechim (**pl.**)   Guests or Visitors.

Parashah/t A section of the Torah.

Pesach A festival commemorating the Exodus from Egypt; also known as Passover.

Purim A holiday celebrating the rescue of the Jewish people from extermination at the hands of the chief minister to the King of Persia (4th century BCE) as related in the biblical Book of Esther.

Rabbi Akiva One of the greatest Rabbis recorded in the Talmud. Died a martyr for the Jewish people c. 135 CE.

Rambam Acronym for Rabbi Moshe ben Maimon (1135–1204). One of the greatest medieval Jewish scholars. Also known as Maimonides and renowned for his codification of Jewish Law and his *Guide to the Perplexed*.

Ramban (Nachmanides) Acronym for Rabbi Moshe ben Nachman (1194–c. 1270). Catalan rabbi, philosopher, physician, Kabbalist, Talmudist and biblical commentator.

Rashi Acronym for Rabbi Shlomo Yitzchaki (1040–1105). The most famous Jewish Commentator who wrote on the entire Torah and Talmud.

Reb/Rebbi Grand Rabbi. This person is the leader of a chassidic community, often believed to have special, mystical power.

Rosh Chodesh The beginning of every Jewish month.

Rosh Hashanah The Jewish New Year.

Rosh Yeshivah The spiritual head of a yeshivah.

Sandek The term used for a person honoured at a Jewish *brit milah* (circumcision) ceremony who holds the baby boy while the *mohel* performs the *brit milah*.

Sarah One of the four matriarchs. Was married to Abraham.

Second Temple Second Holy Temple in Jerusalem which was destroyed by the Romans in 70 CE.

Selichot Special prayers for forgiveness, said on fast days and also during the period preceding Yom Kippur.

Shabbat (pl. Shabbatot) The Jewish Sabbath.

Seder The Passover *seder* is a Jewish ritual feast that marks the beginning of the Jewish holiday of Passover.

Sefer Torah (pl. Sifrei Torah)   A Torah Scroll.

Shaliach Tzibur   A Jewish prayer leader in the Synagogue also known as *Chazzan* (Cantor).

Shalom   Peace. Also used as a greeting of welcome.

Shavuot   Pentecost. A festival celebrating the day God gave the Jews the Torah at Mount Sinai.

Shechinah   The English transliteration of a Biblical Hebrew word meaning dwelling or settling, and denotes the dwelling or settling of the Divine Presence of God, especially in the Temple in Jerusalem.

Shema Yisrael   Listen [O] Israel. – The first two words of a section of the Torah, and the title of a prayer that serves as a centerpiece of the morning and evening Jewish prayer services. It is the quintessential Jewish declaration of faith.

Shiur   A lesson or lecture on any Torah topic.

Shiva   Literally means 'seven' and refers to the initial seven days of mourning (inclusive of the day of burial) observed by a mourner.

Shlep (pl. Shlepping)   Yiddish word meaning 'to carry with great effort'.

Shochet   A person officially certified as competent to kill cattle and poultry for food in the manner prescribed by Jewish law.

Shul   Yiddish word for 'synagogue'.

Simchah   Joy. Also used to describe a happy occasion.

Simchat Torah   Festival of the Rejoicing of the Torah when we celebrate the completion of the Torah reading for that cycle and immediately begin reading a new cycle, reading it again from the start.

Sinai (Sinaitic)   It is situated between the Mediterranean Sea and the Red Sea. Mount Sinai is the mountain on which the Torah was given to the Jewish people after the Exodus from Egypt.

Sivan   Third Hebrew month.

Sodom   Sodom is a city mentioned in the Book of Genesis which was destroyed by fire.

Succah   The temporary dwelling lived in during the festival of *Succot*.

Succot   A festival commemorating God's protection in the wilderness and also the final harvest; also known as the Feast of Tabernacles or the Festival of Ingathering.

Talmud Torah   A name for a Jewish Primary School.

Talmud/Talmudic   The most significant collection of the Jewish Oral Tradition interpreting the Torah.

Talmid Chacham   Wise student. An honorific title given to one well versed in Jewish law, in effect, a Torah scholar.

Tanach   An acronym made up of the first letters of the three sections of the Hebrew Bible, namely *Torah* (Pentateuch), *Nevi'im* (Prophets) and *Ketuvim* (Writings). Also known as the Written Law.

Tefillah   Prayer or Service.

Tefillin   Biblical passages on parchment scrolls placed in small leather boxes and affixed with leather straps; worn during morning prayer by adult men other than on *Shabbat* or *Yom Tov*.

Teshuvah   Repentence. The way of atoning for sin in Judaism.

Tisha Be-Av   The ninth day of the Jewish month of Av. The destruction of both Temples, as well as much other Jewish suffering, happened on this day throughout history.

Torah   In its narrowest sense, the first five books of the Bible: Genesis, Exodus, Leviticus, Numbers and Deuteronomy, sometimes called the Pentateuch; in its broadest sense, Torah is the entire body of Jewish teachings.

Tosafot/Tosafist   Tosafists were rabbis from France and Germany in the medieval period who wrote commentaries on the Talmud.

Tzaddik   Righteous person.

Written Law   See *Tanach*.

Yam Suf   The sea that God miraculously split at the culmination of the Exodus from Egypt.

Yeshivah   An academy of religious study.

Yishuv   Settlement. Referring to the body of Jewish residents in Palestine, before the establishment of the State of Israel. The term came into use in the 1880s and continued to be used until 1948.

Yizkor   Memorial service held on certain Holy Days in honour of deceased relatives and members of the Community.

Yom Kippur   The Day of Atonement; a day set aside for fasting, prayer and repenting for the sins of the previous year.

Yom Tov (**pl. *Yamim Tovim***)   A festival and holy day, namely Rosh Hashanah, Yom Kippur, *Pesach*, *Shavuot* and *Succot*.

Yom Yerushalayim   Jerusalem Day. Celebrating the reunification of Jerusalem during the Six Day War of 1967.

Yud   Tenth Letter of the hebrew alphabet.

Zeide   Yiddish word for grandfather.

Zohar   The Zohar is the foundational work in the literature of Jewish mystical thought known as Kabbalah

Z"l (*Zichrono Livracha*)   "Of blessed memory." Written after the name of deceased Jews of good character.

יד ושם
Yad Vashem

Let No Holocaust Victim Be Forgotten!

יד ושם
Yad Vashem

Through your participation in **"70 Days for 70 Years"** you have demonstrated your commitment to commemorate the life of a Shoah victim.

Over four million names and short biographies of Jews murdered in the Holocaust are recorded in Yad Vashem's Central Database of Shoah Victims' Names. The names of millions of victims remain unknown – and time is running out.

You can help complete this historic task by submitting a Page of Testimony for any Holocaust victim you have information about.

Pages of Testimony are available online or by request. For assistance and more information, please contact: names.outreach@yadvashem.org.il

DONATE NOW on the Yad Vashem Website to support the ongoing efforts to collect, digitize, catalogue and upload the names and life stories of Shoah victims, so they will always be remembered.

 www.yadvashem.org/database

March OF THE LIVING UK

An experience you'll never forget.

(Which is the whole idea)

Join us for a very special March of the Living in 2015, commemorating the 70th anniversary of the liberation of Auschwitz.

On 16 April 2015, thousands of Jewish people will march three kilometers from Auschwitz to Birkenau, the largest concentration camp complex built by the Nazis during World War II.

The March commemorates Yom Hashoah, Holocaust Remembrance Day. You can be there – along with over 10,000 participants from more than 40 countries.

Prior to the March, you will travel as part of a small group, visiting the concentration camps of Auschwitz-Birkenau and Majdanek, as well as historic Jewish sites in Poland.

Like previous Marchers, you will find that the trip has a profound impact, giving you a new sense of self. It will be an experience that will remain with you for a lifetime.

March of the Living 12-17 April 2015

To read more about this unique experience visit: marchoftheliving.org.uk